australia

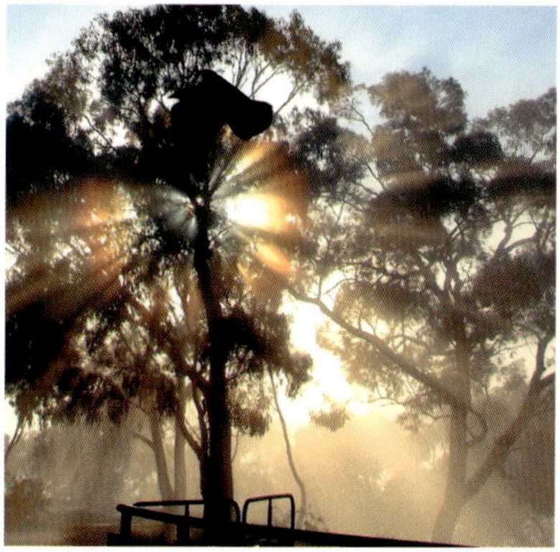

a photographic essay. peter emanuel's
impressions of australia. thankyou God
for your creation

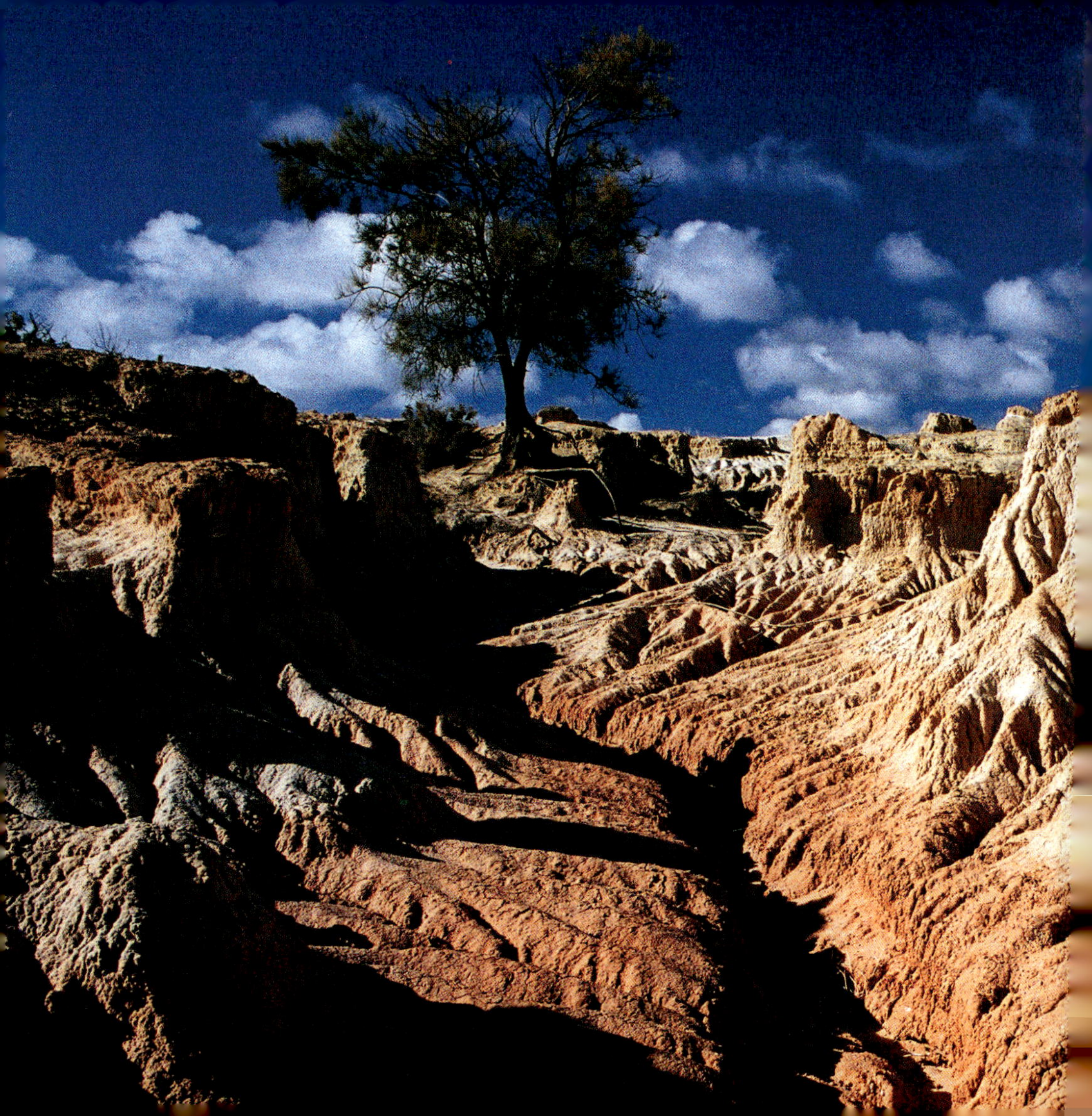

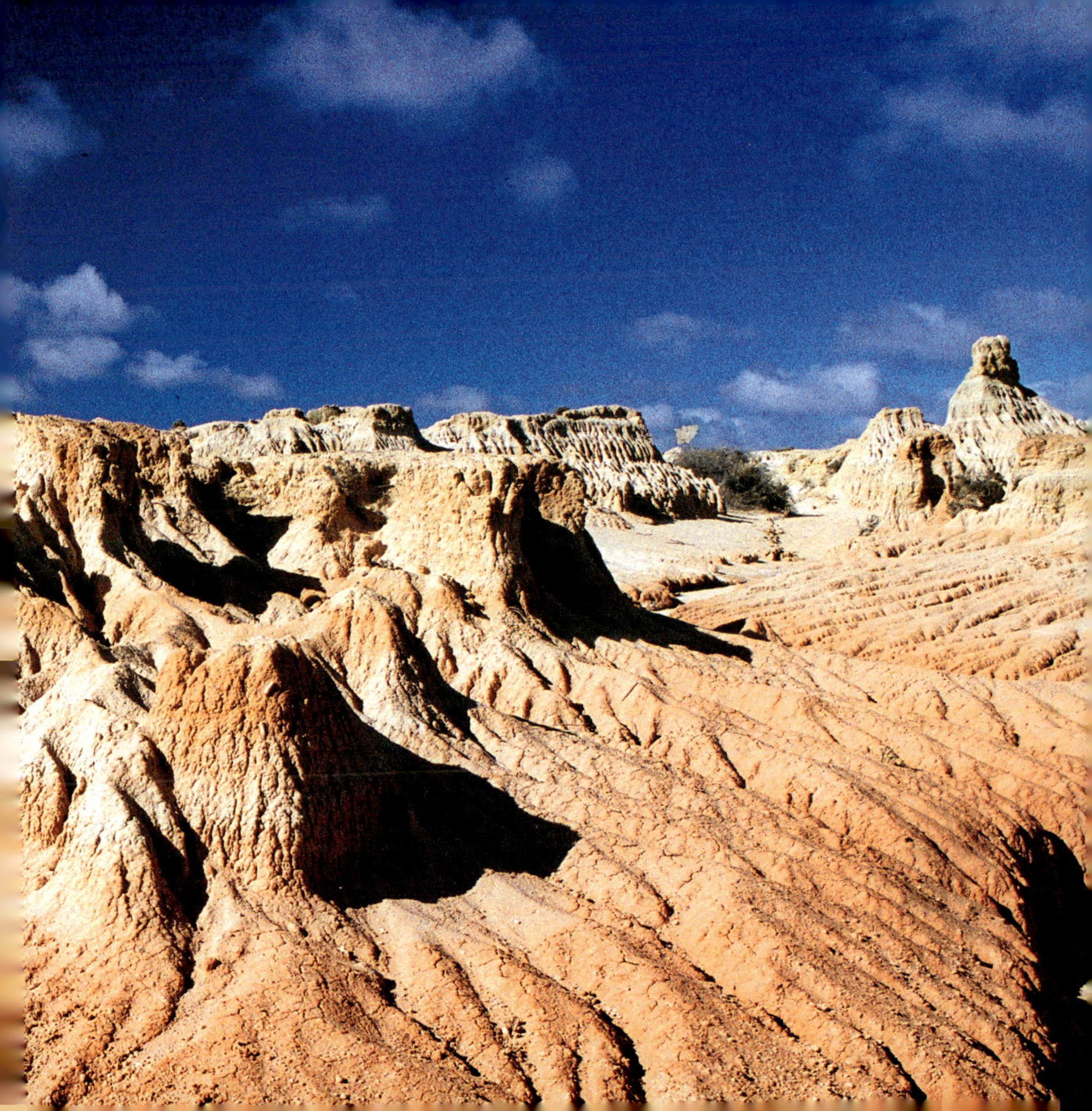

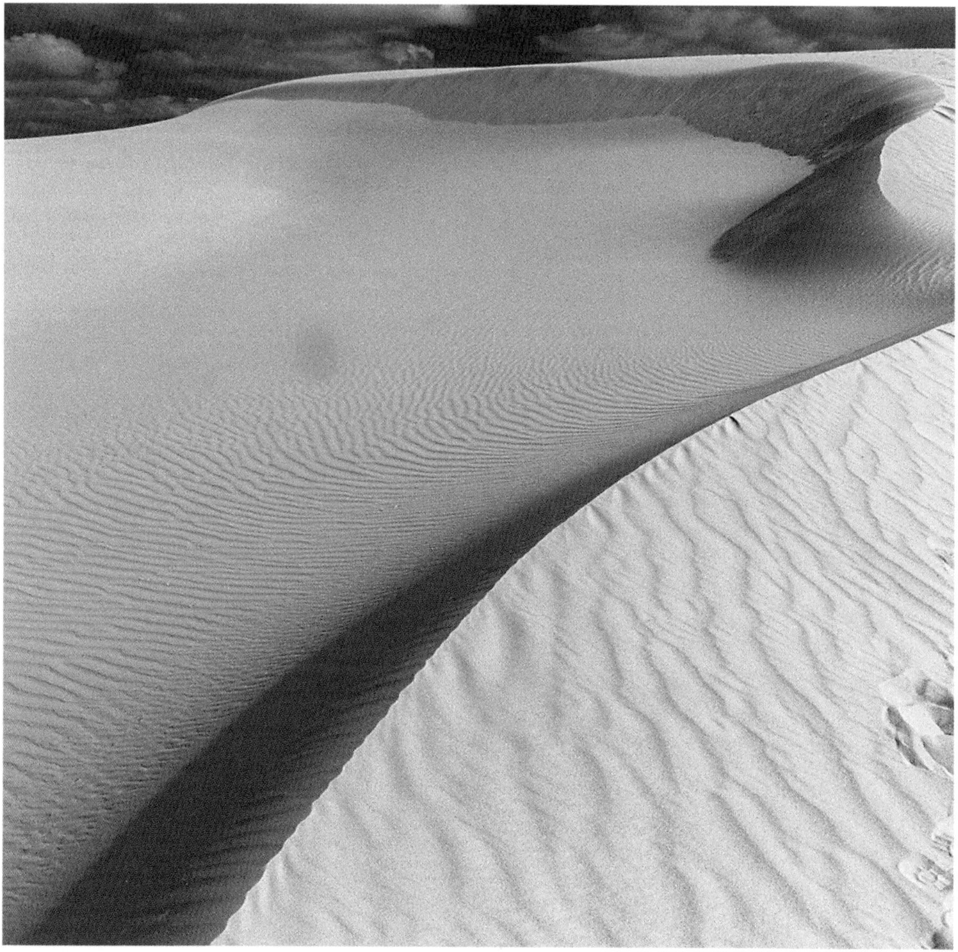

previous page. walls of china, mungo national park

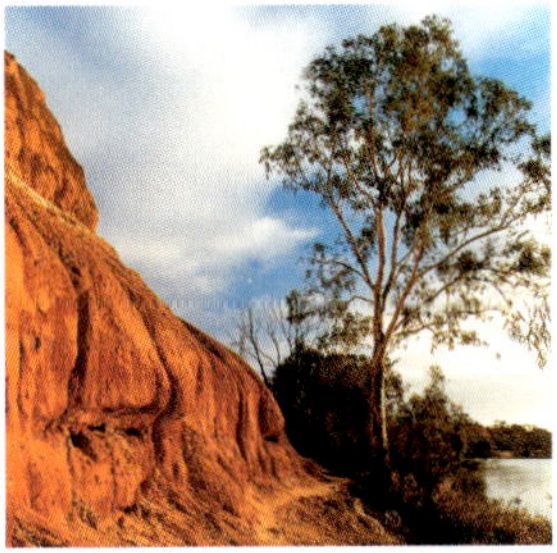
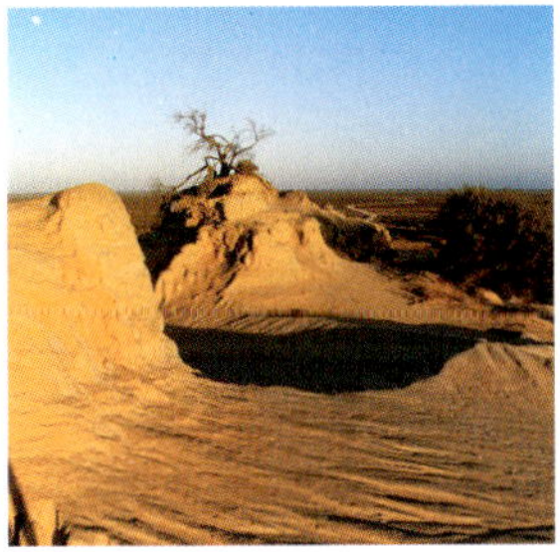
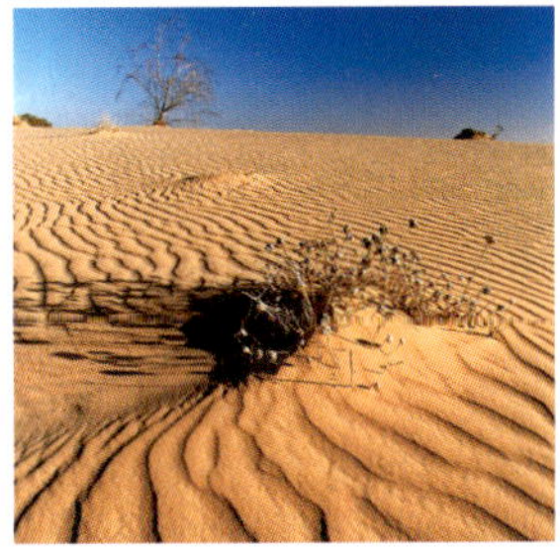

next pages. darling river near wentworth

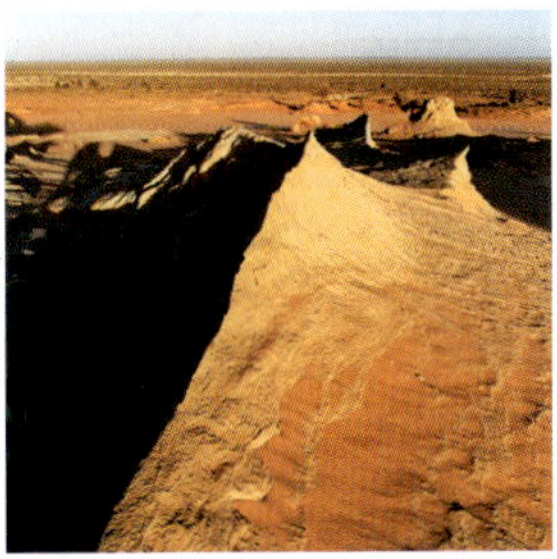
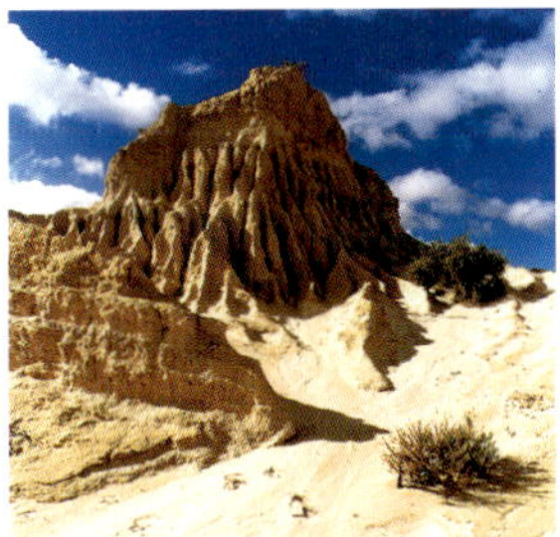
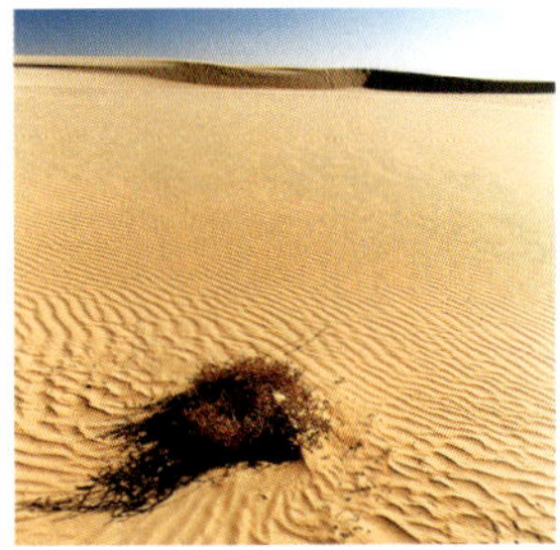
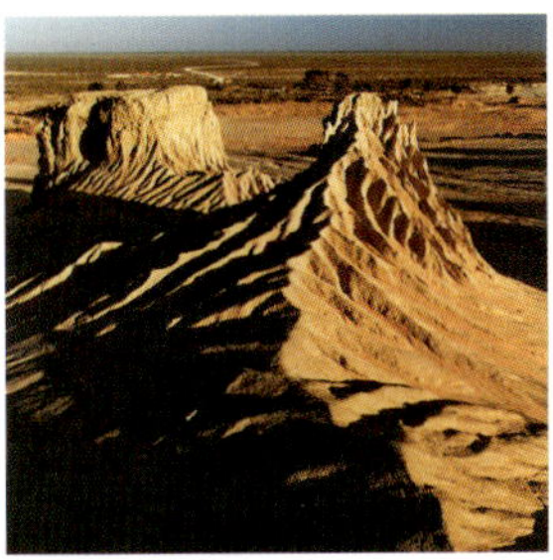
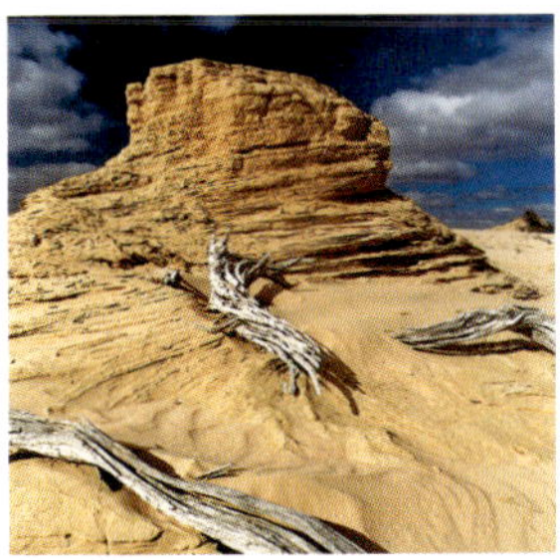
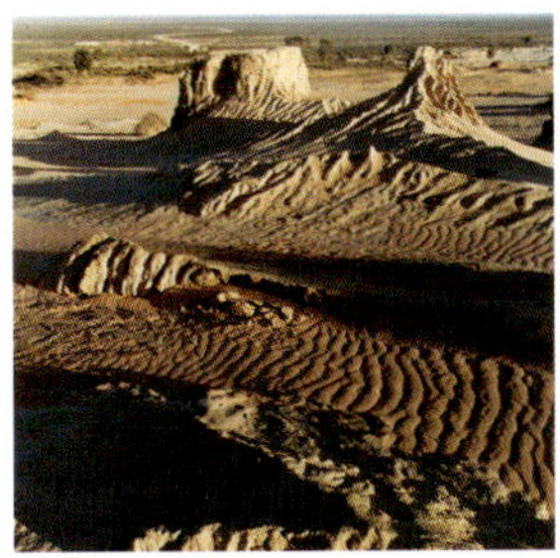

a. red cliffes, murray river b-i. mungo national park

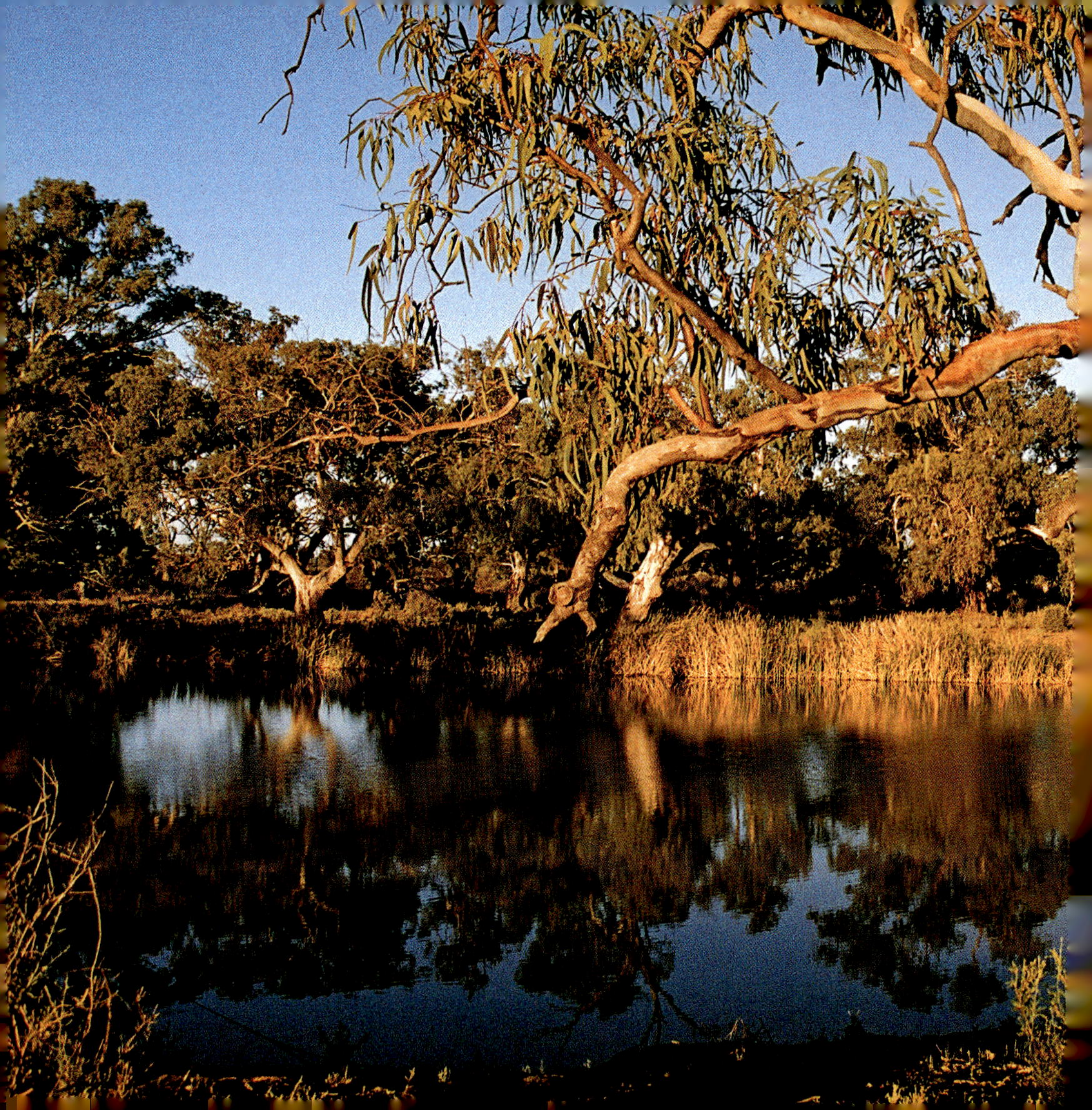

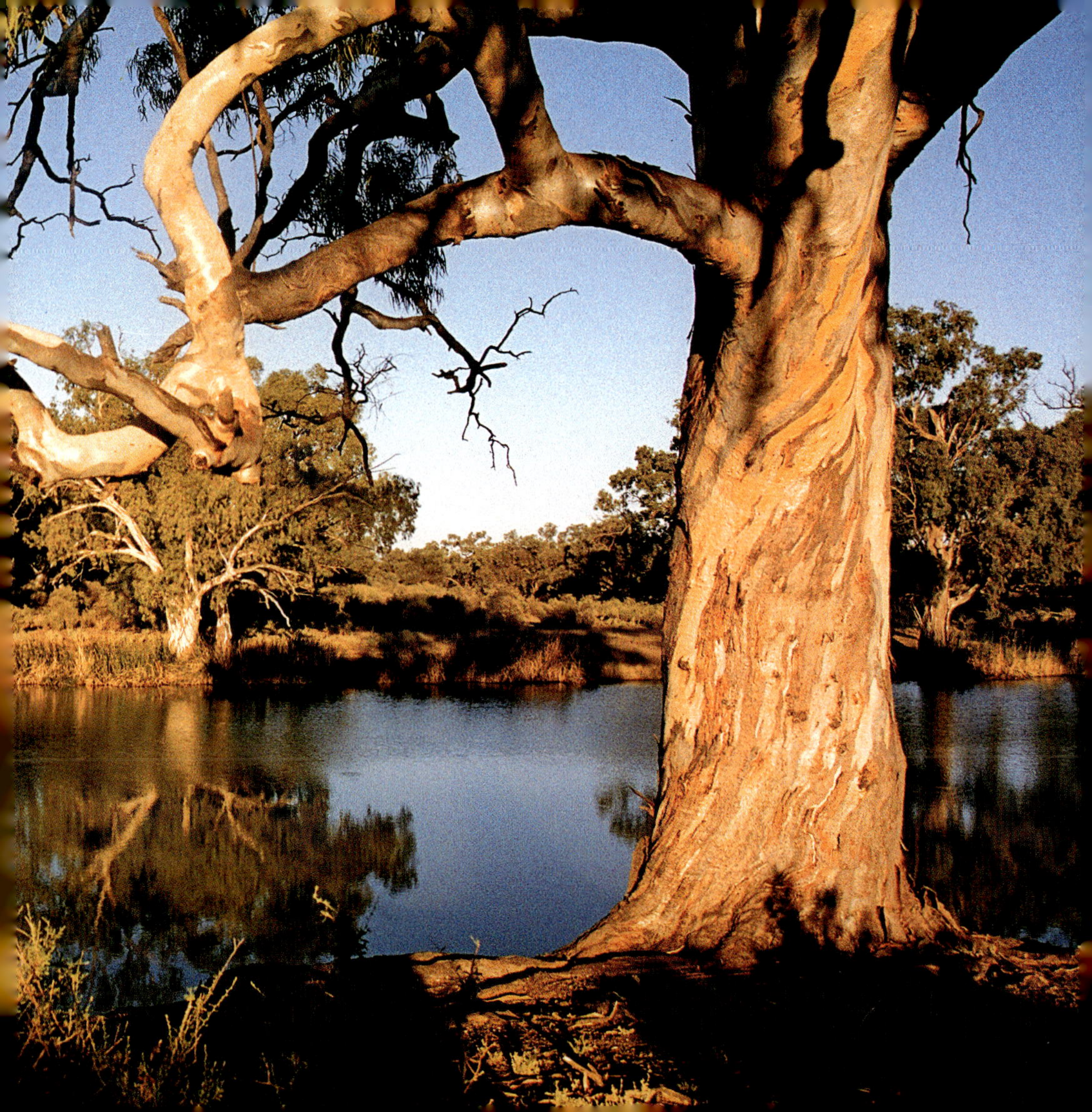

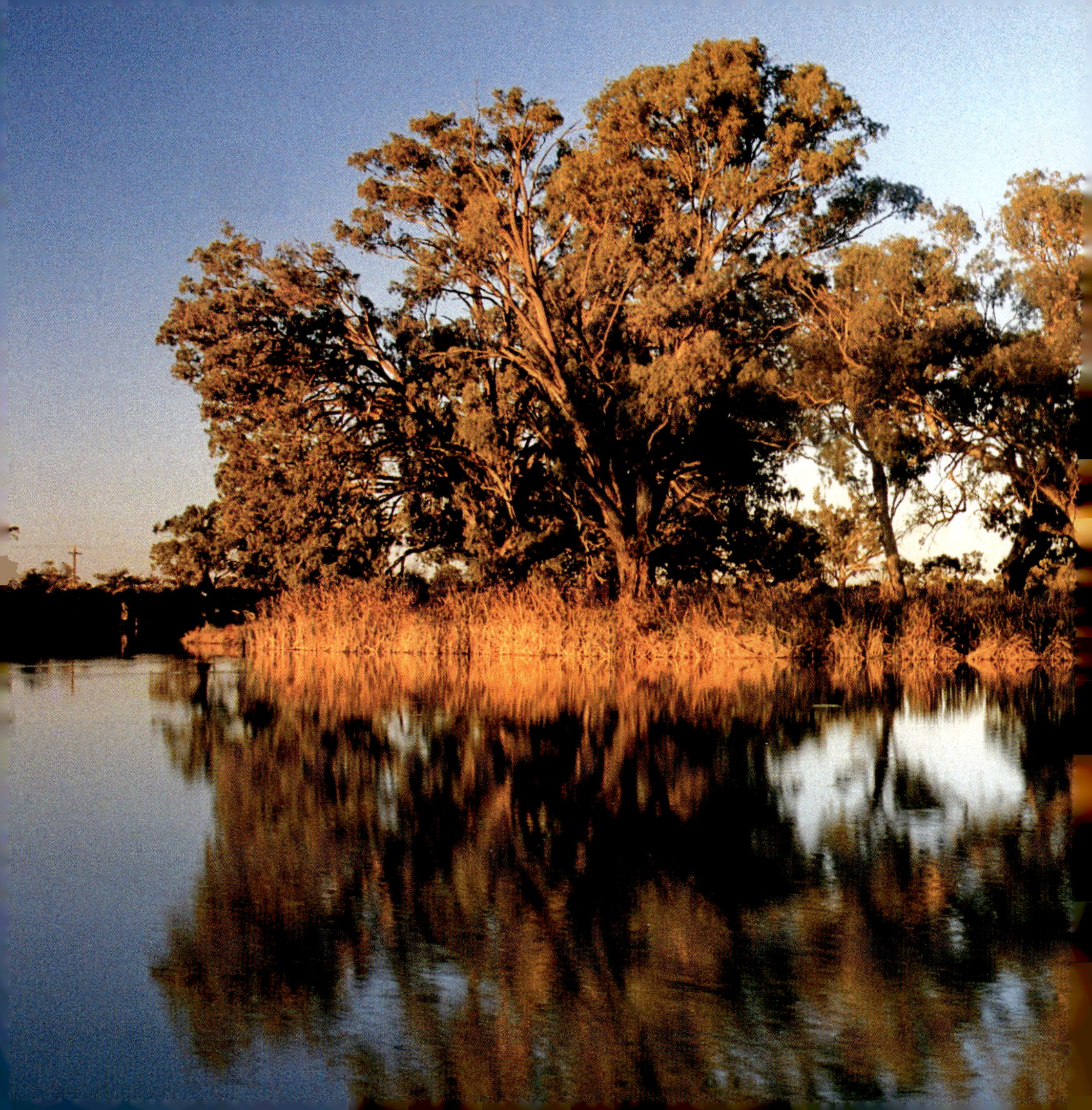

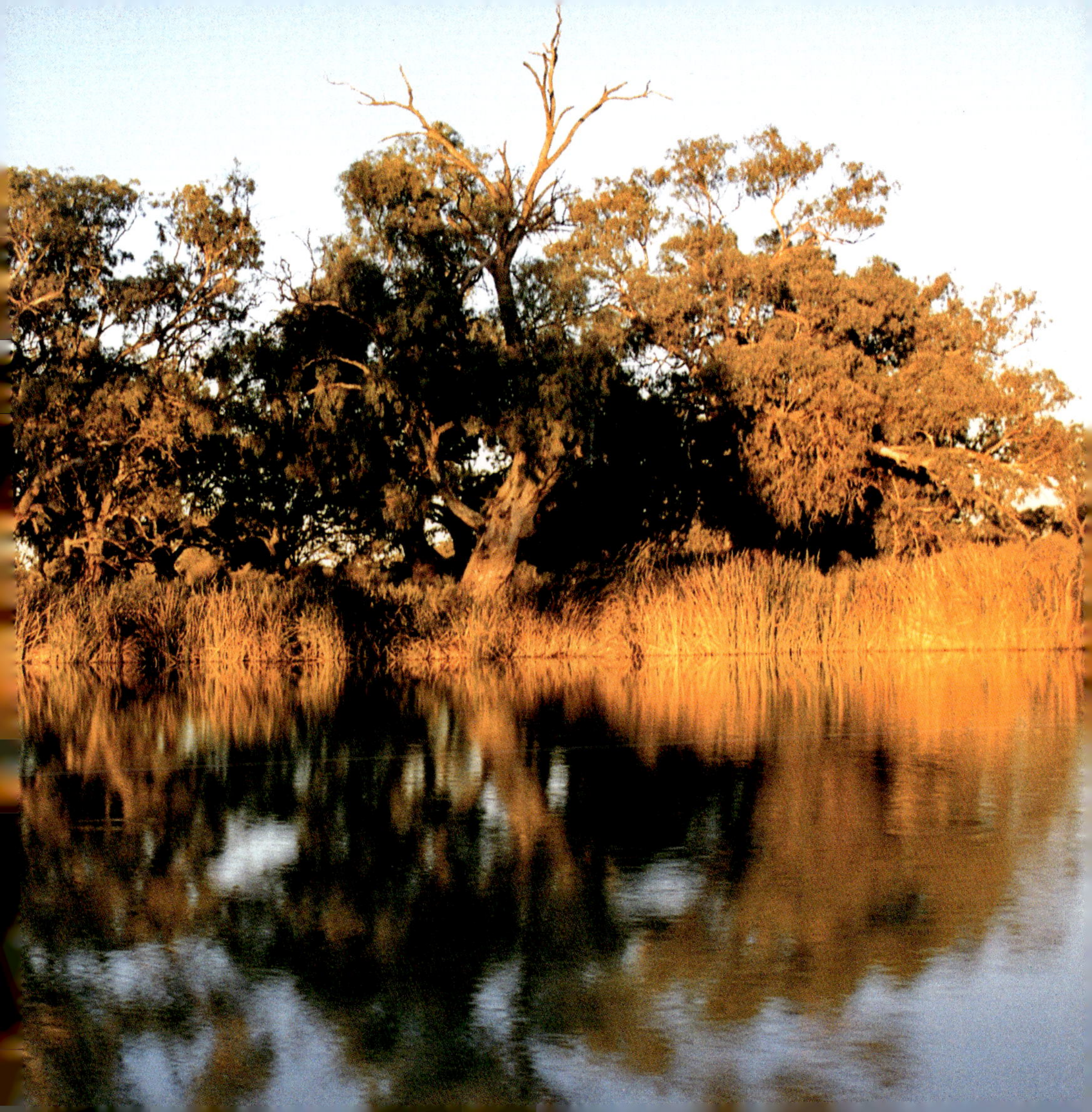

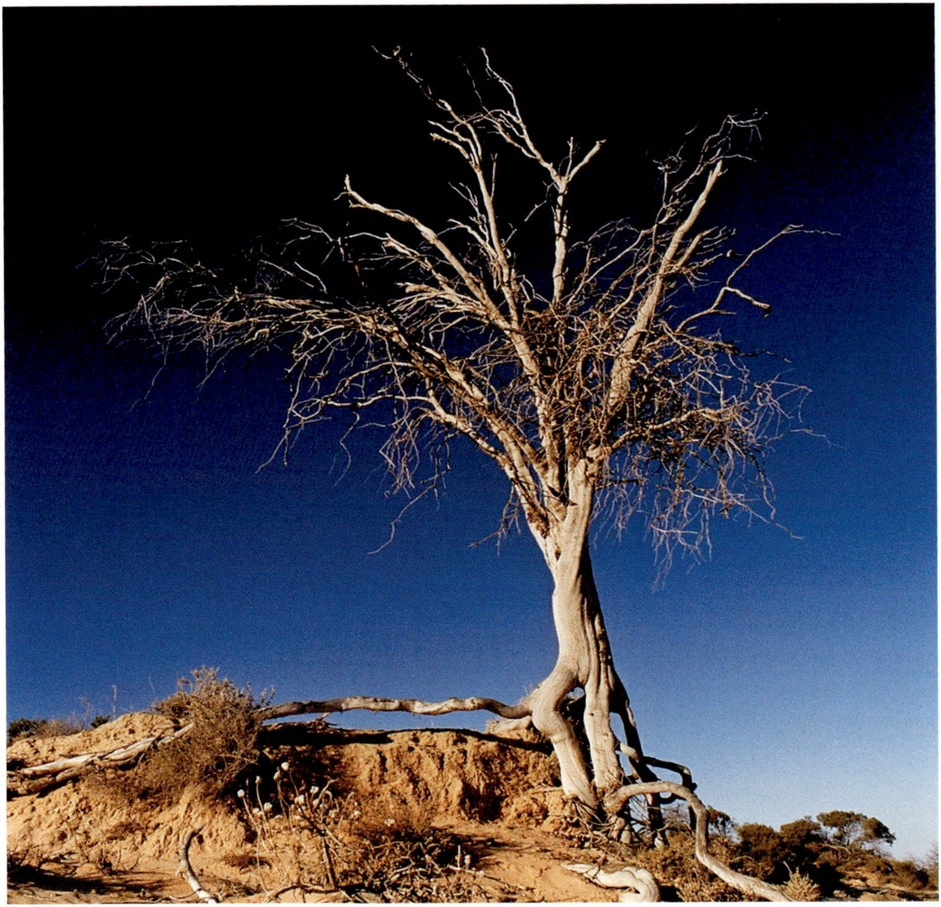

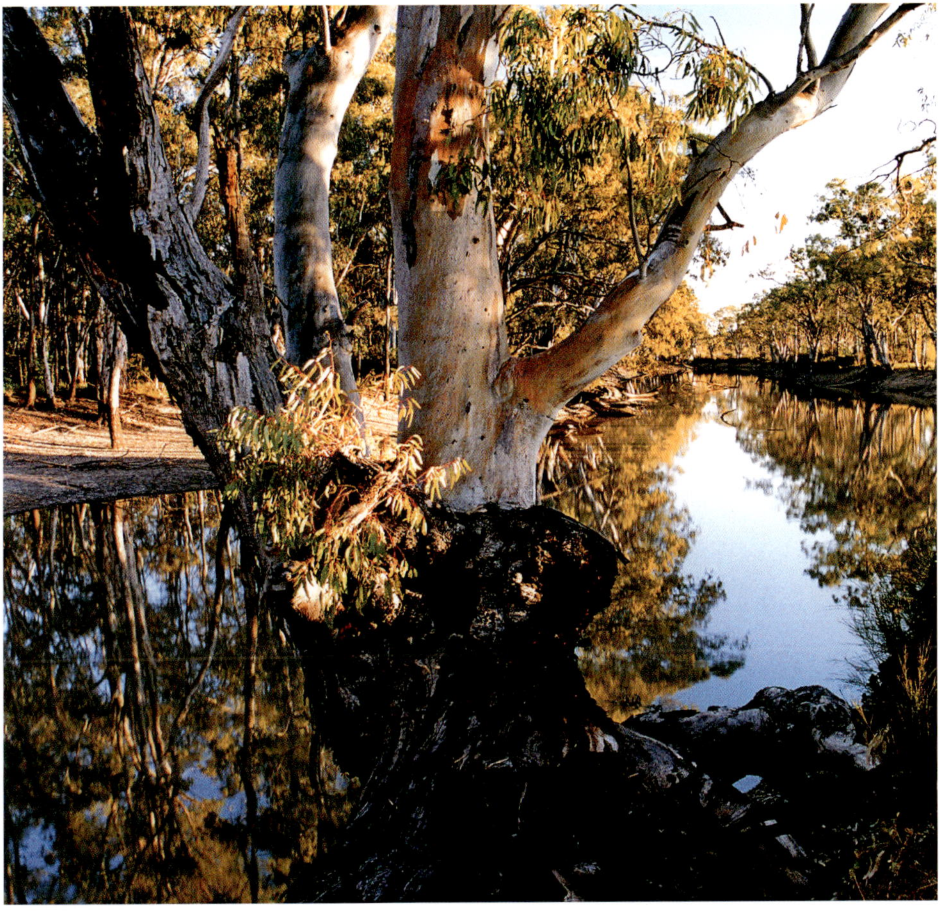

next page. red gum bridge, koondrook; following page, pyap, swan hill

murray river lagoon, barham-koondrook

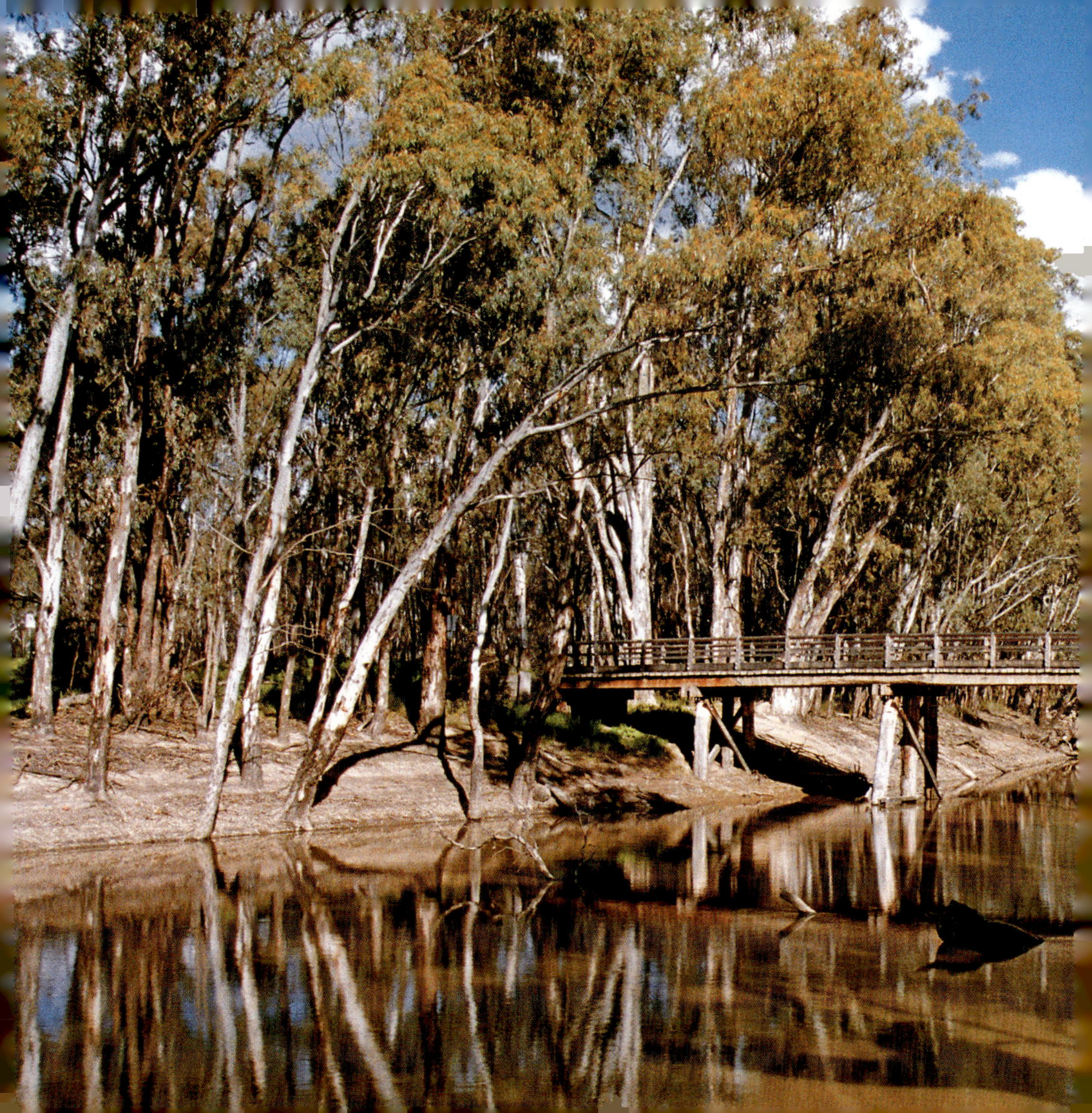

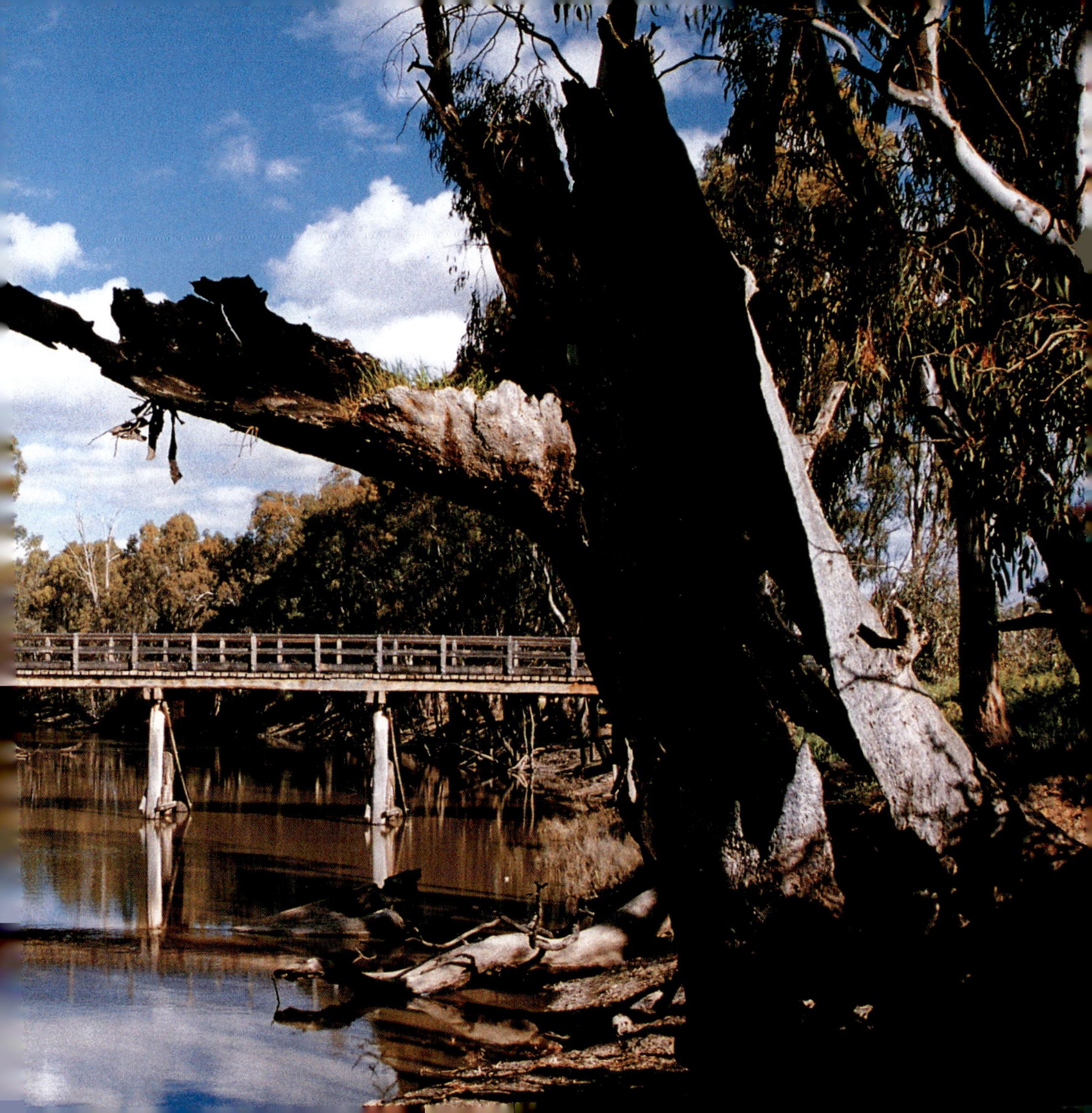

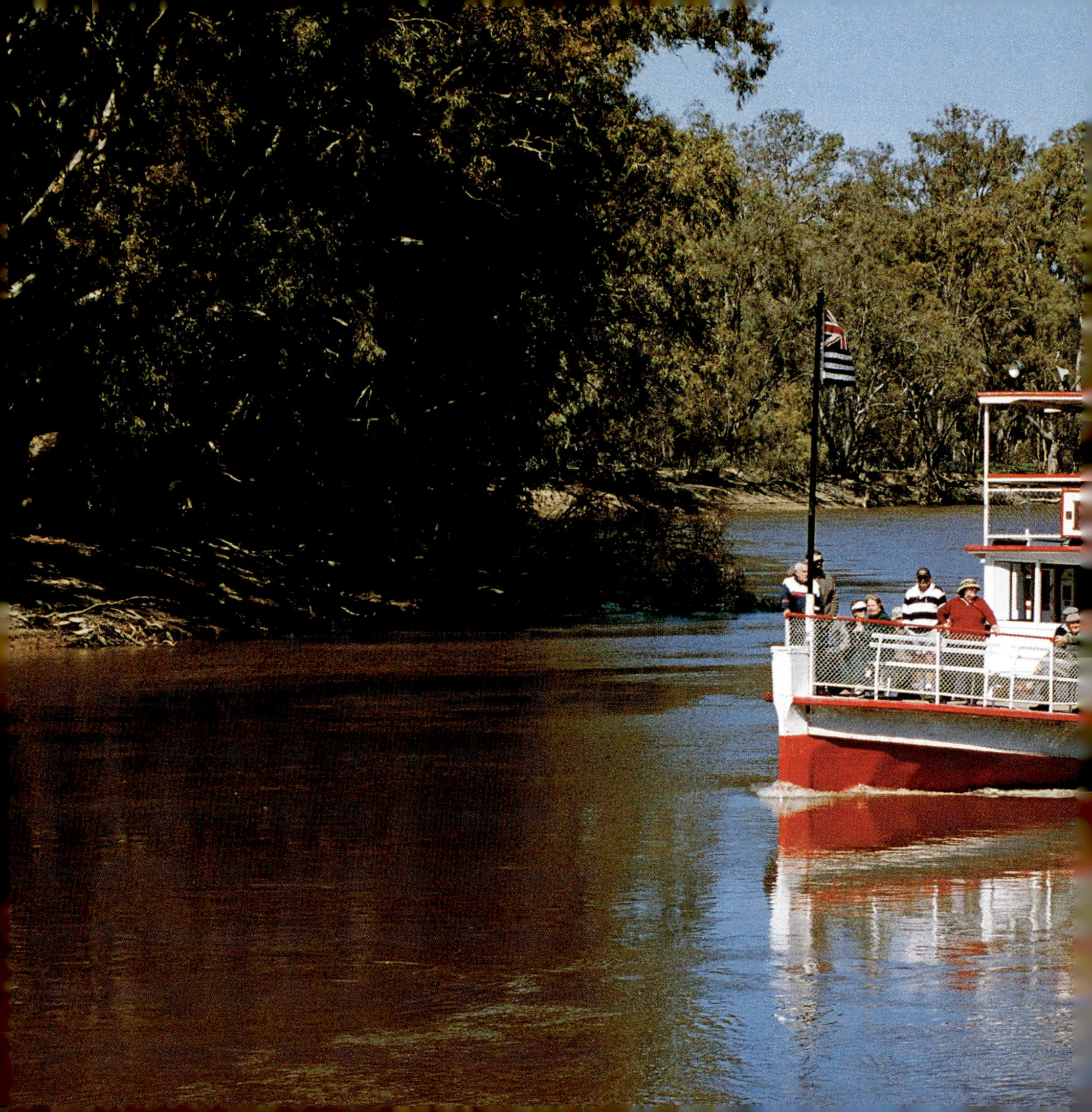

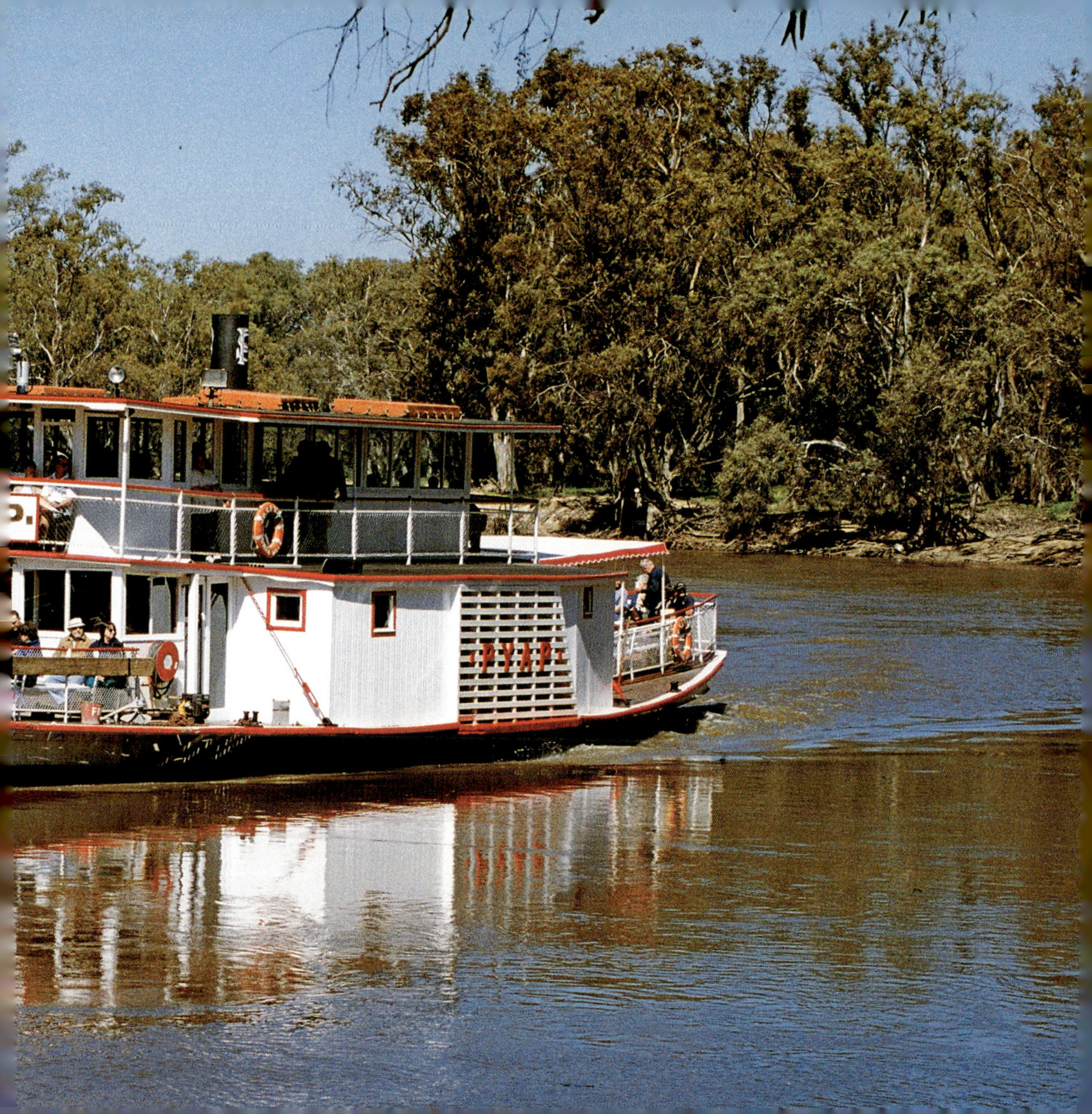
PYAP

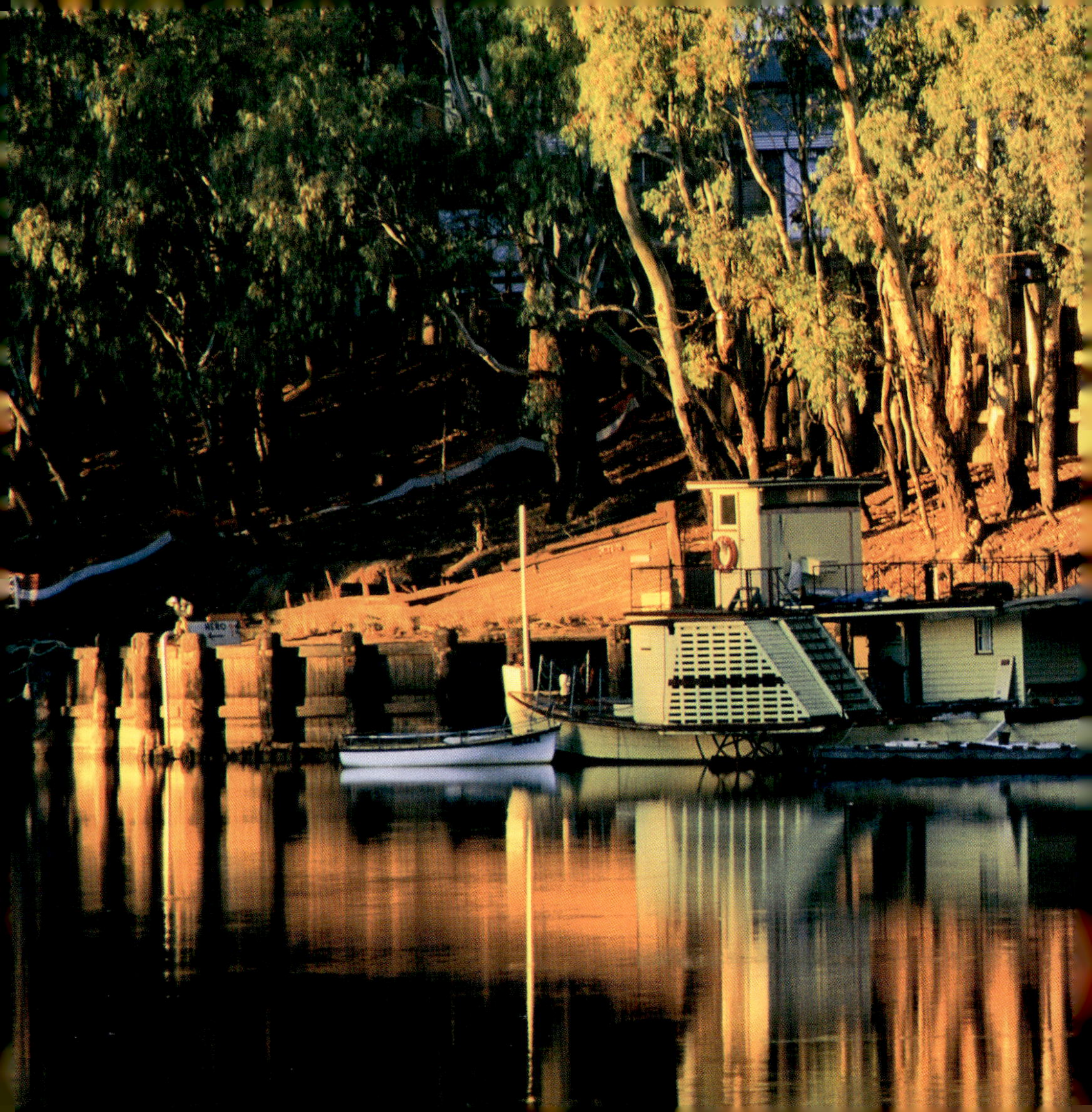

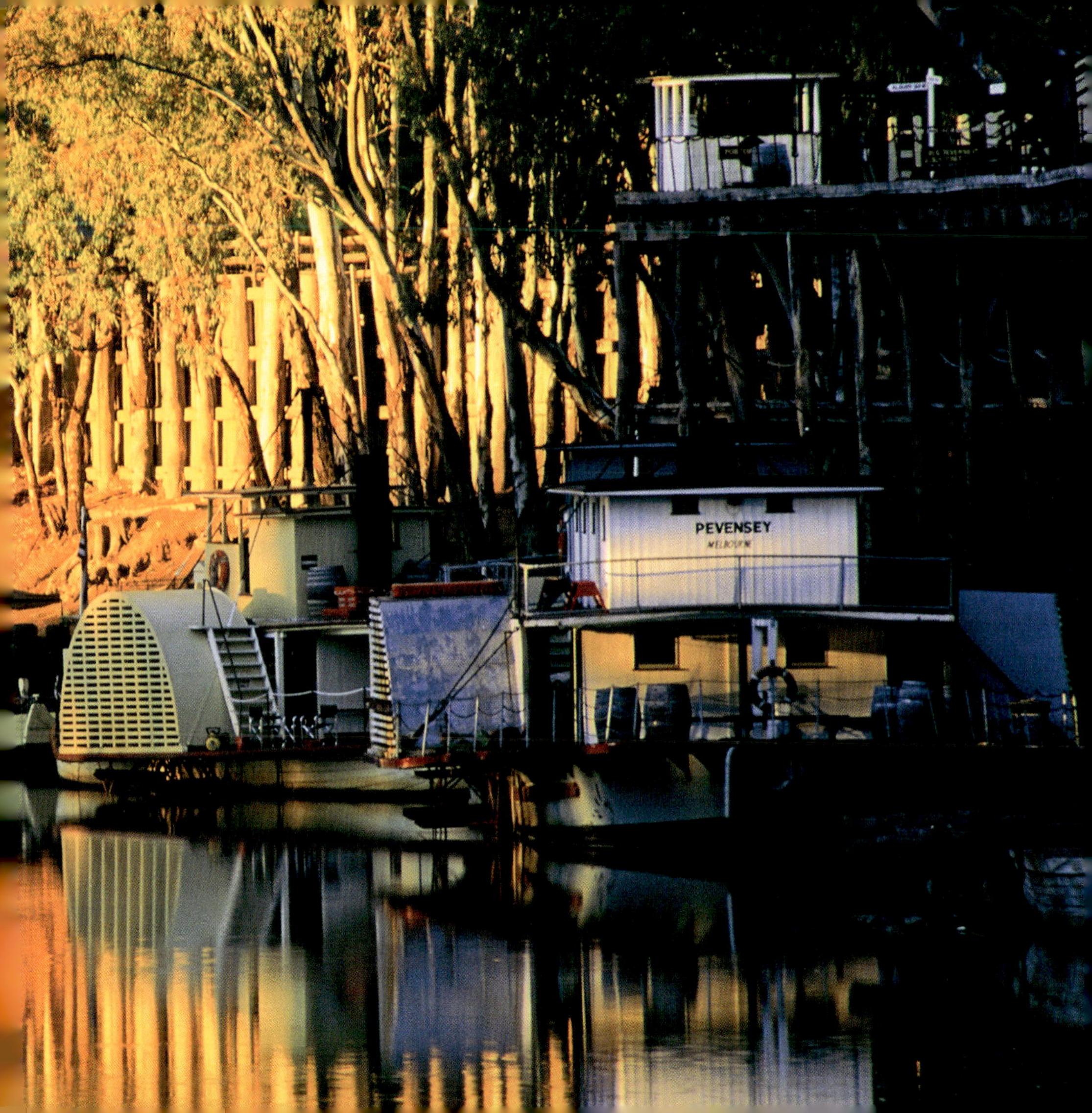
PEVENSEY
MELBOURNE

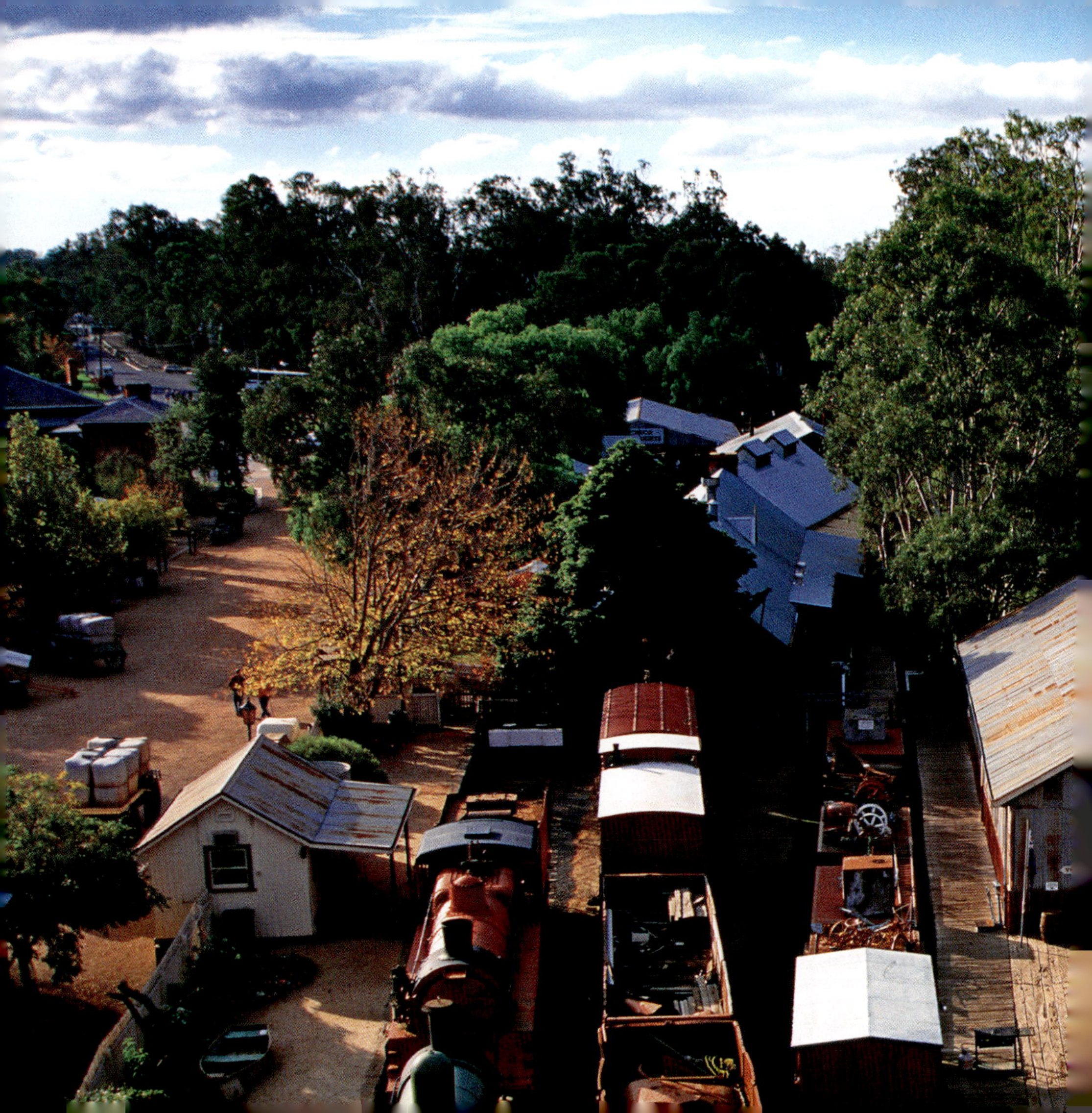

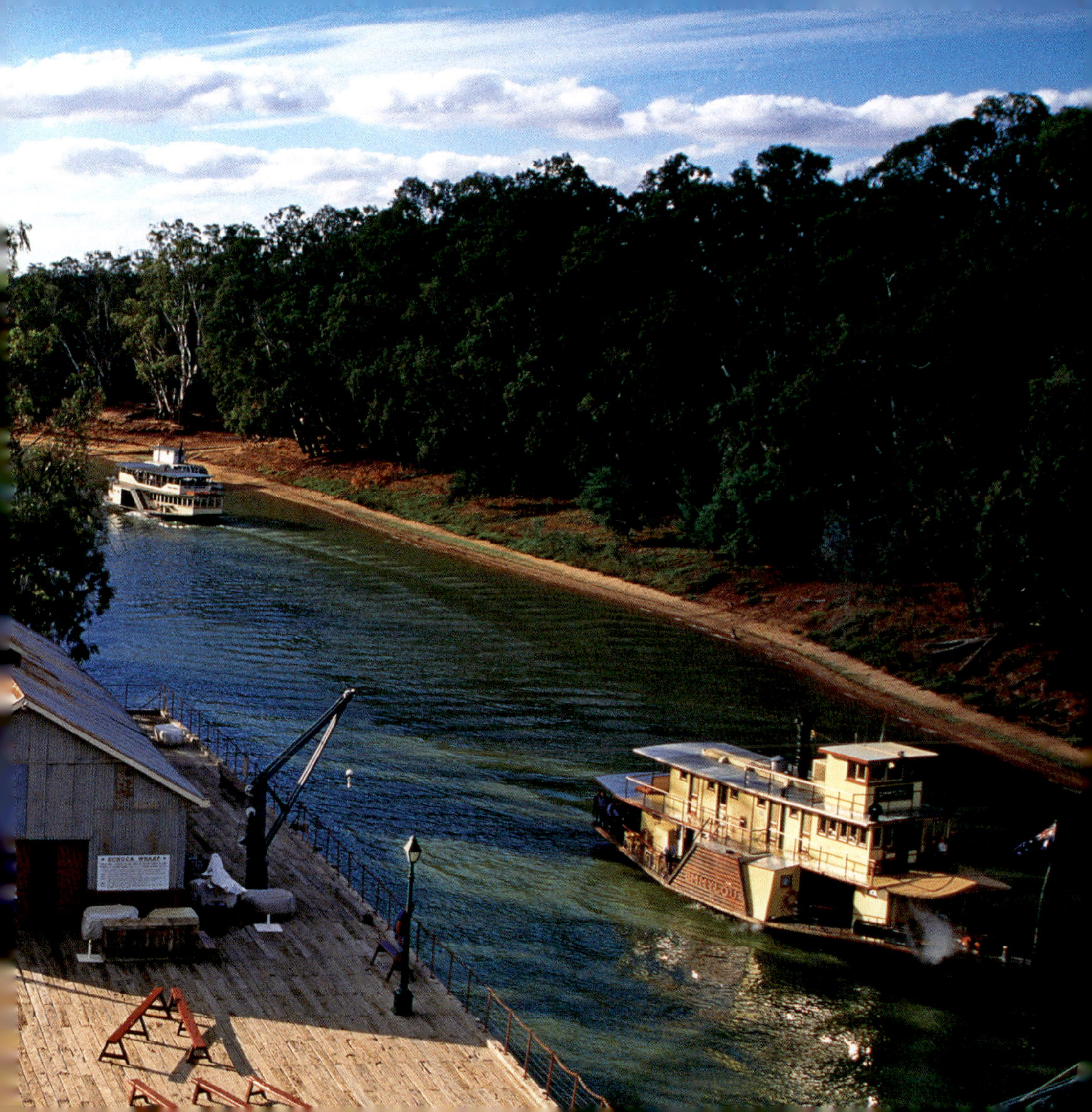
ECHUCA WHARF

previous pages. echuca

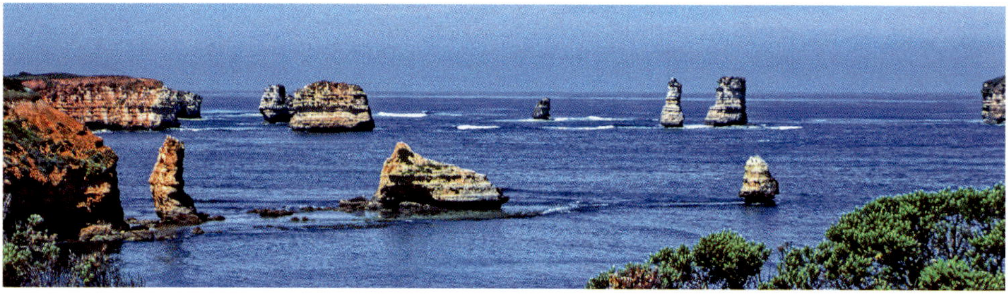

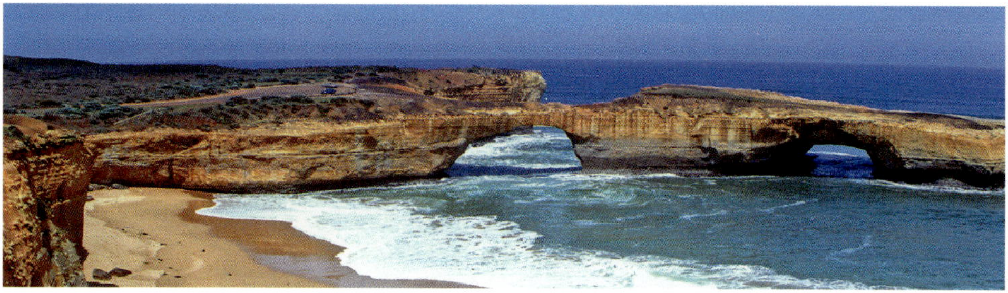

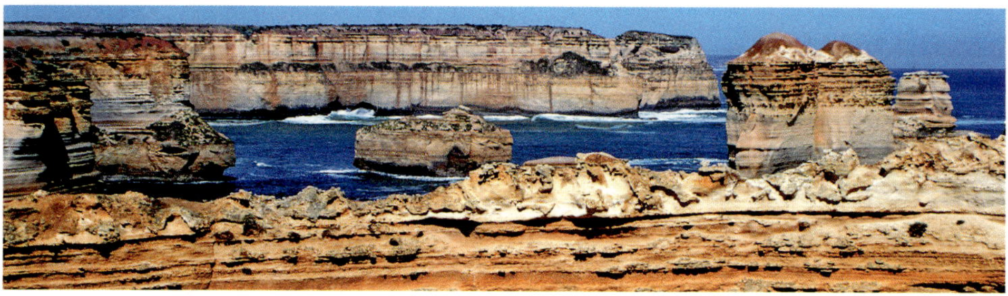

 port campbell, great ocean road

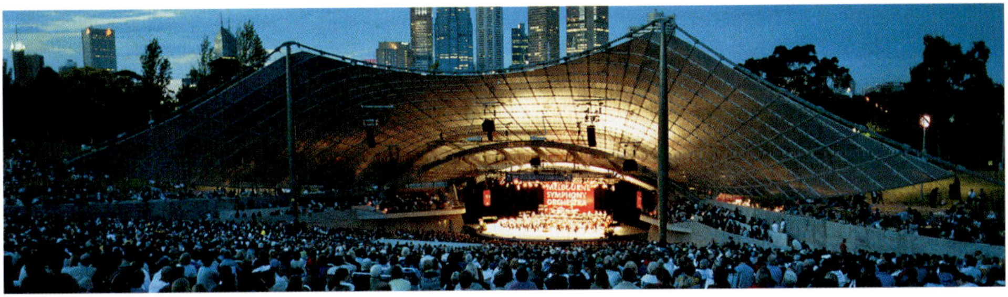

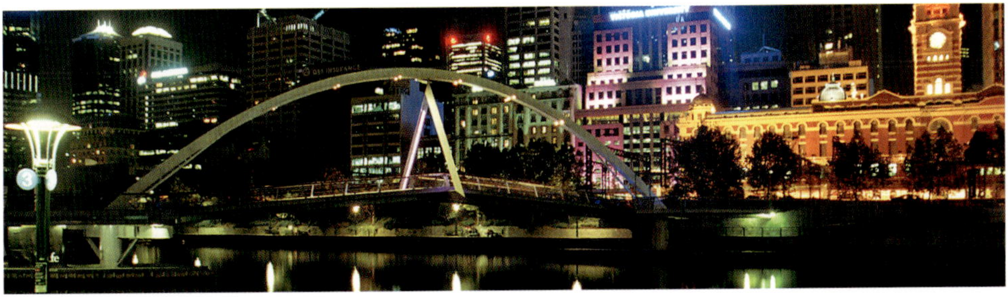

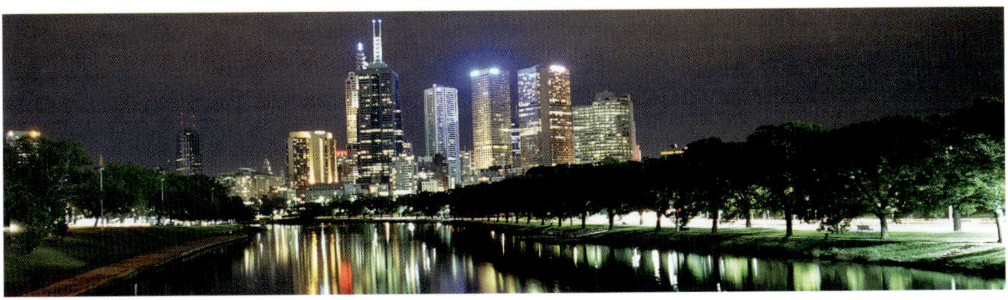

a. sidney myer music bowl b&c. yarra river, melbourne

next page. st kilda beach, albert park and melbourne skyline

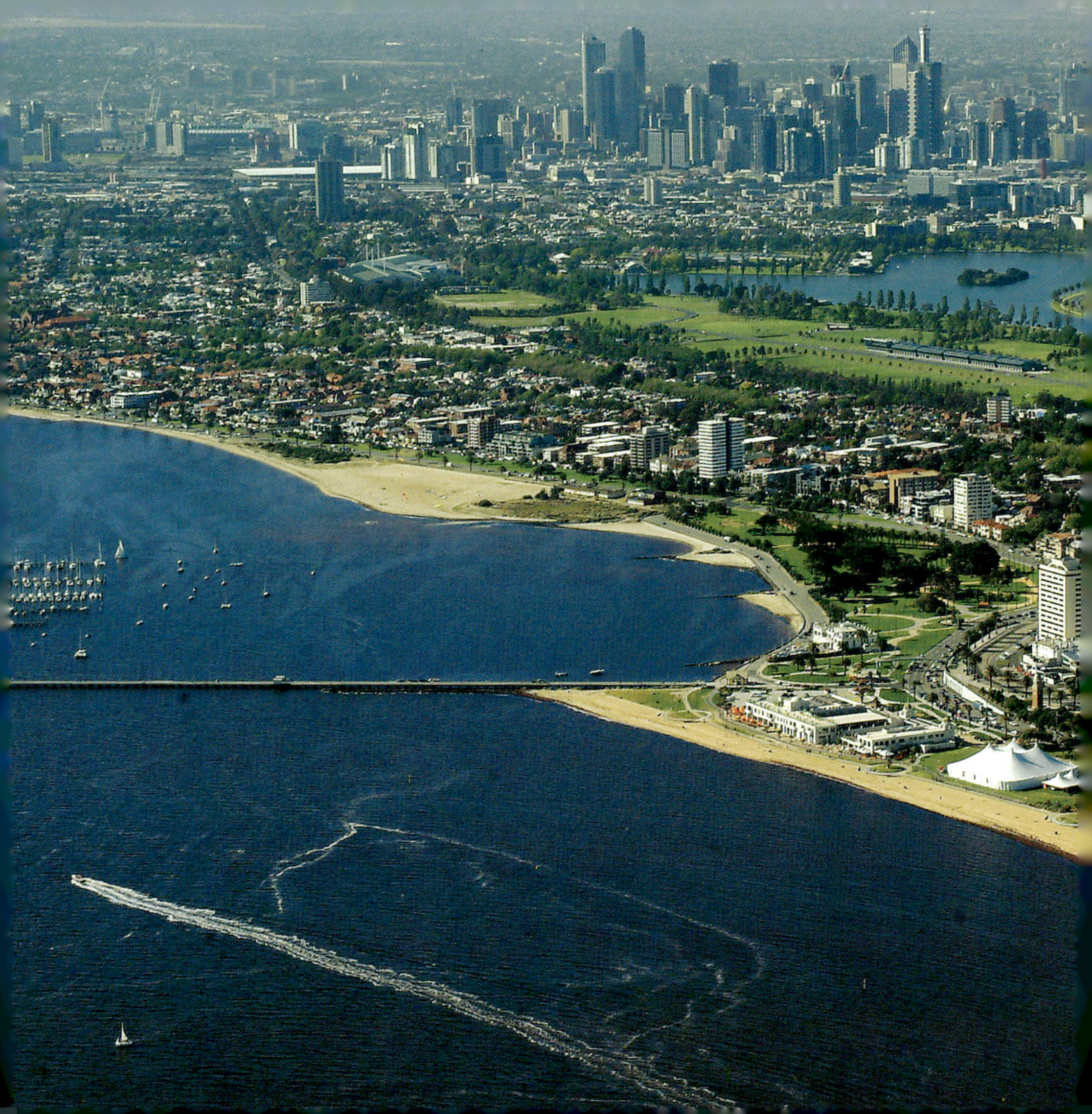

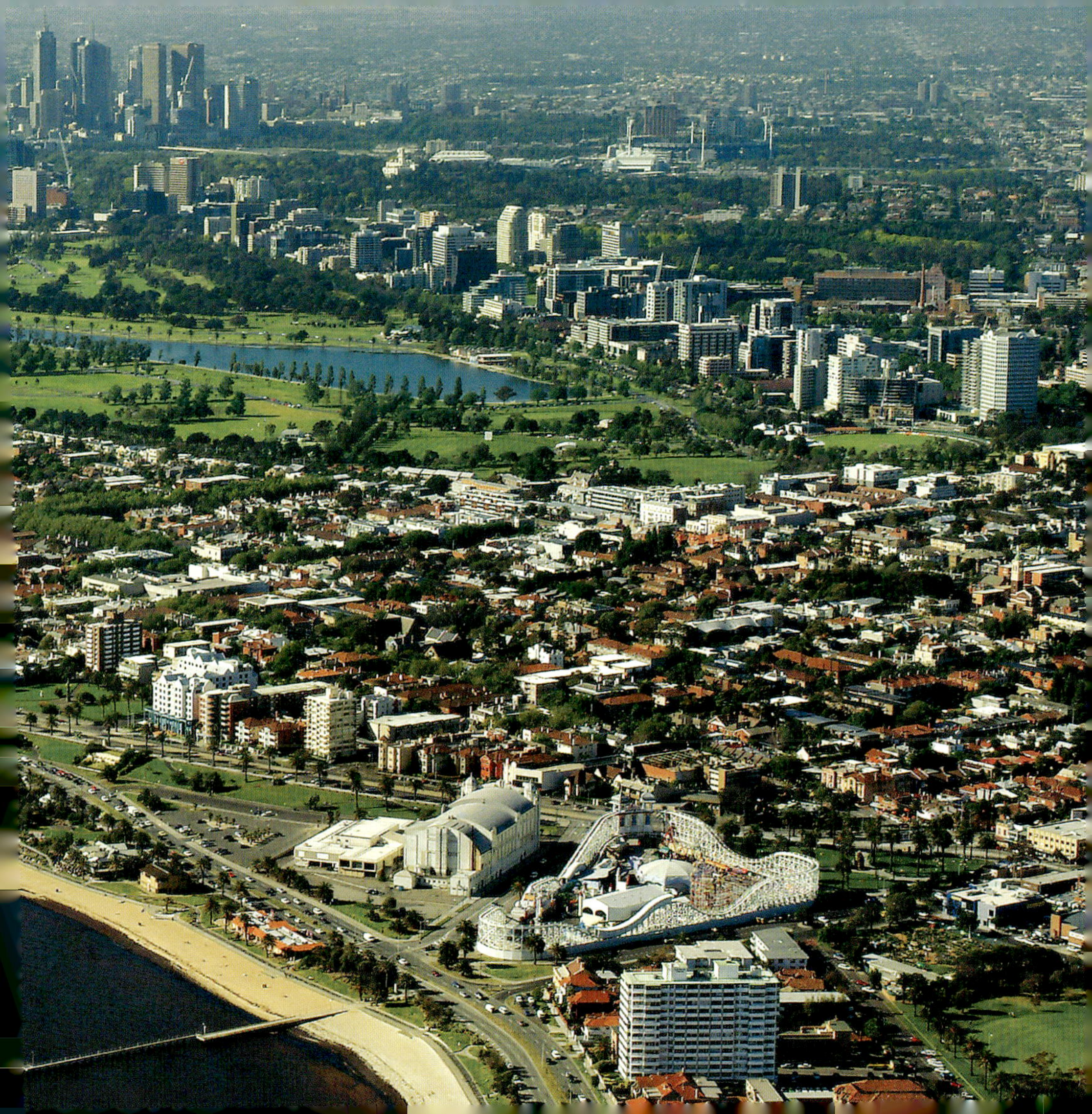

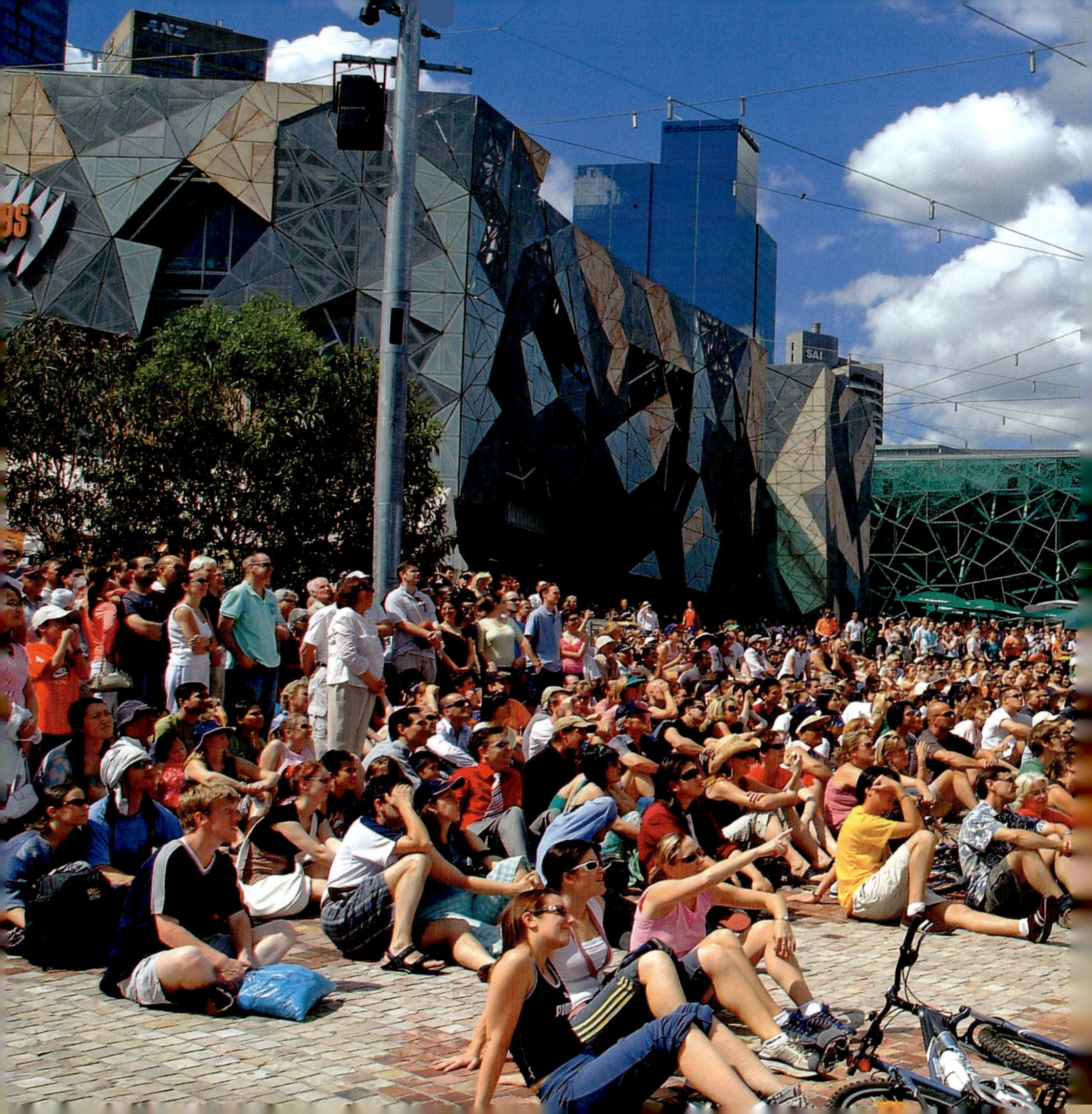
ANZ
SAI

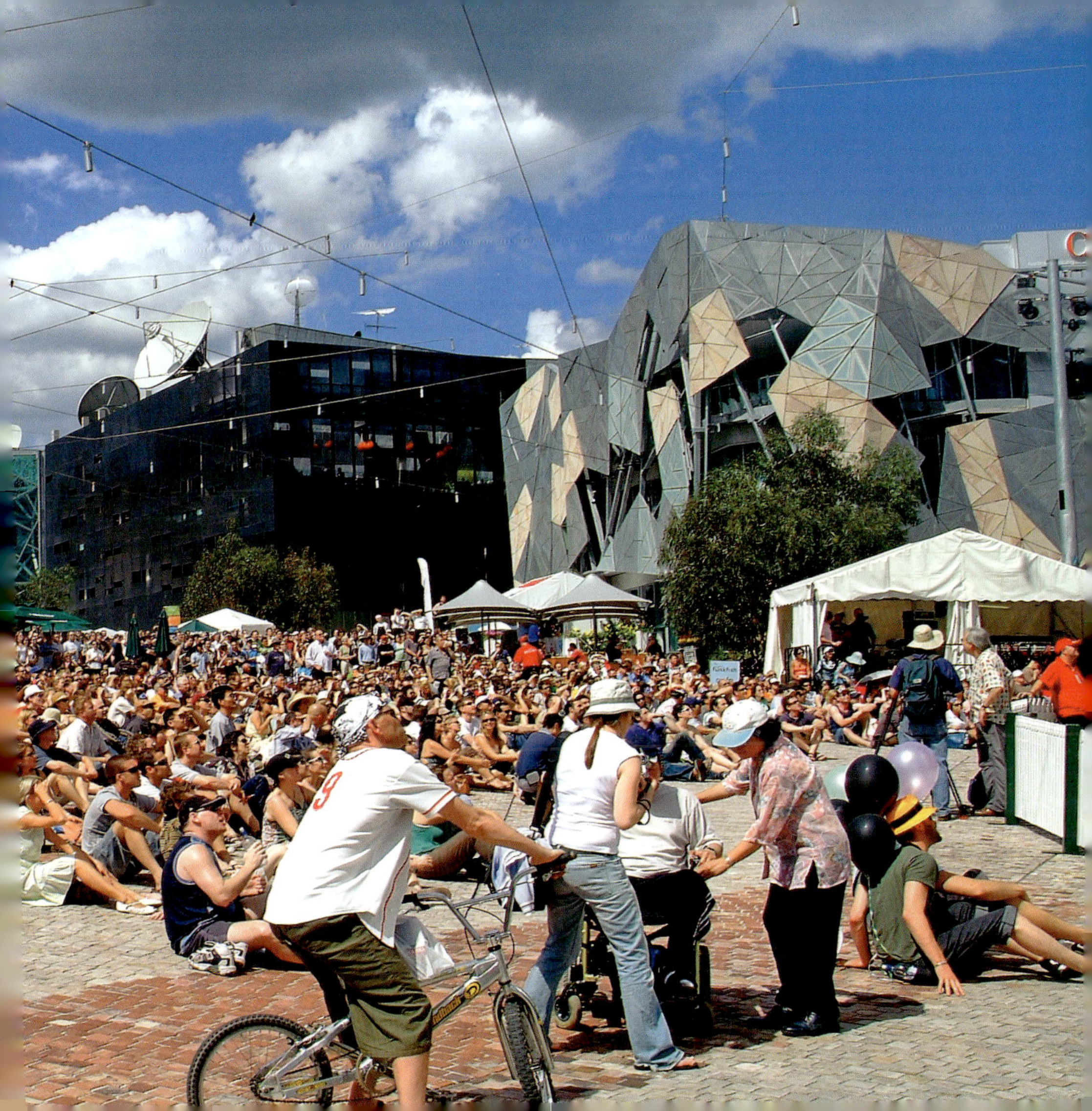

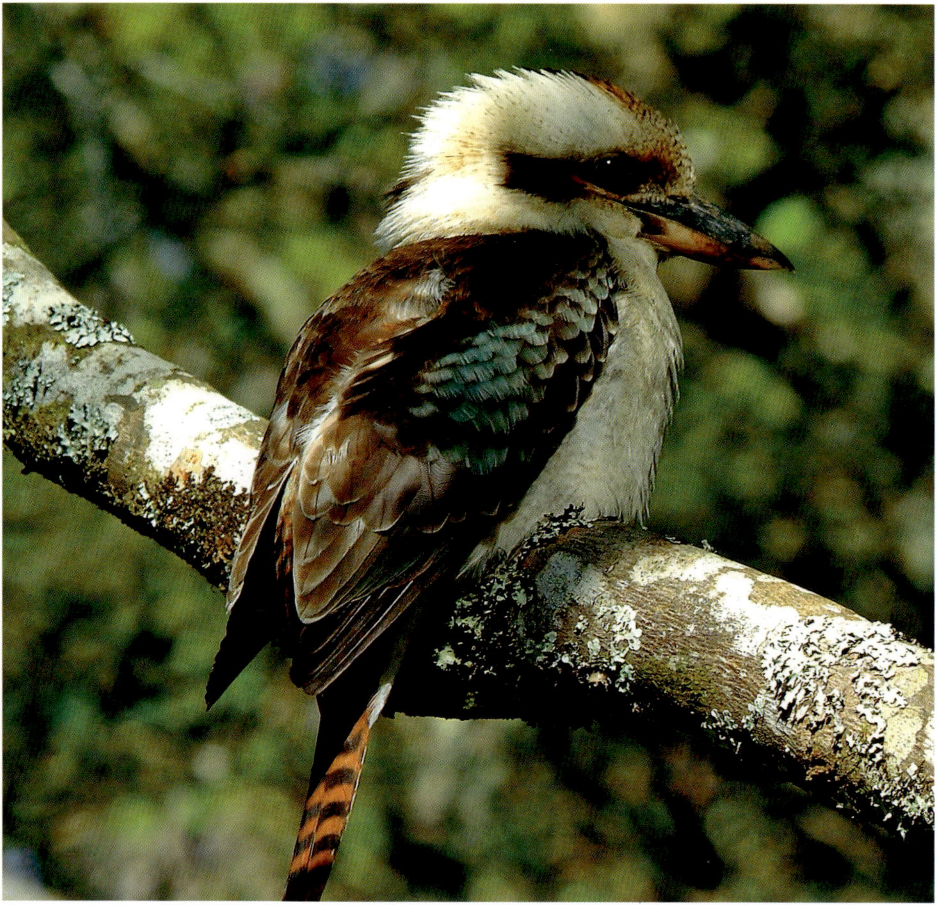

previous page. federation square, melbourne

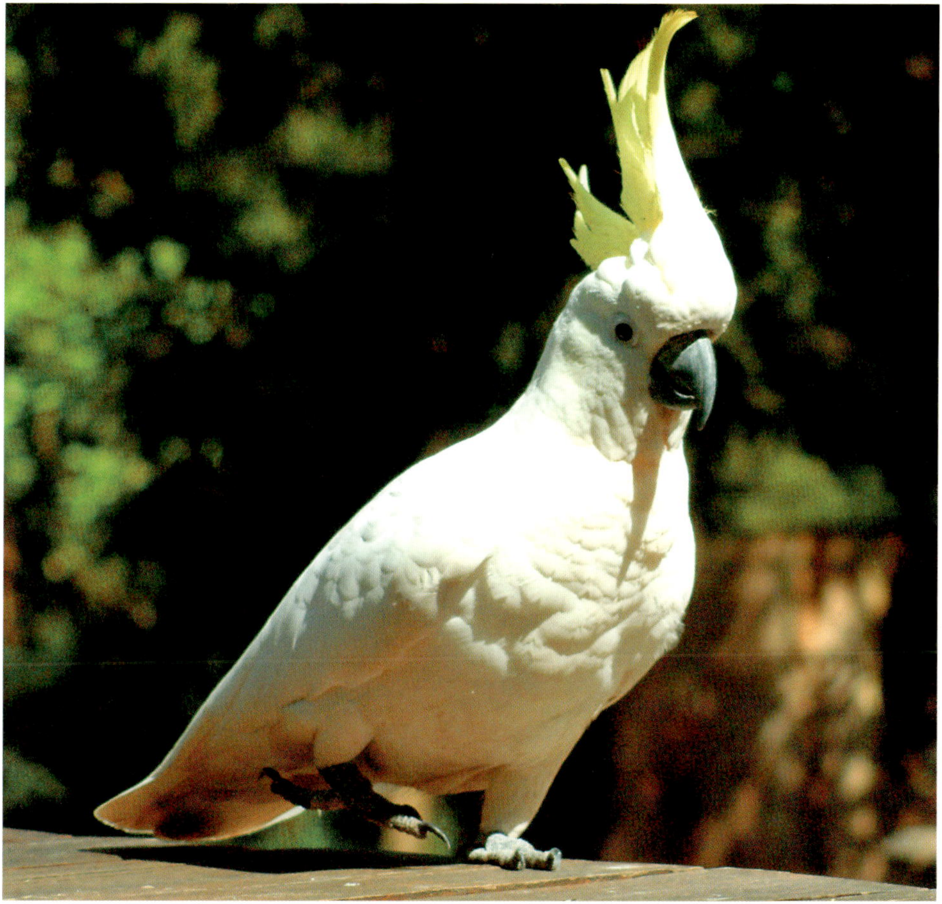

next page. sherbrooke forest, dancenong ranges

cockatoo

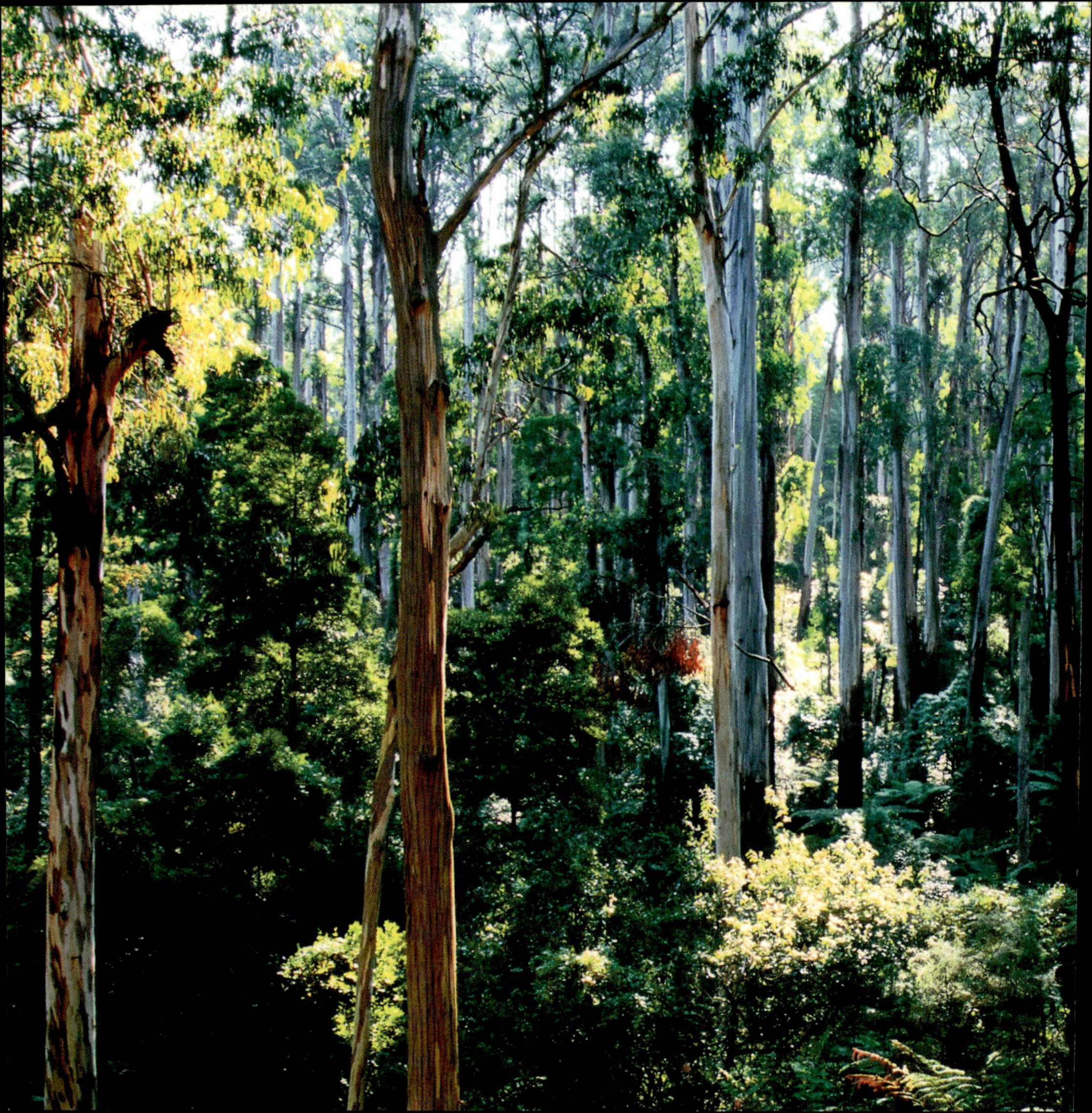

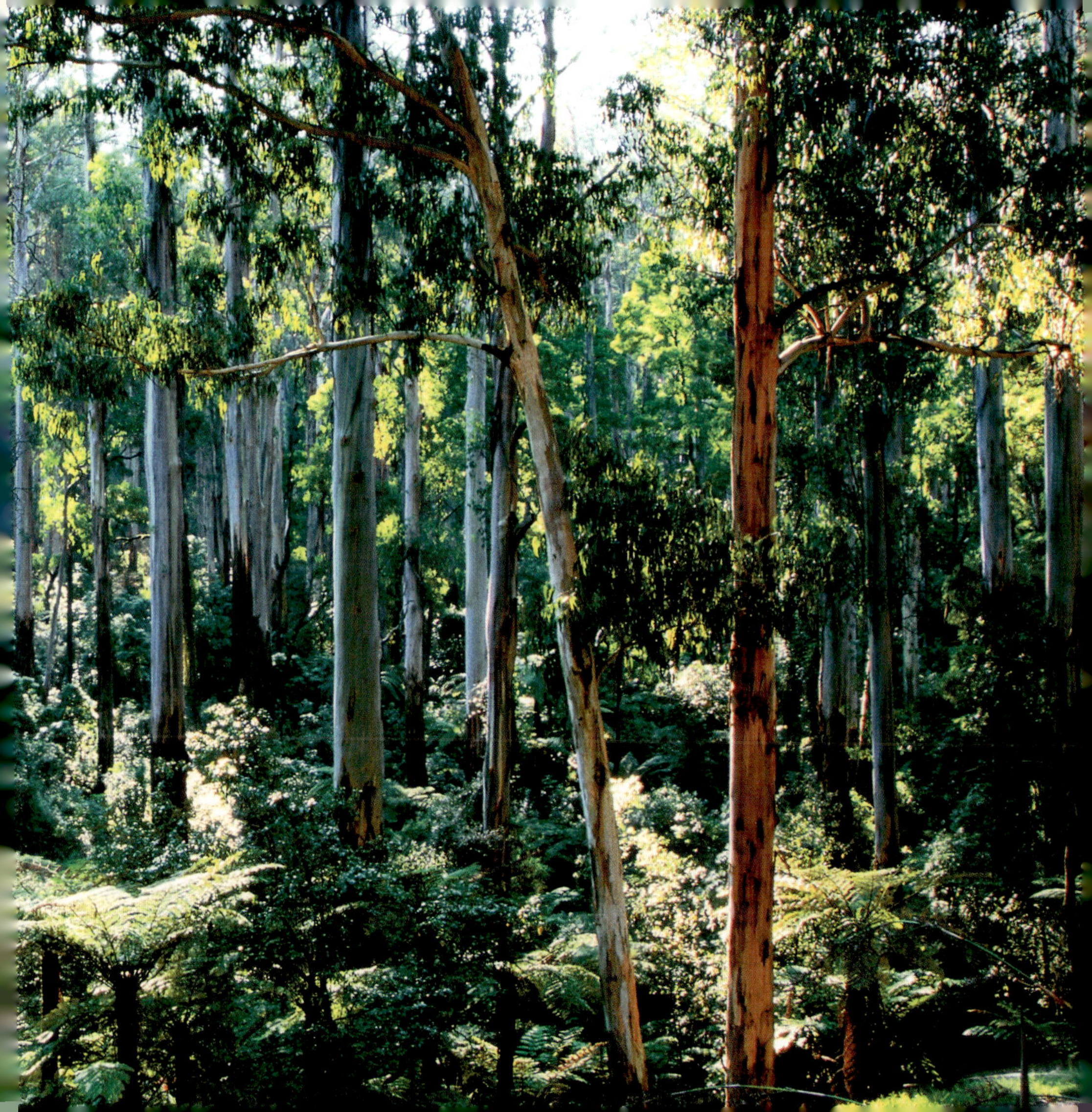

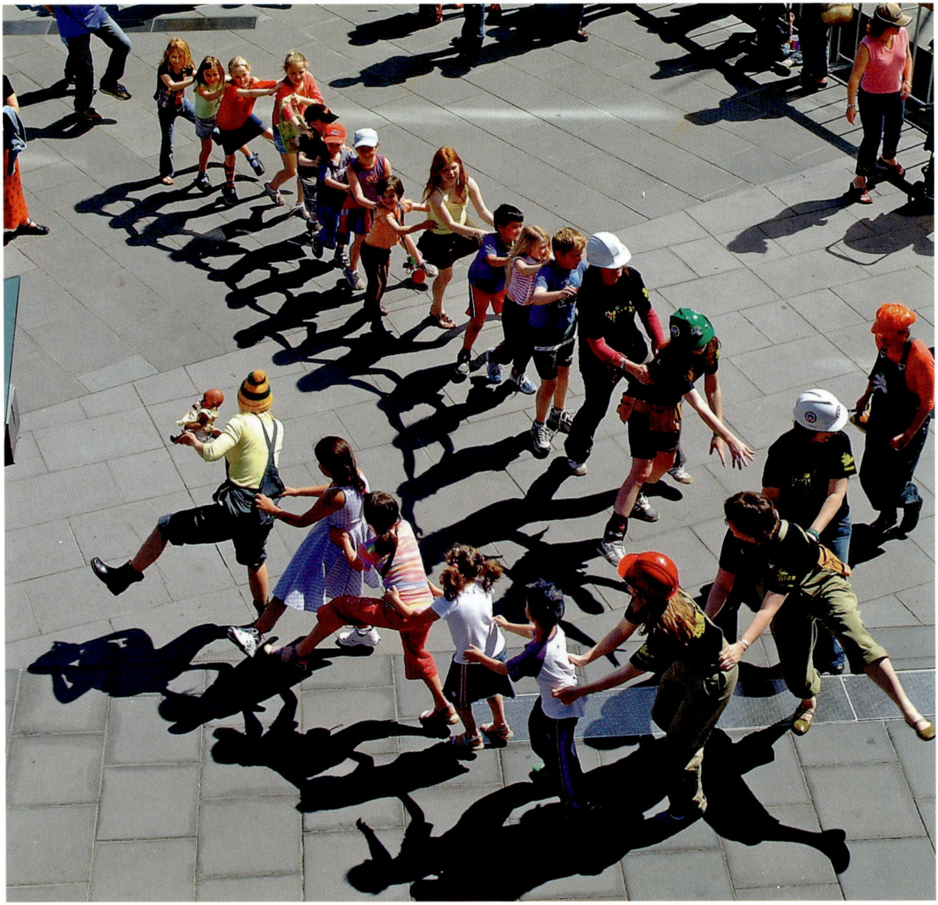

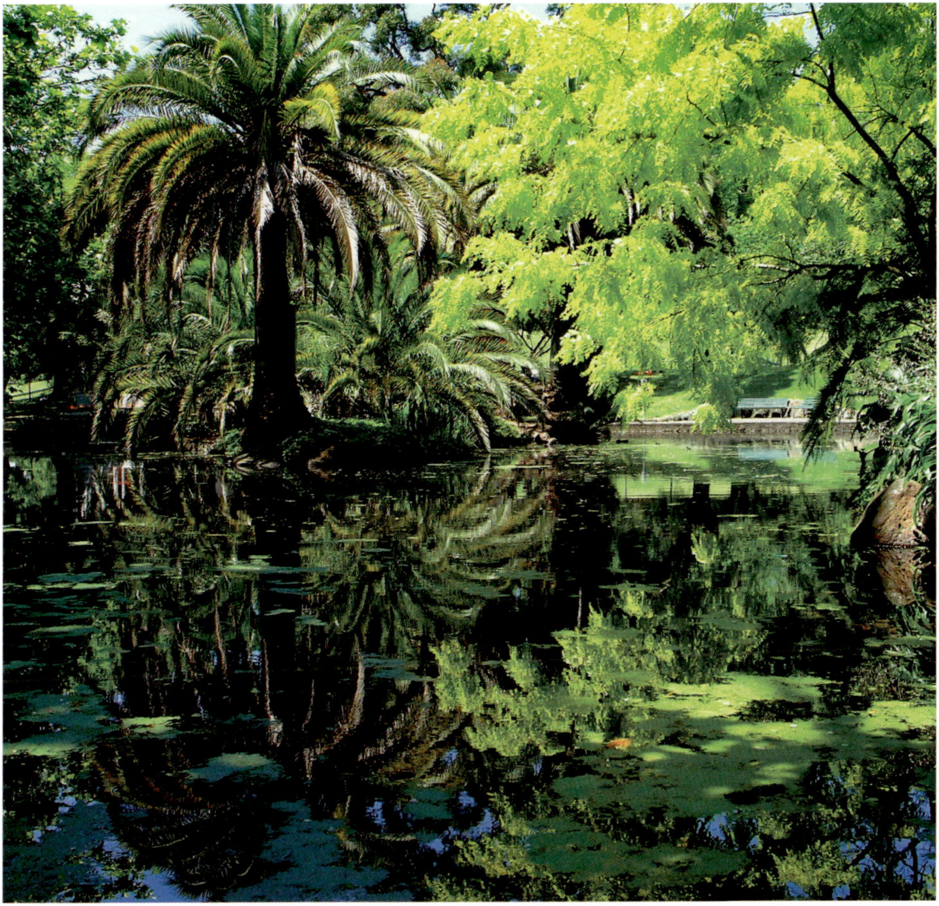

next page. alfred nicholas gardens

queen victoria gardens, melbourne

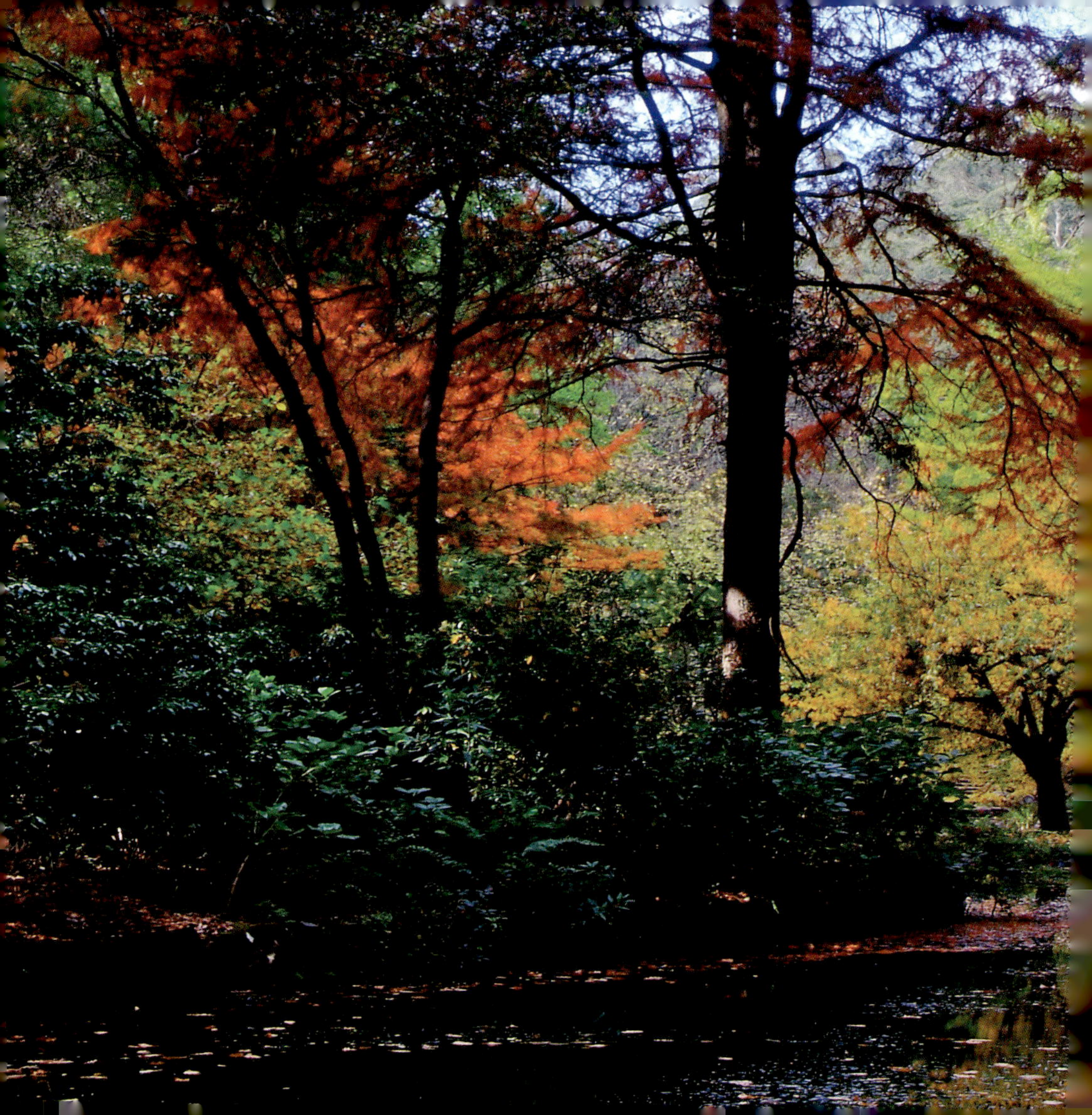

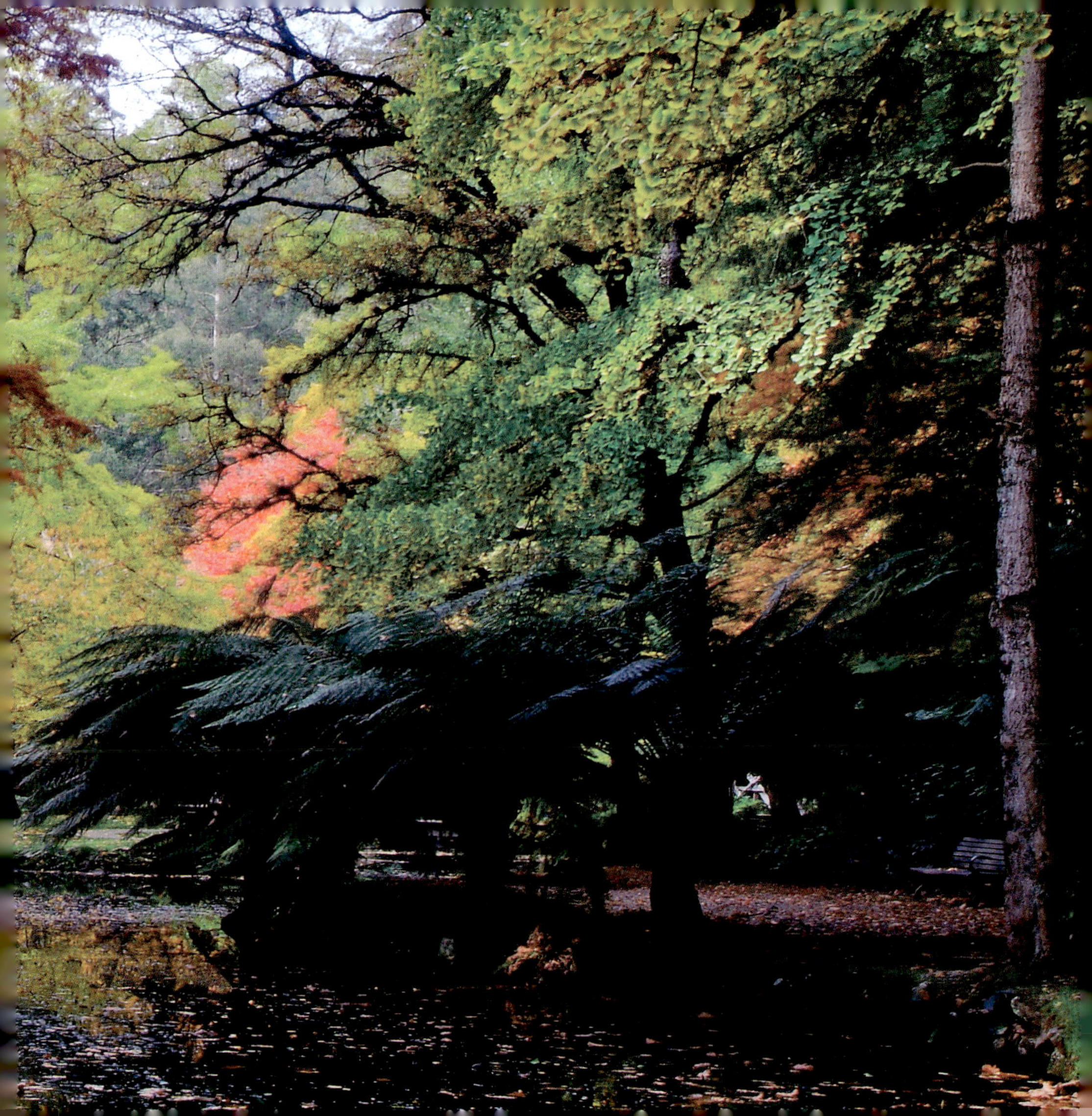

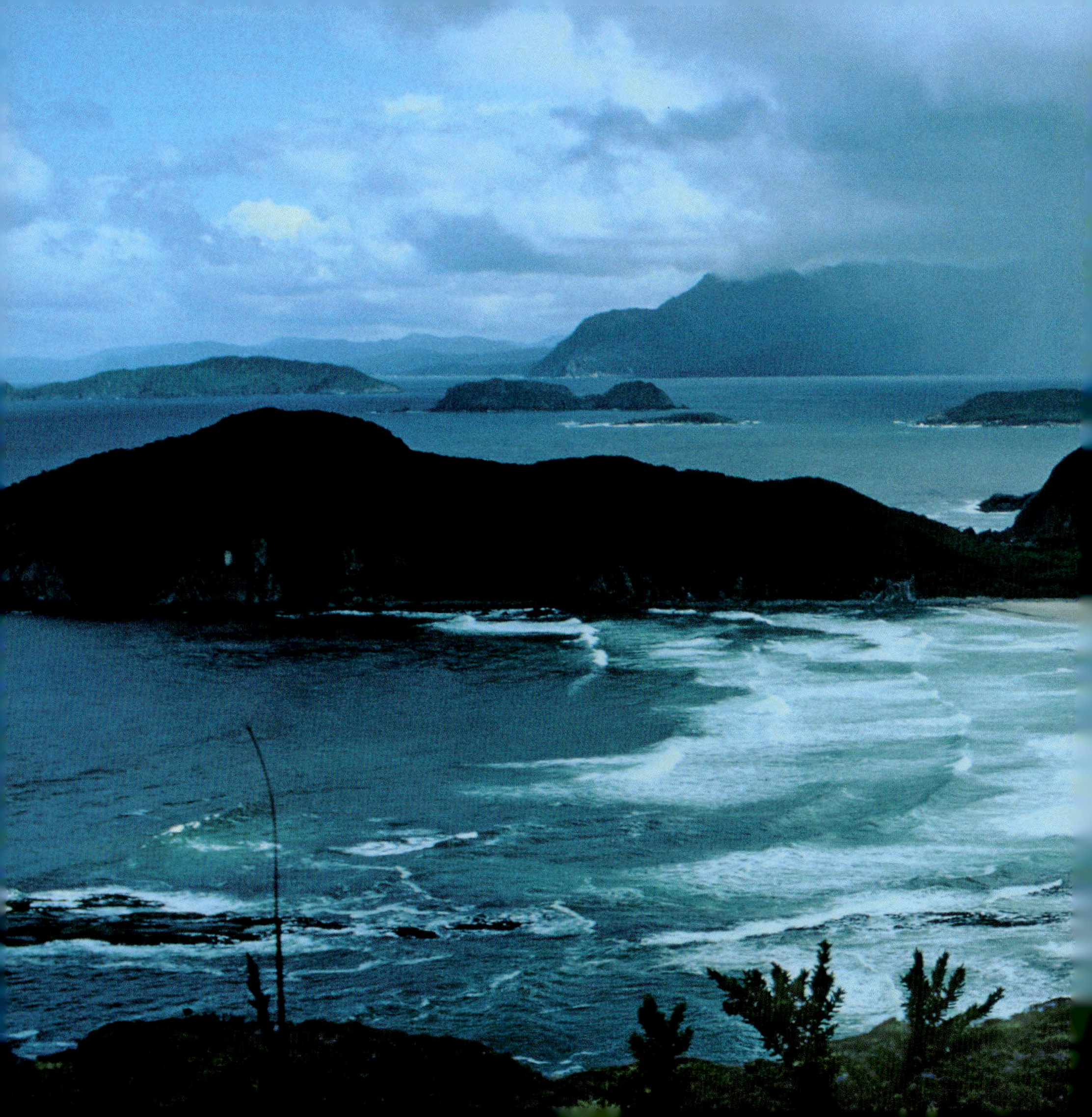

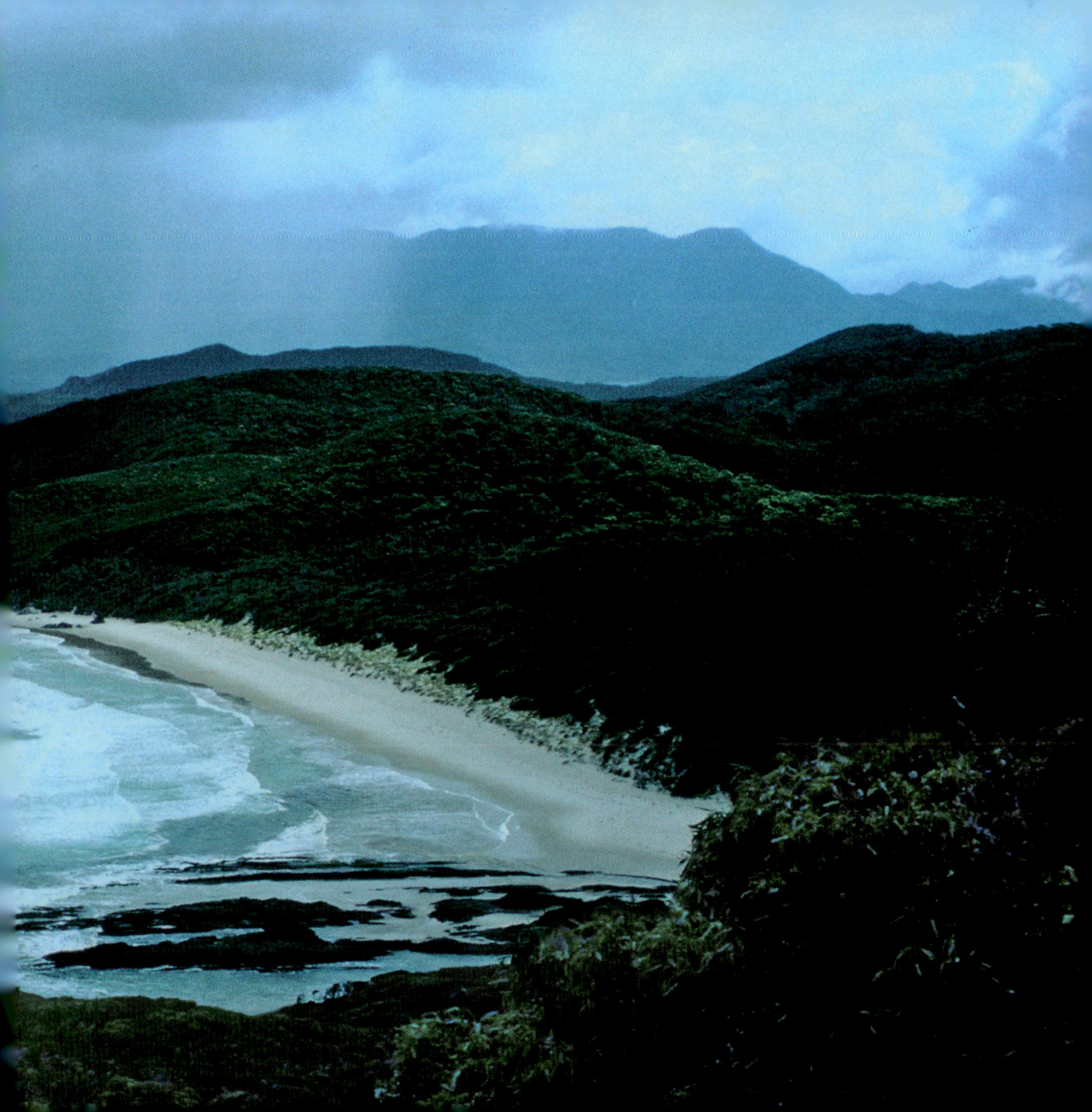

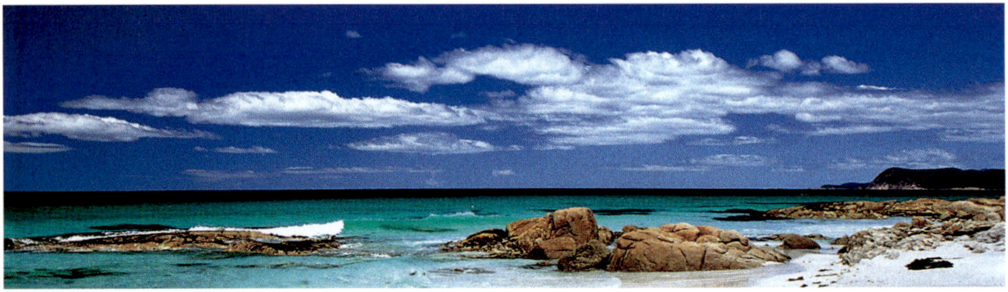

surprise beach, south coast of tasmania

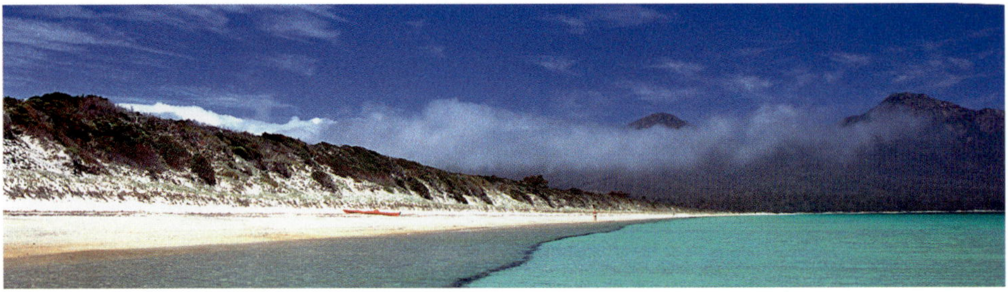

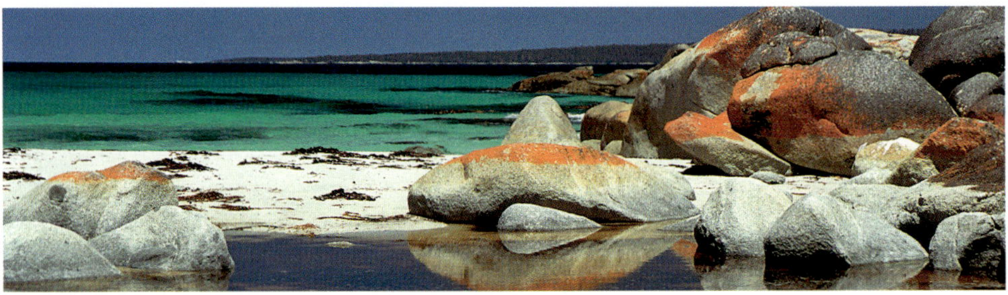

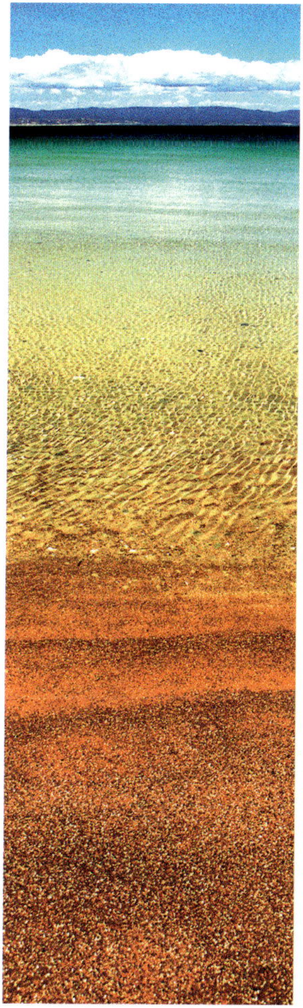
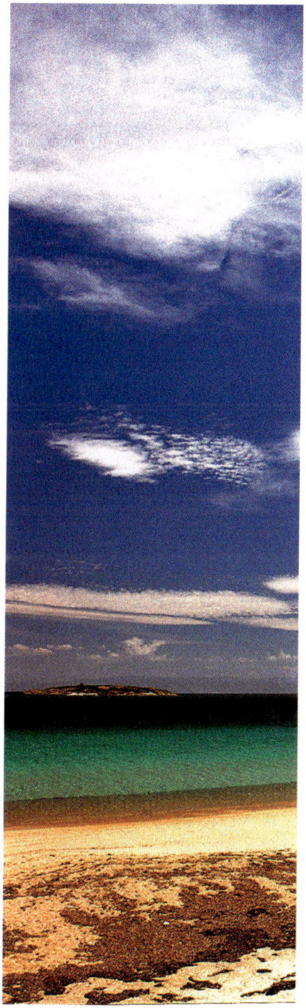
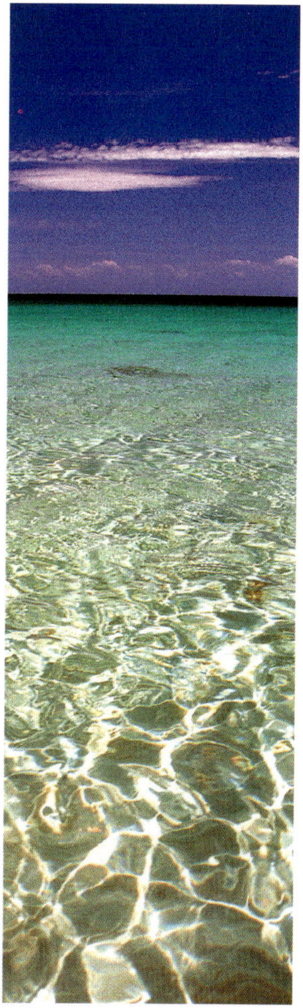

next page. cradle mountain, tasmania

east coast tasmania

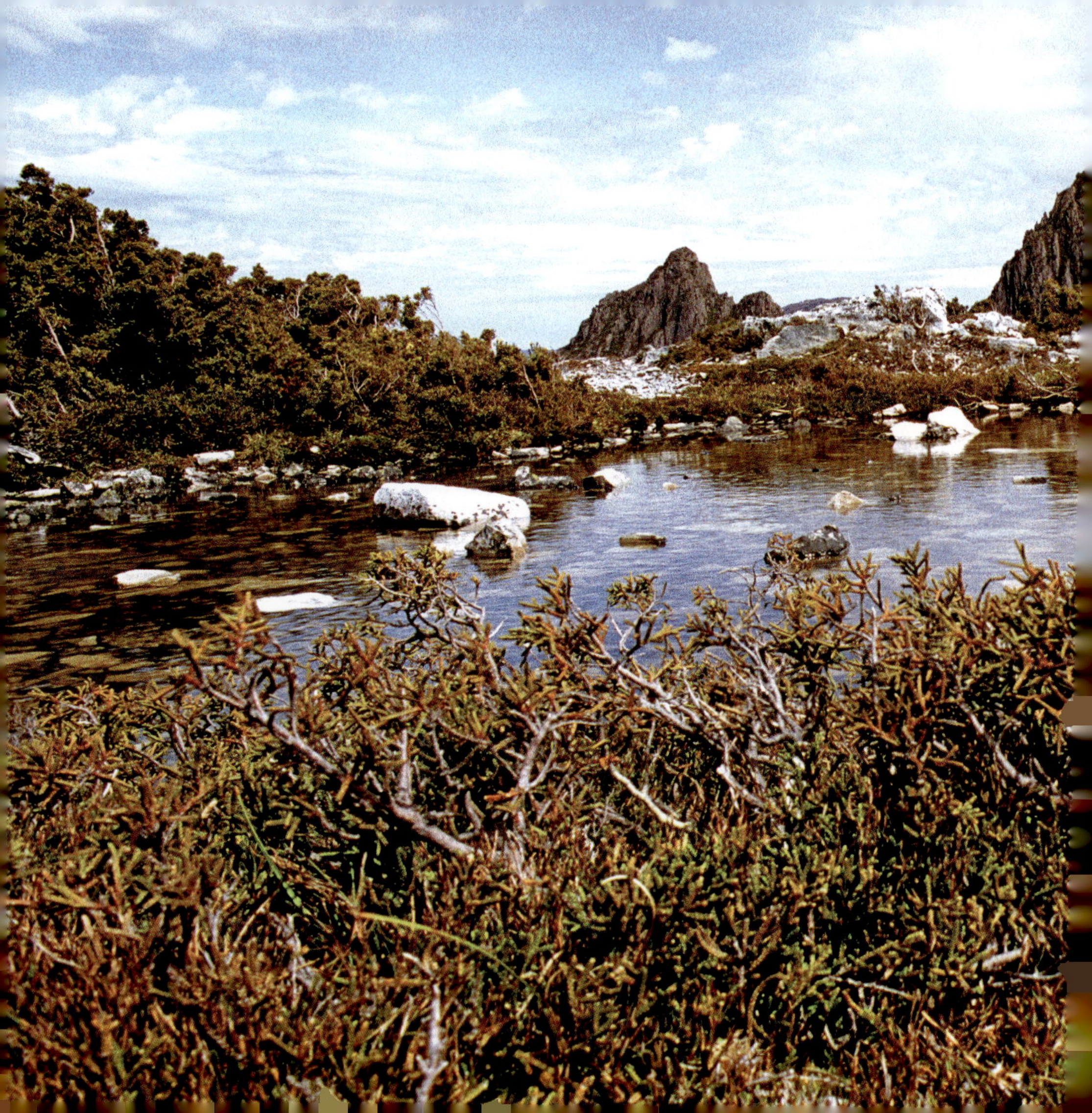

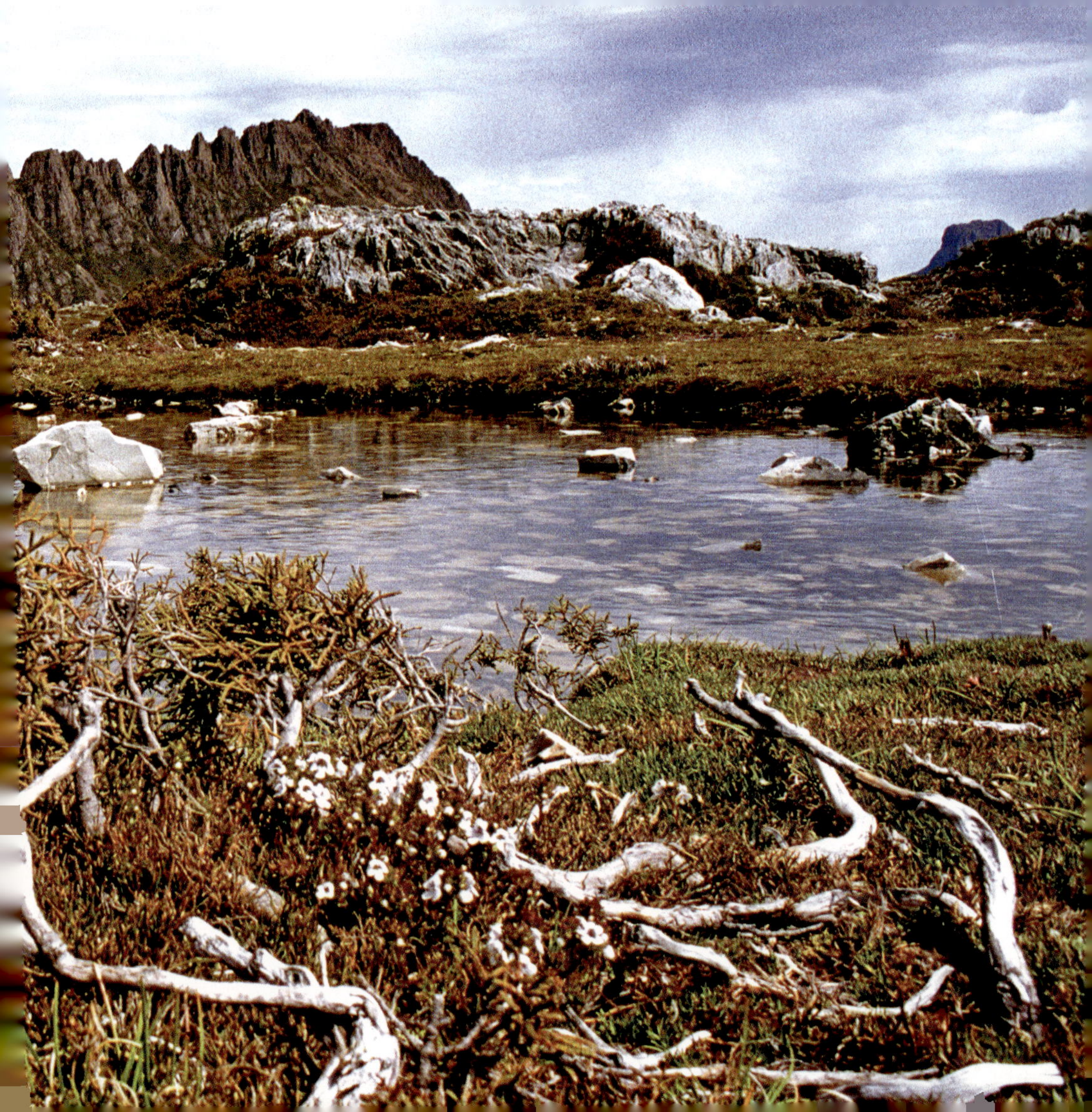

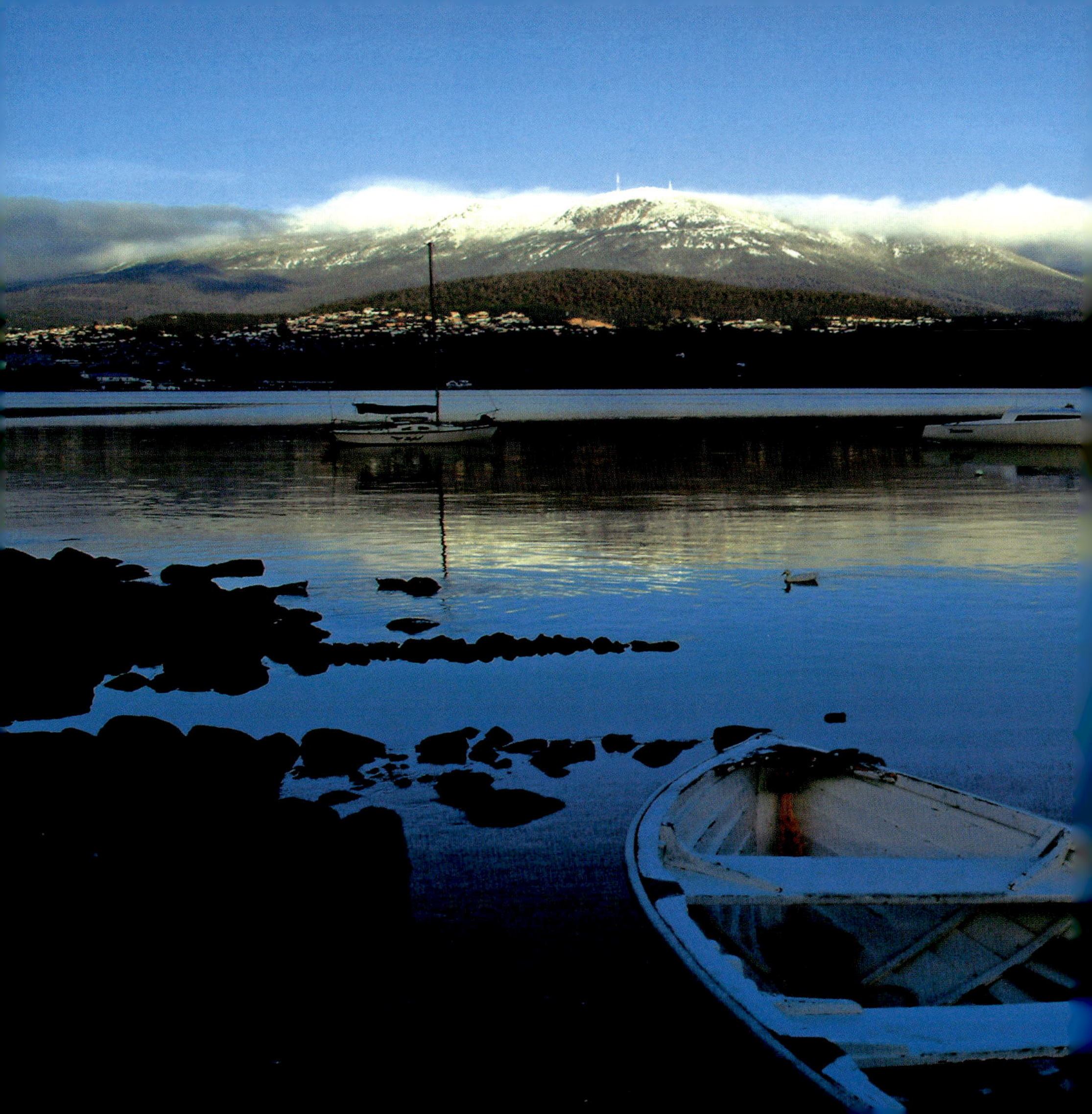

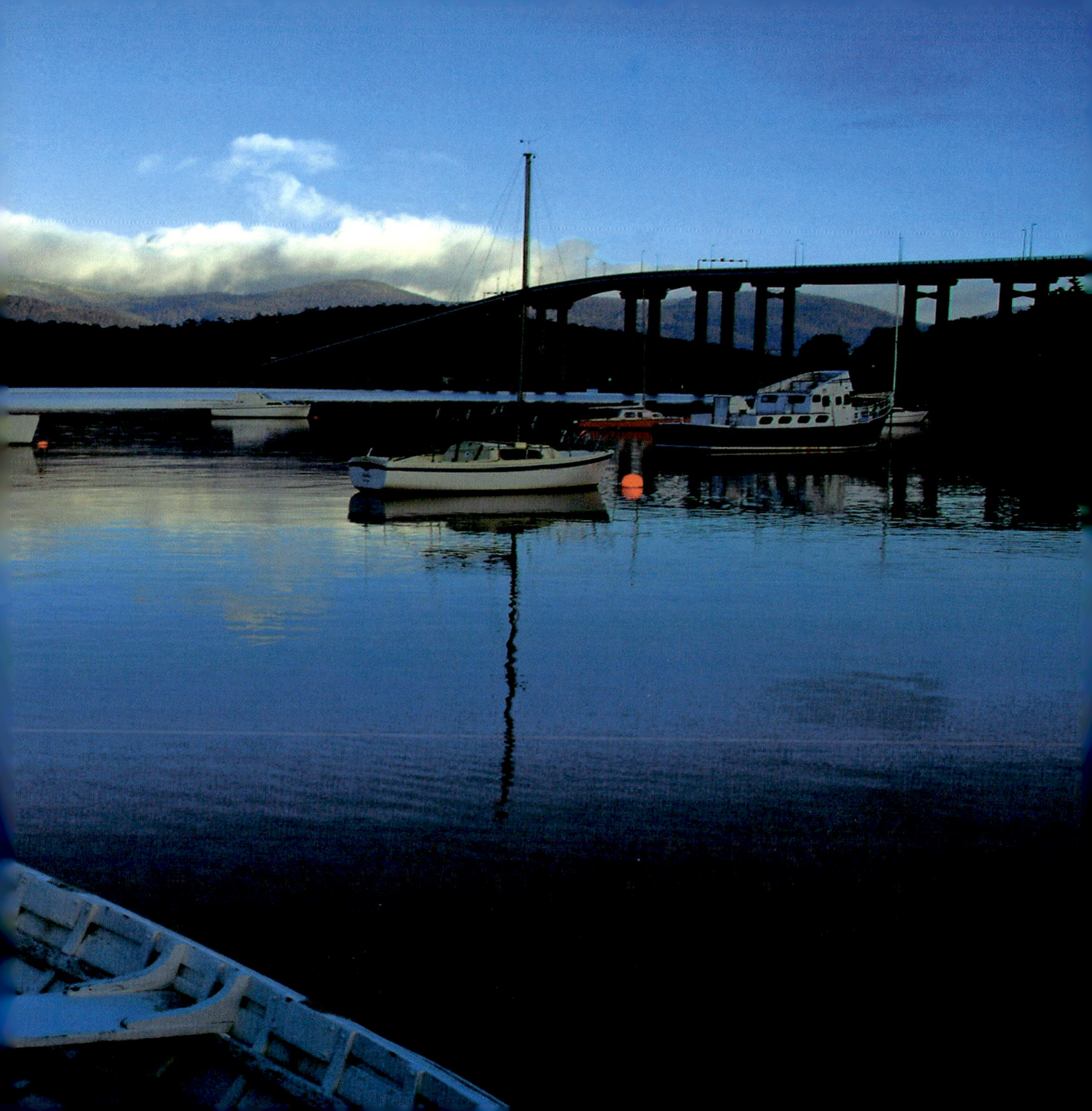

previous page. derwent river, hobart, tasmania

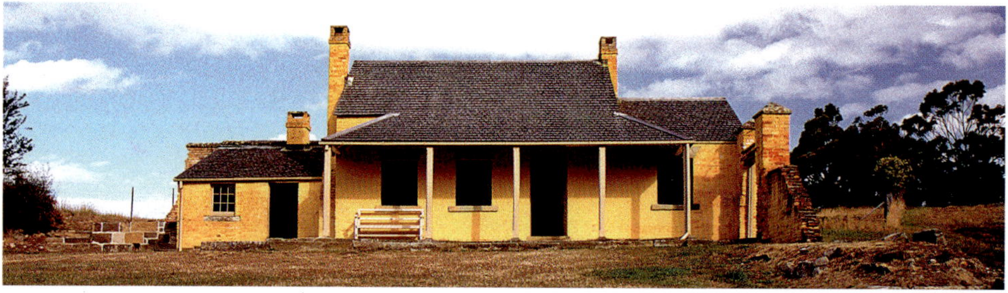

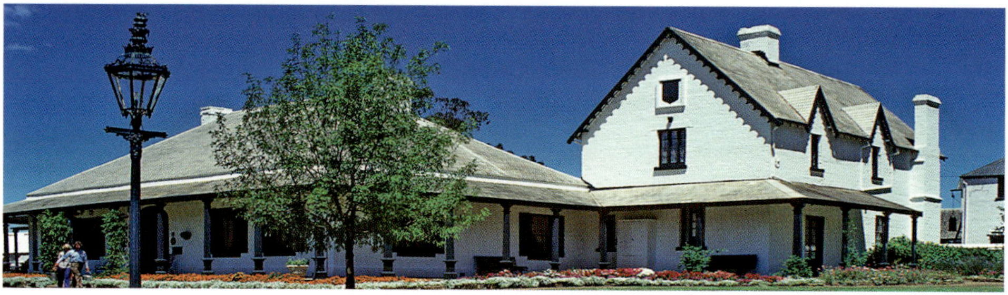

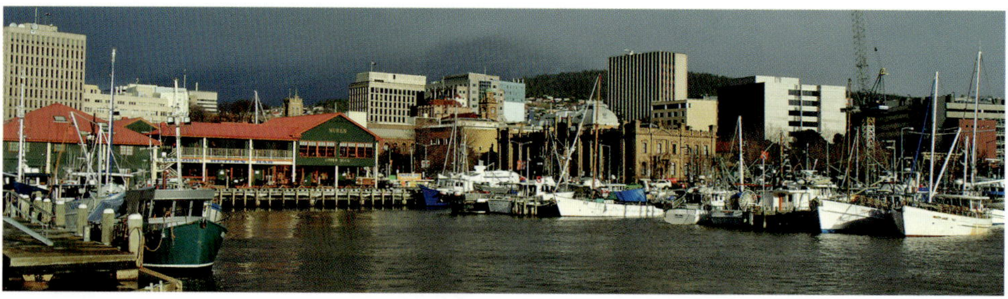

 a. port arthur b. entally house c. constitution dock, tasmania

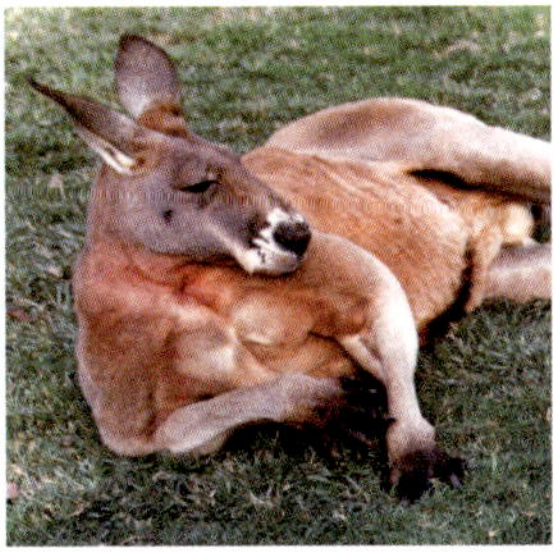
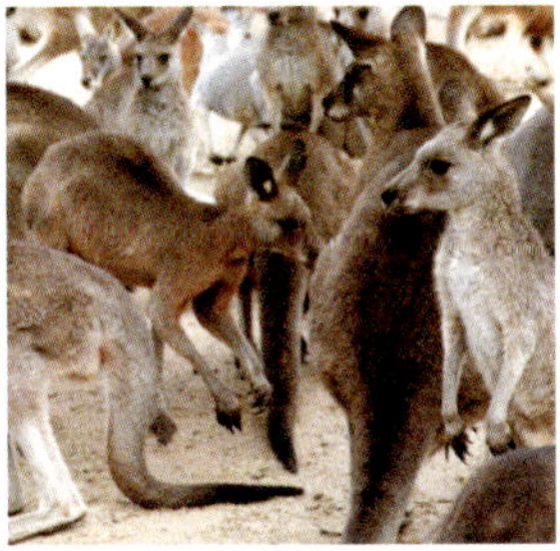
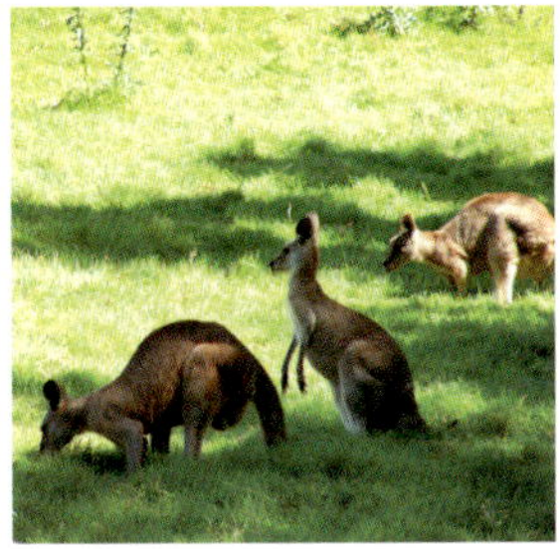
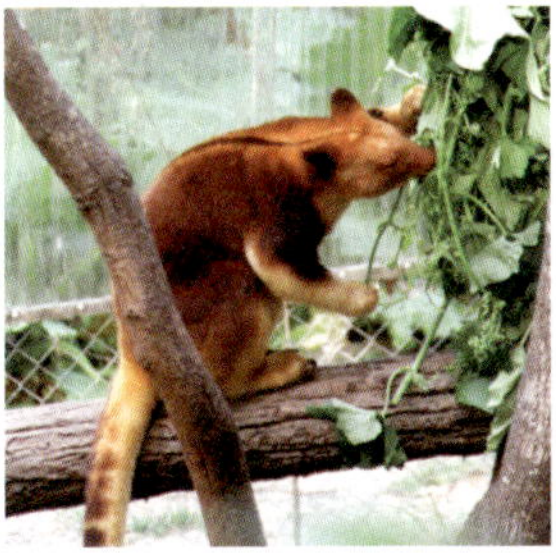
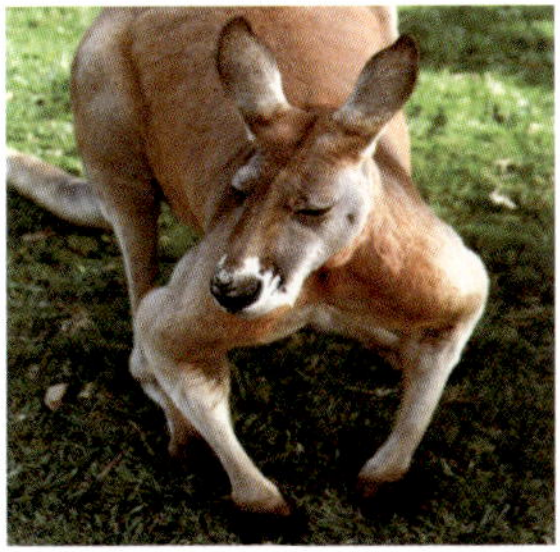
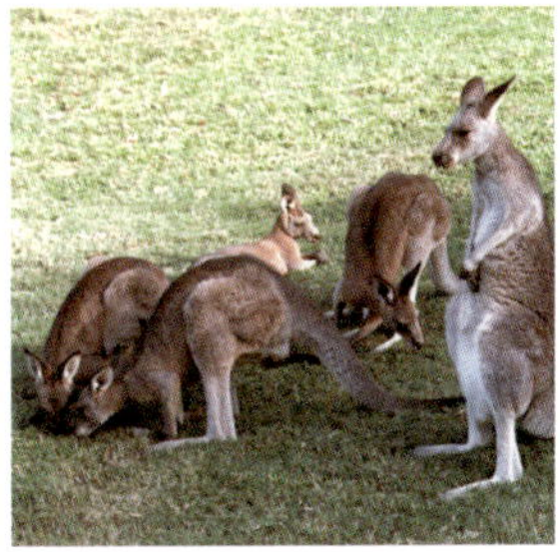
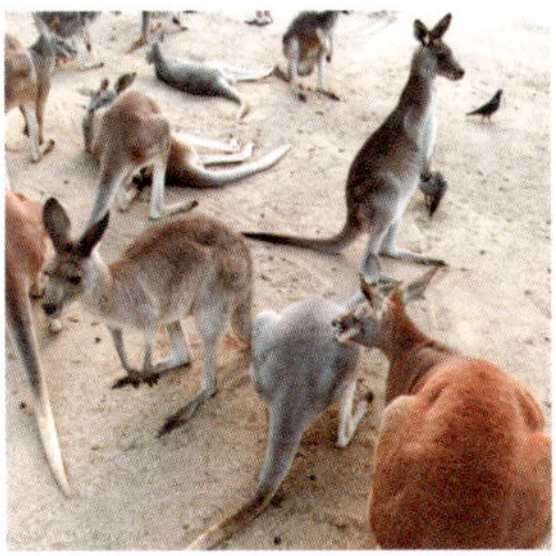
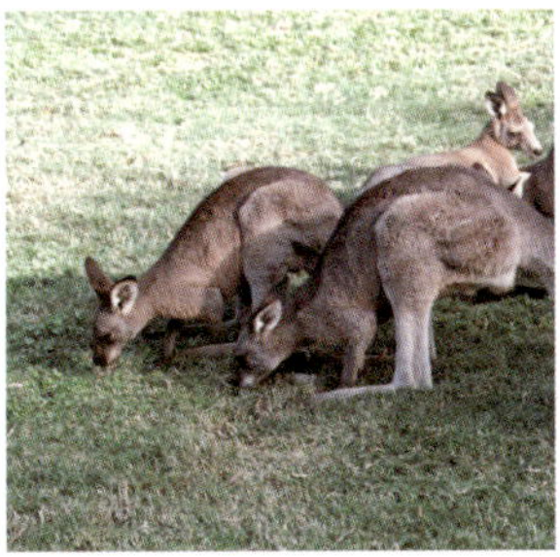
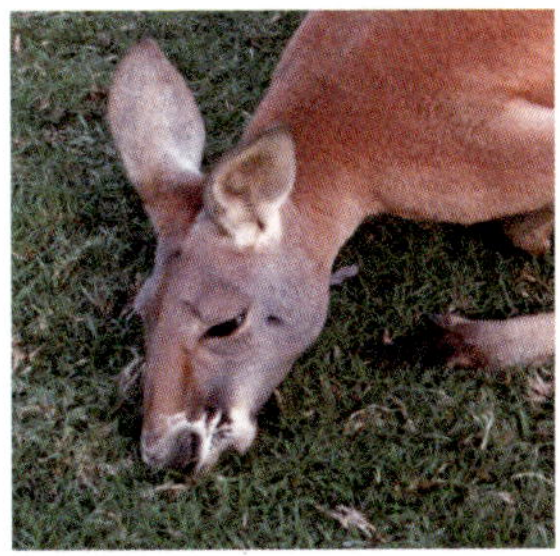

next page. kangaroos on top of mount anslie, canberra. following page. canberra

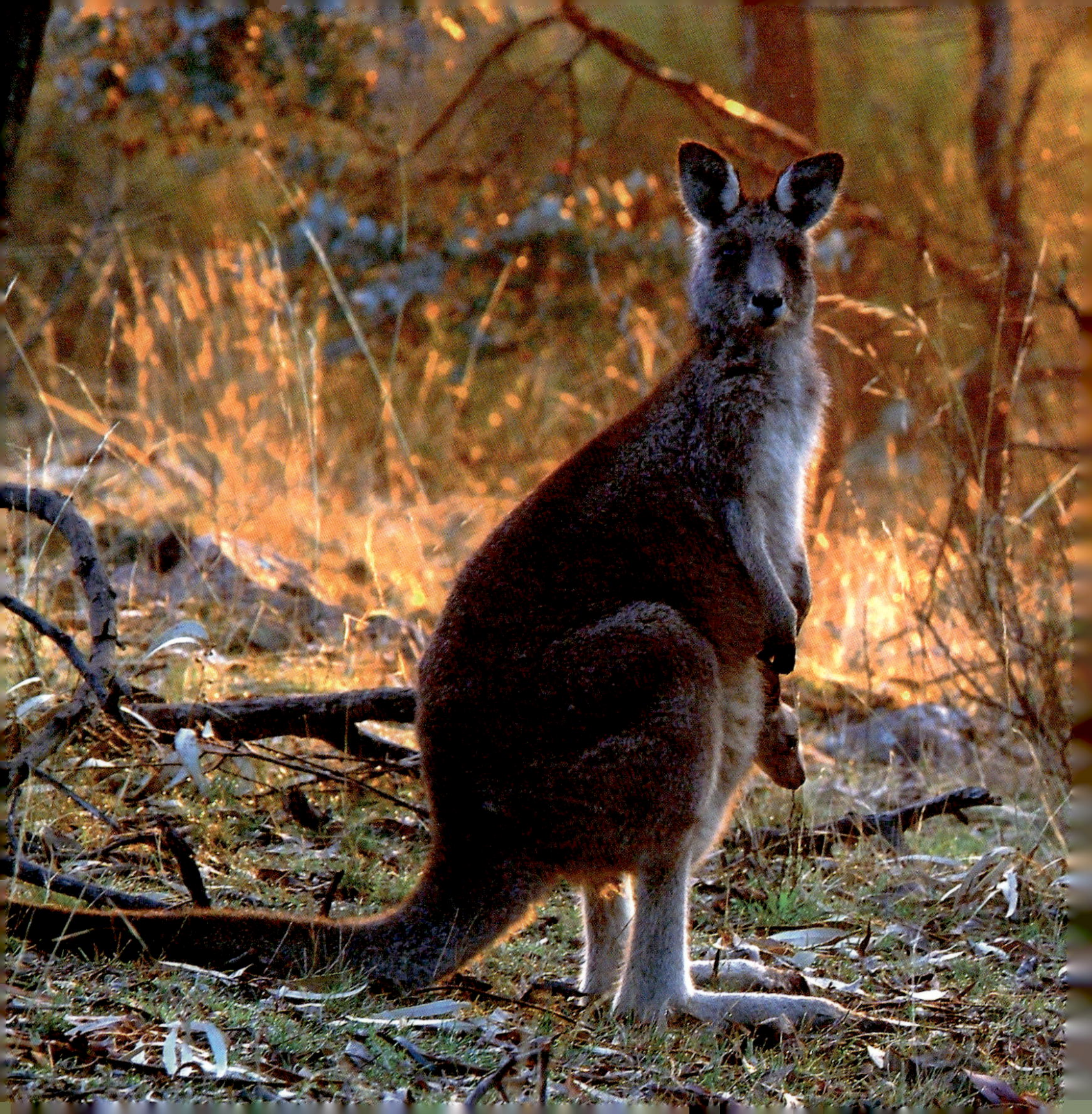

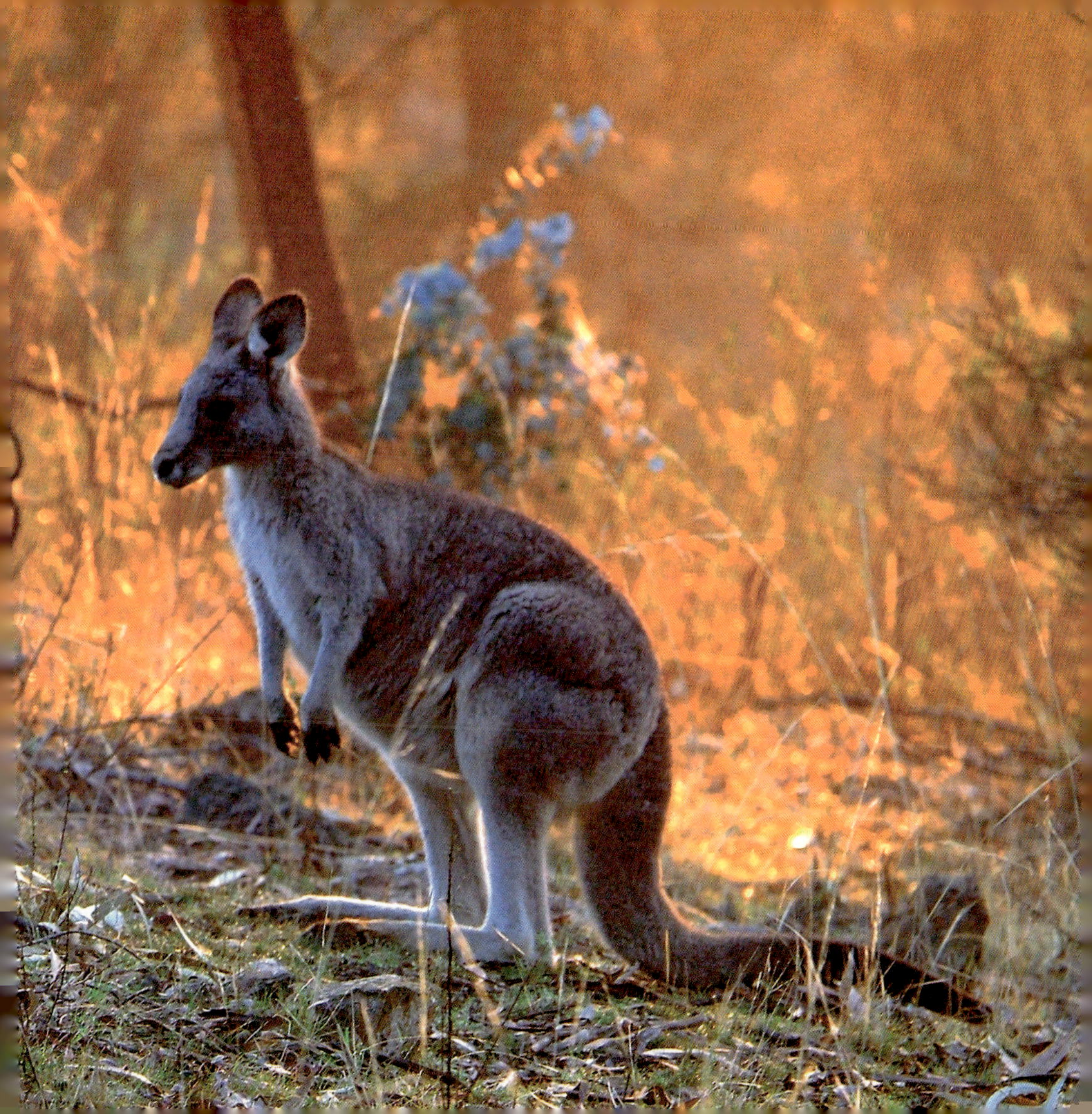

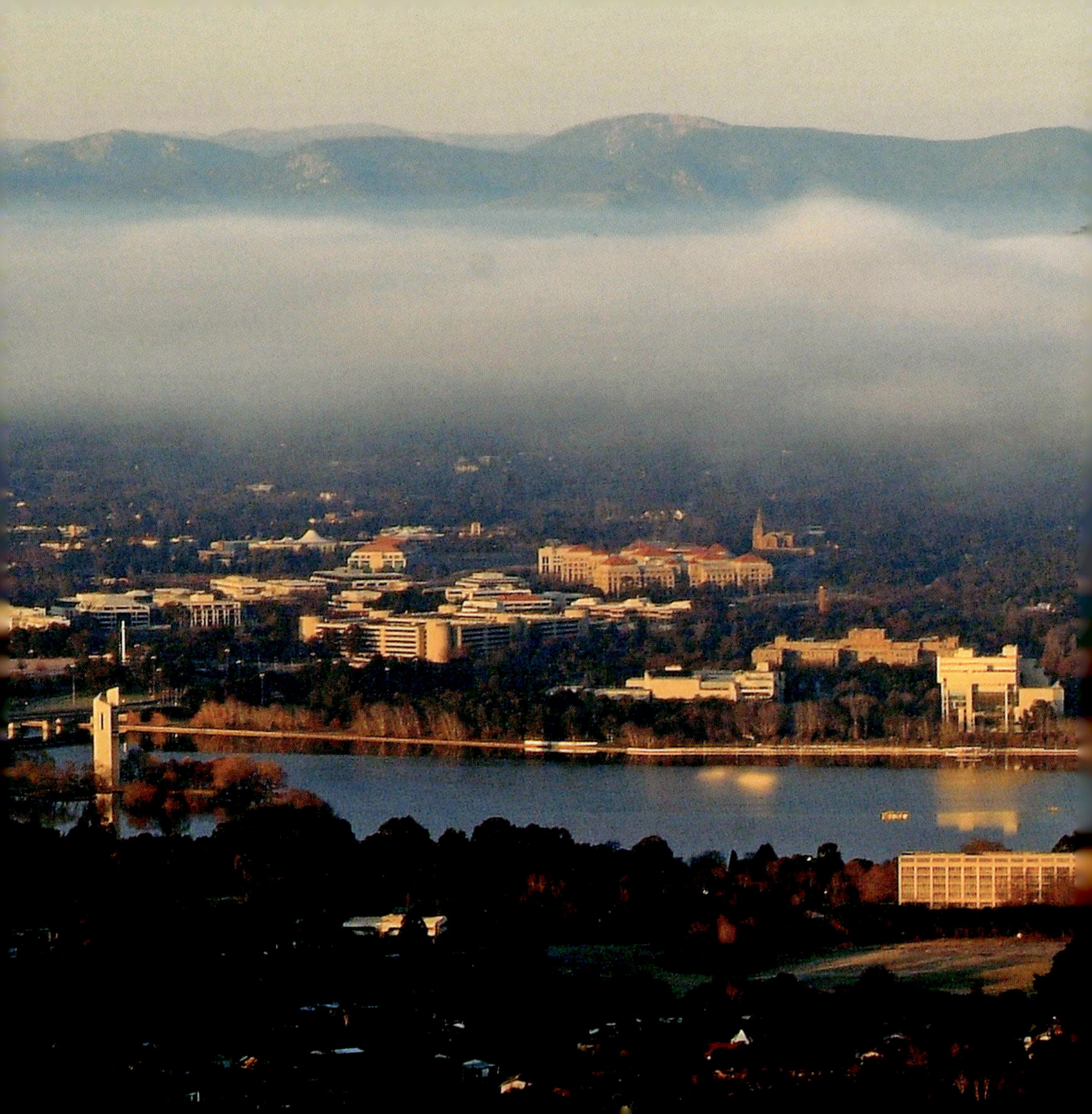

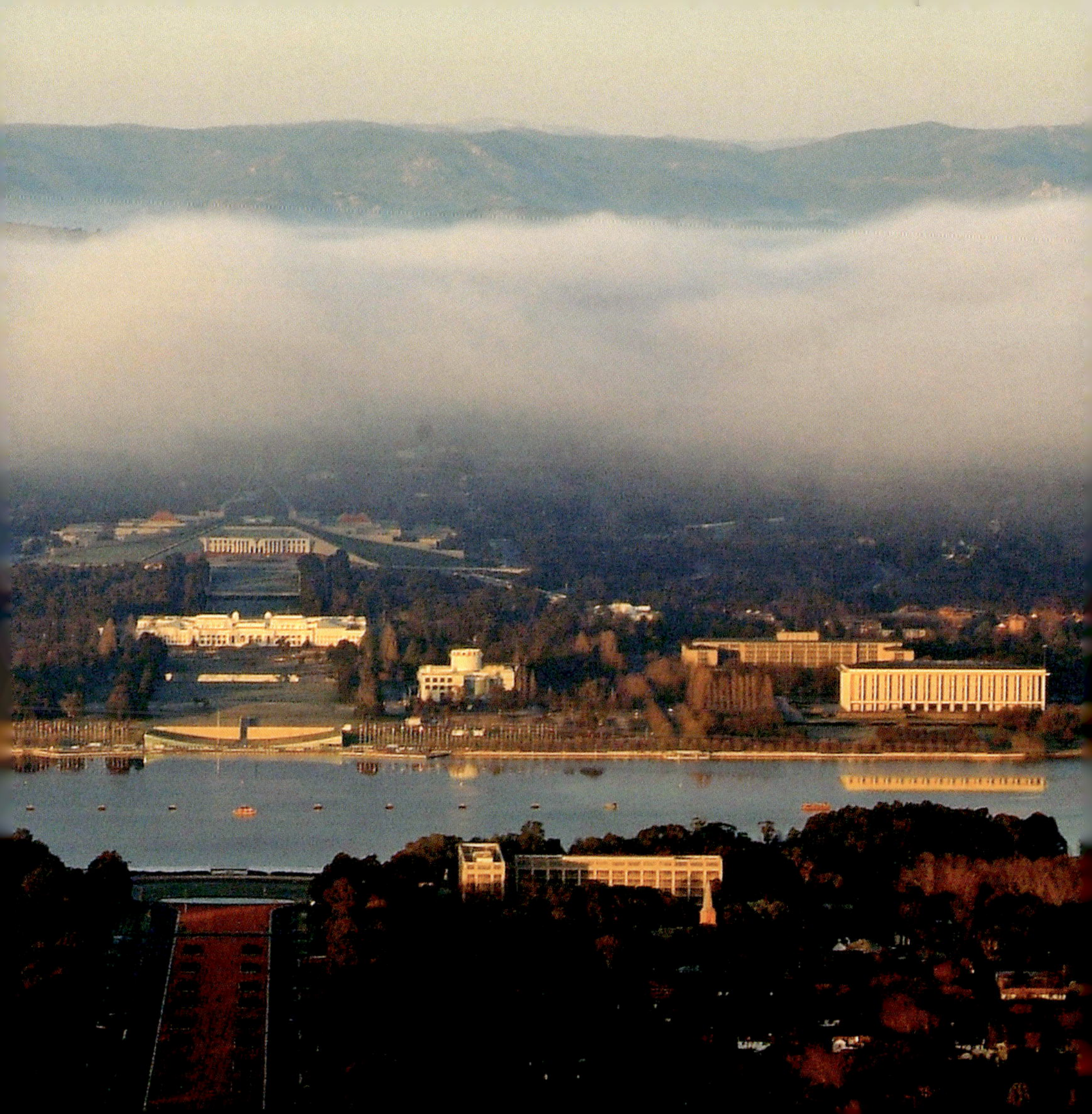

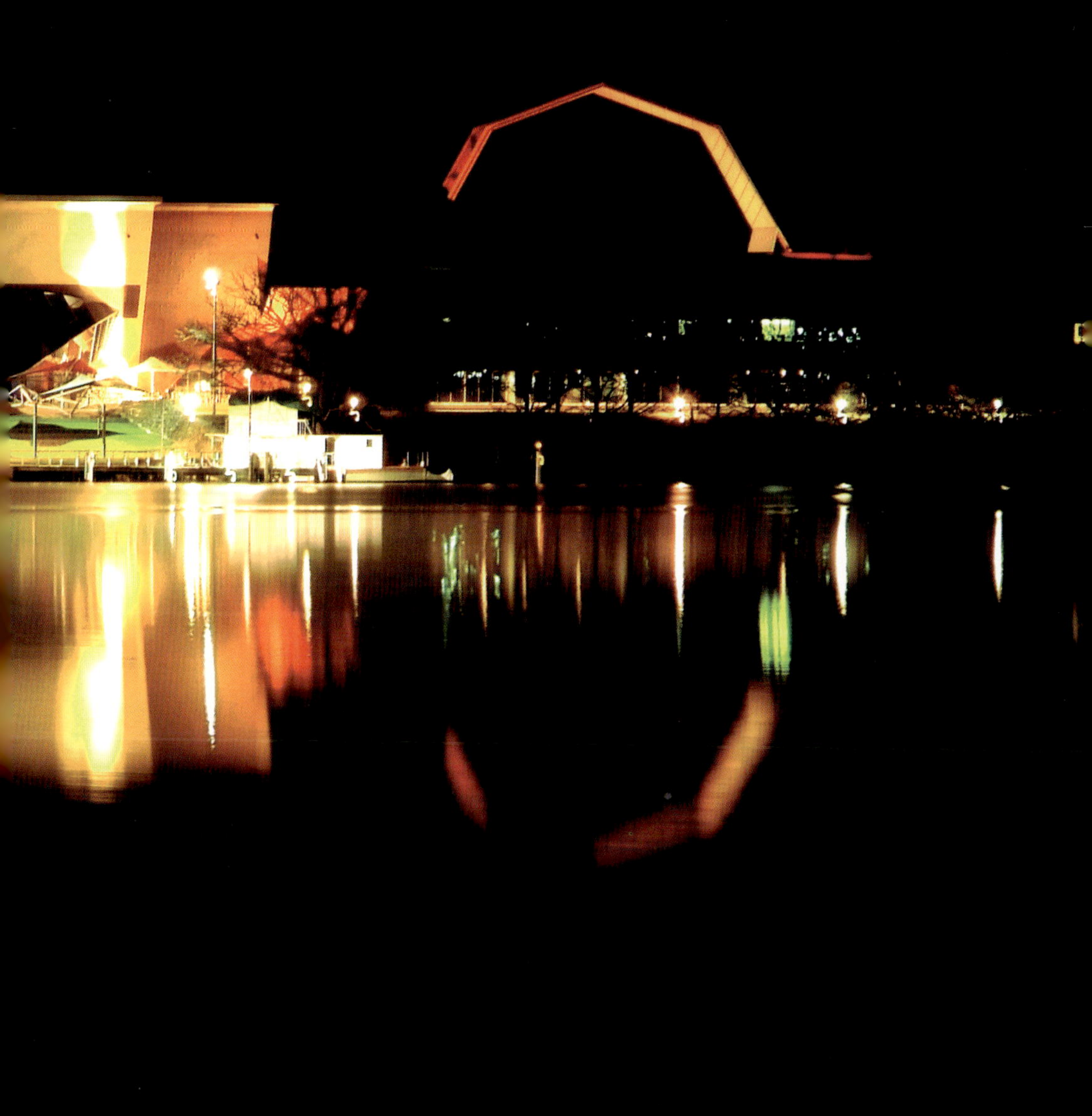

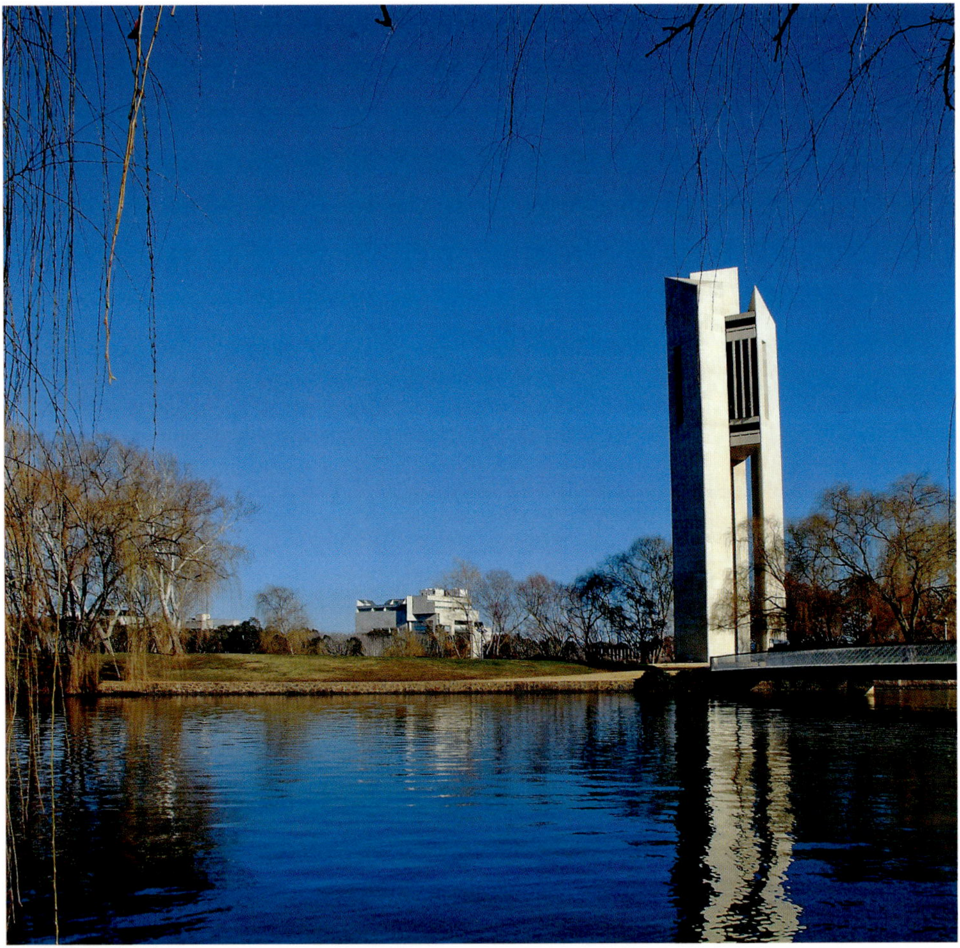

previous page. australian museum

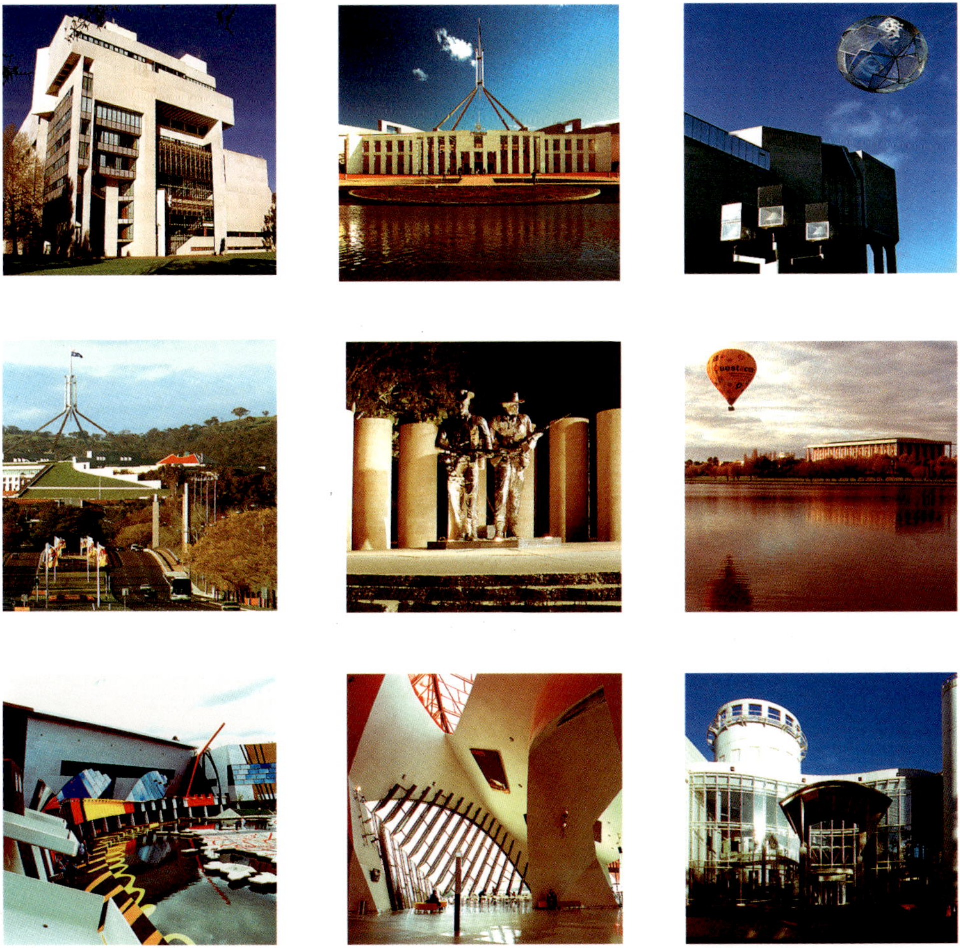

a. high court b. parliament house c. national art gallery d. commonwealth avenue e. anzac memorial f. national library g&h. national museum i. questacom, canberra

next page. lake burley griffin, camberra

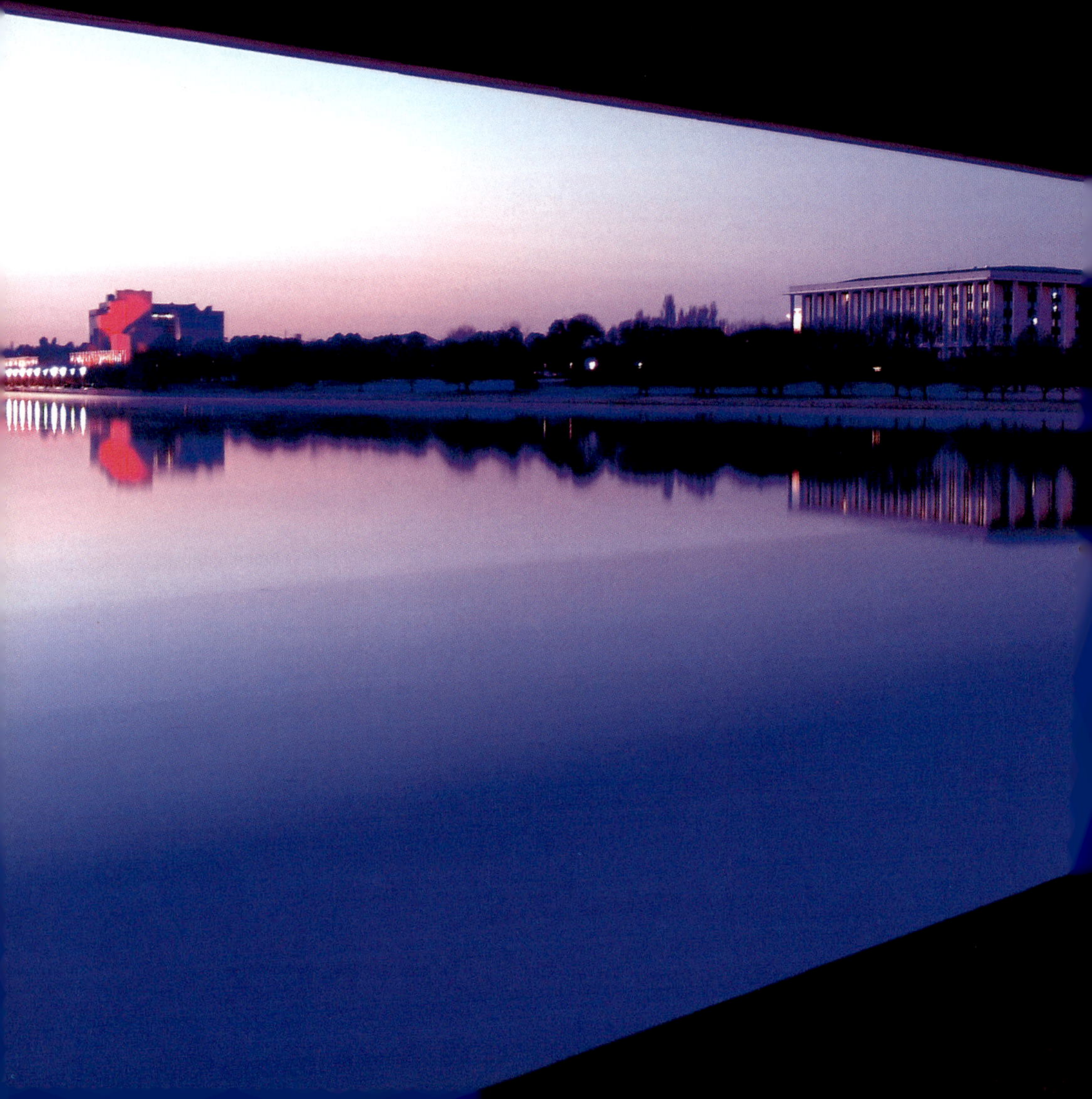

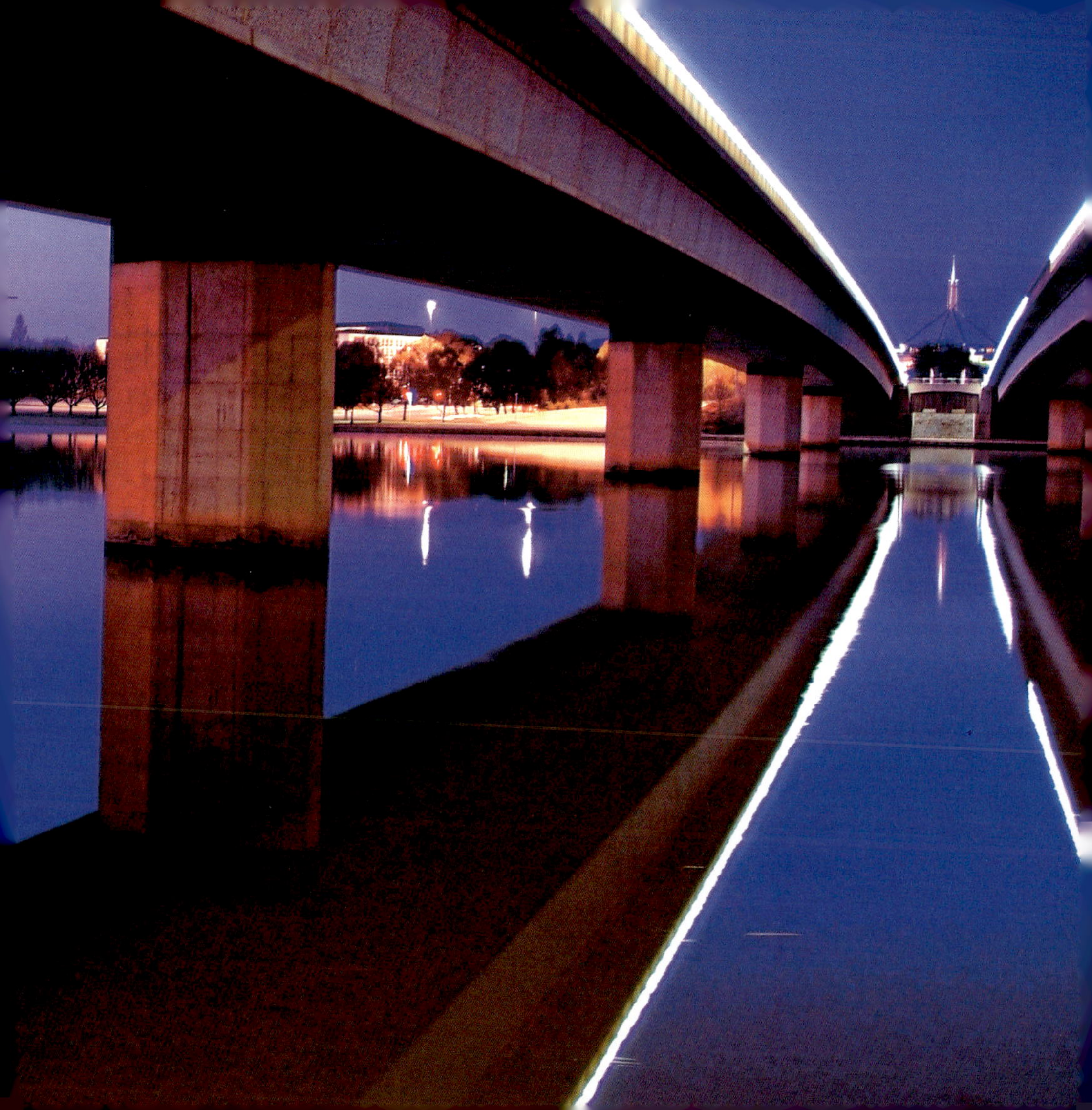

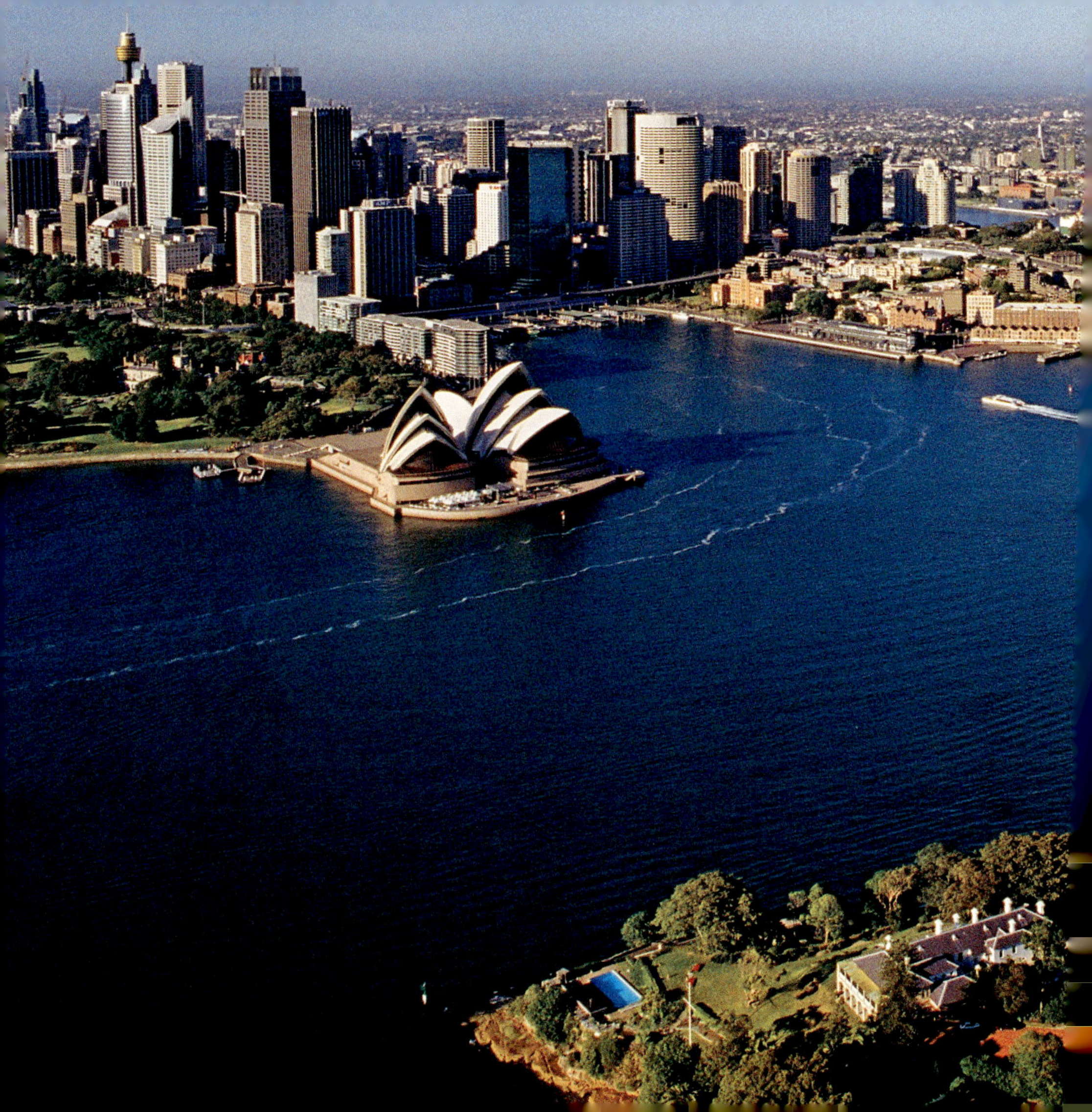

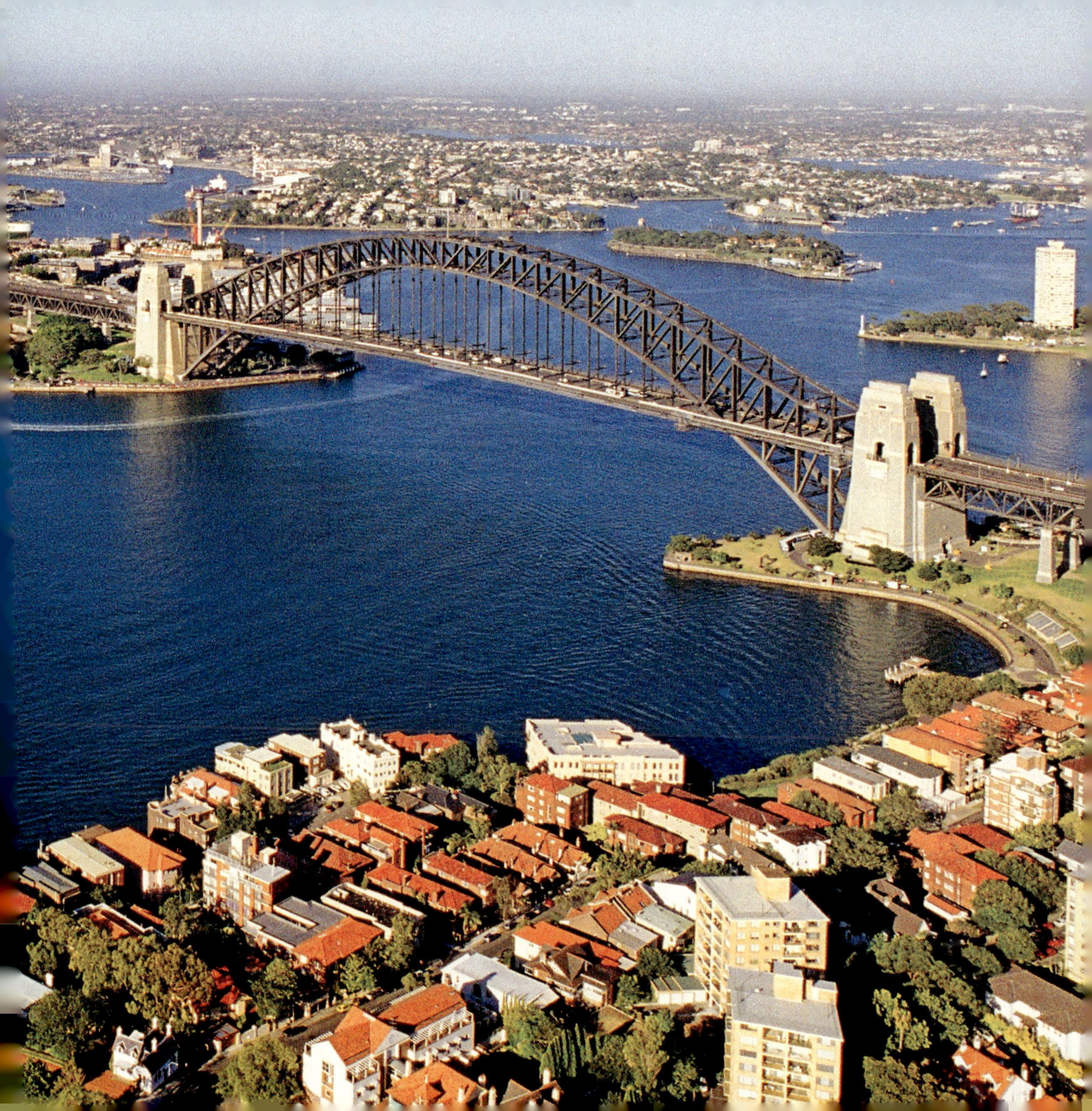

previous page. sydney viewed from kirribilli

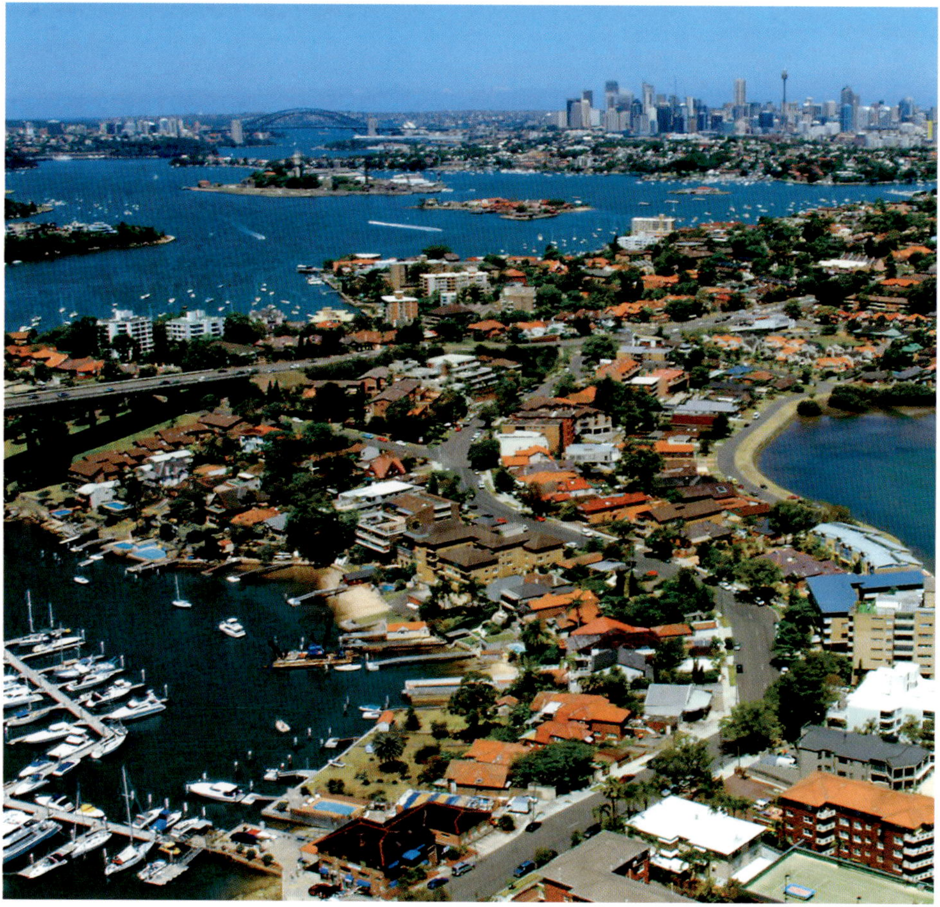

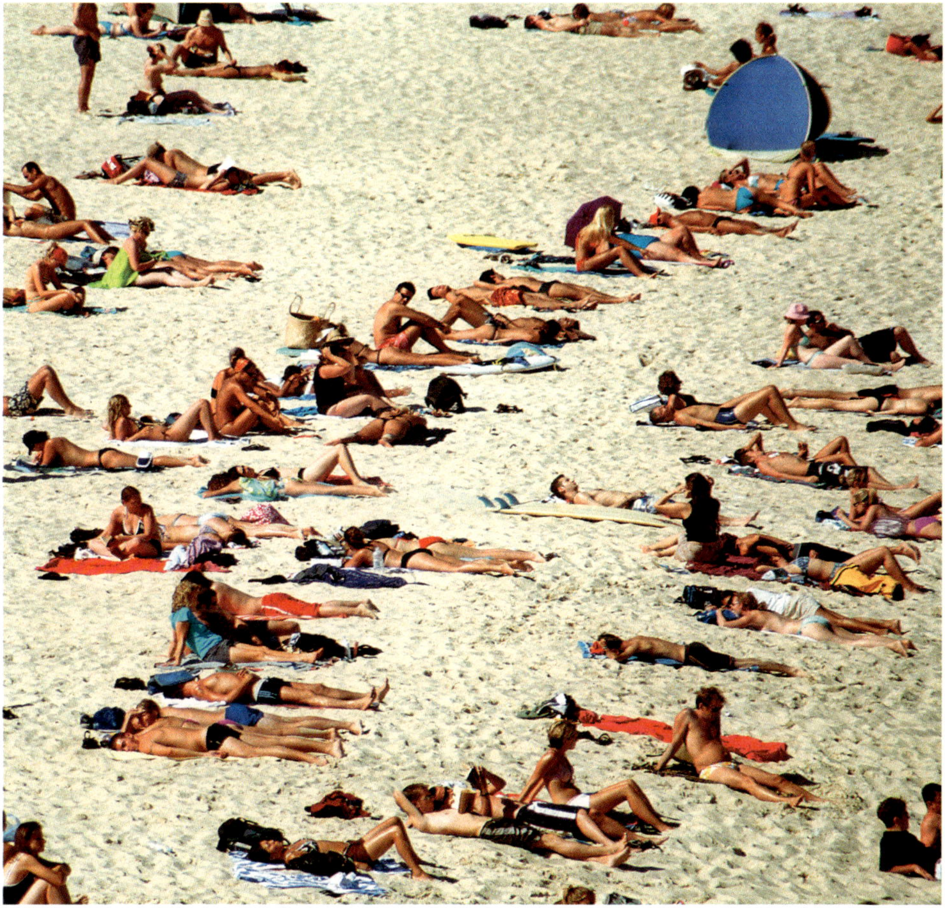

next page. darling harbour, sydney

bondi beach

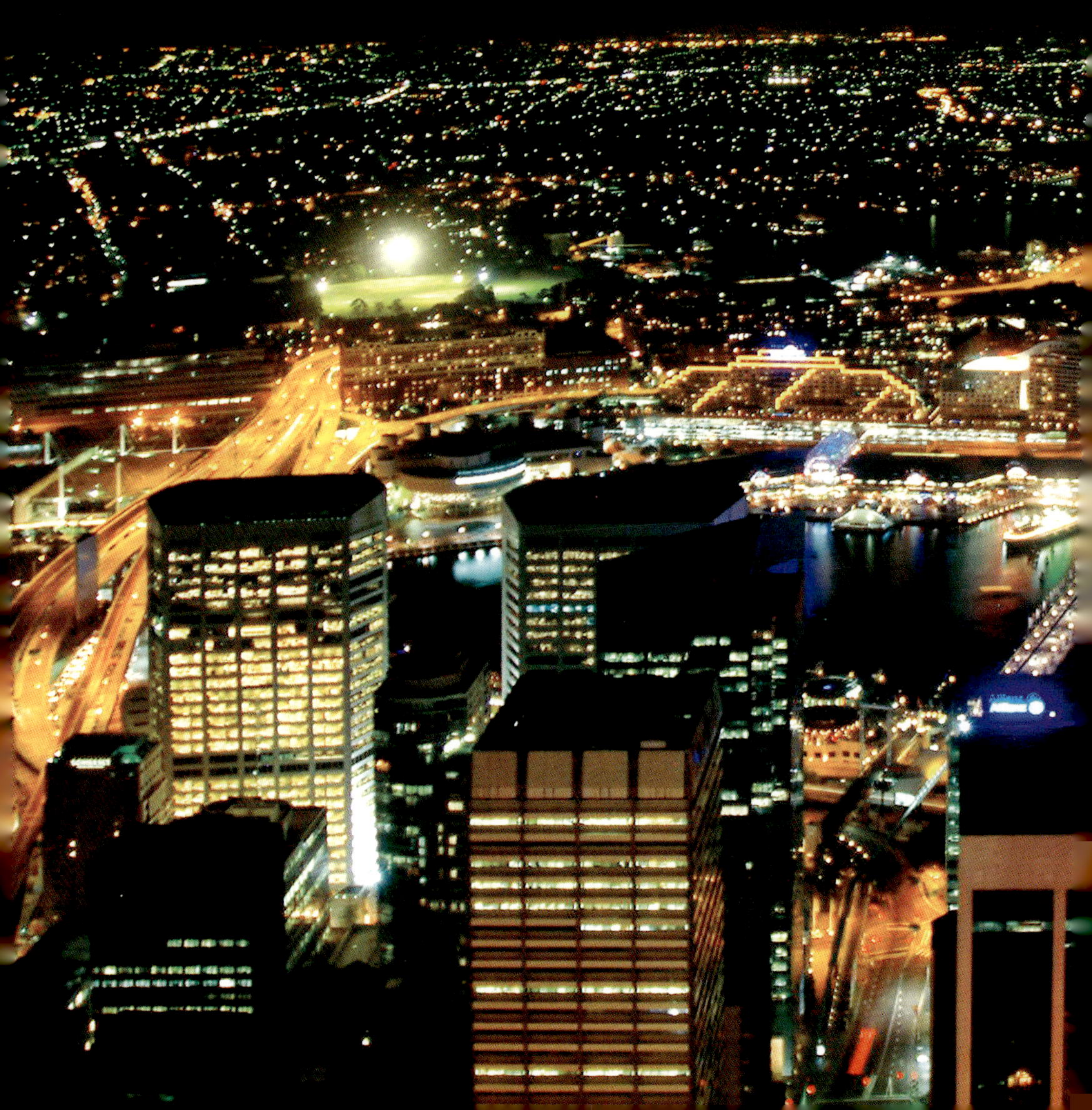

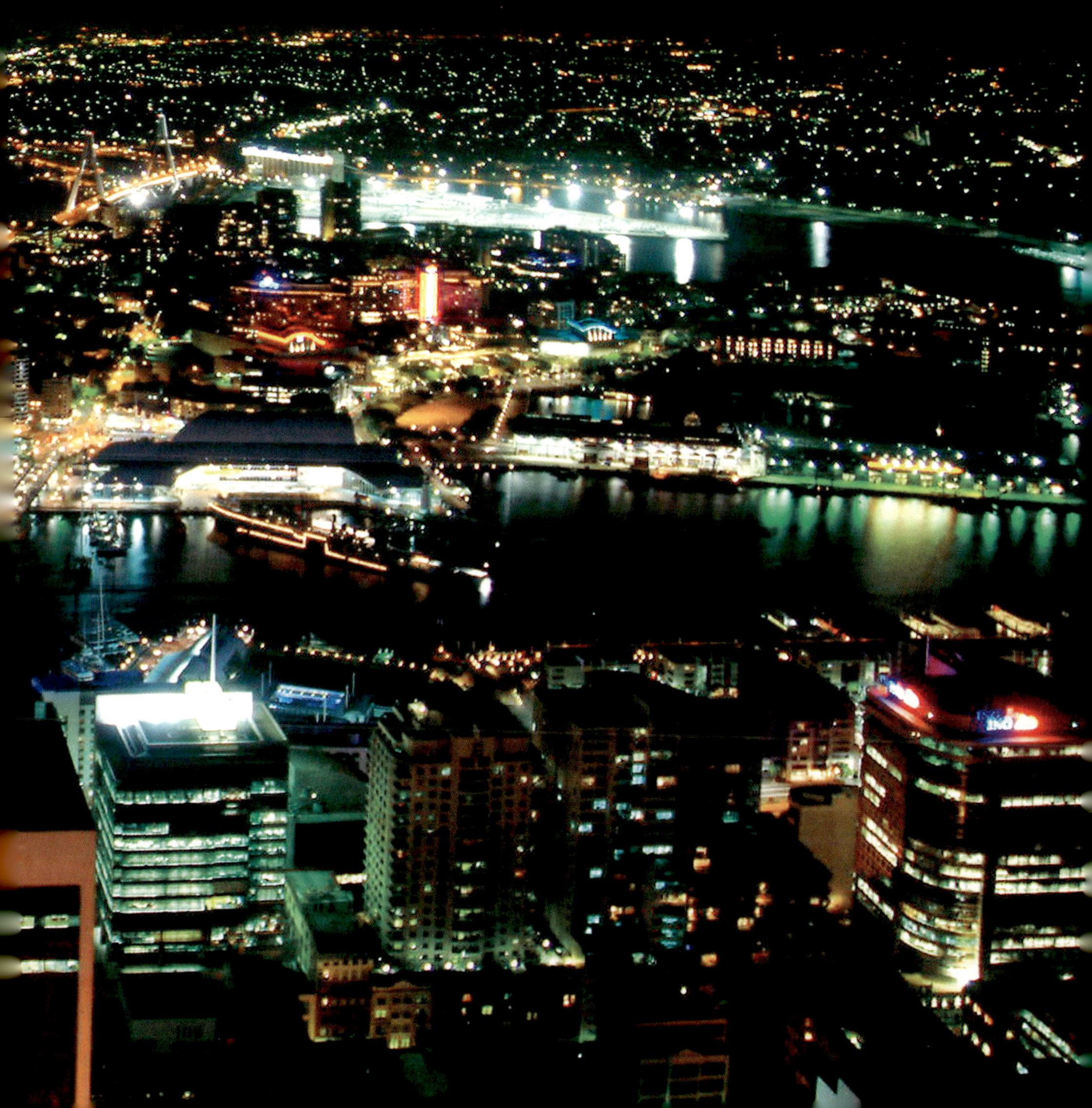

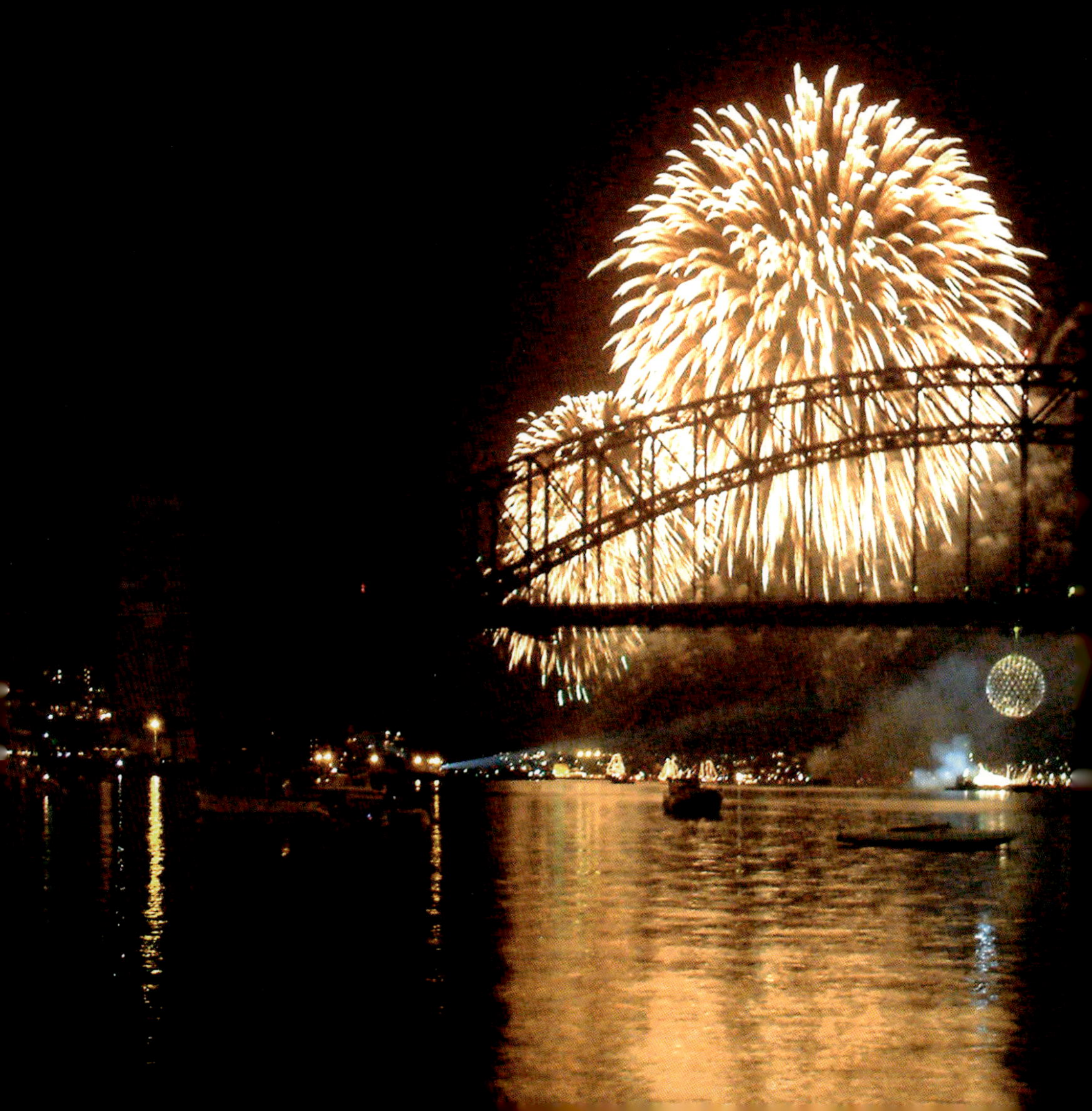

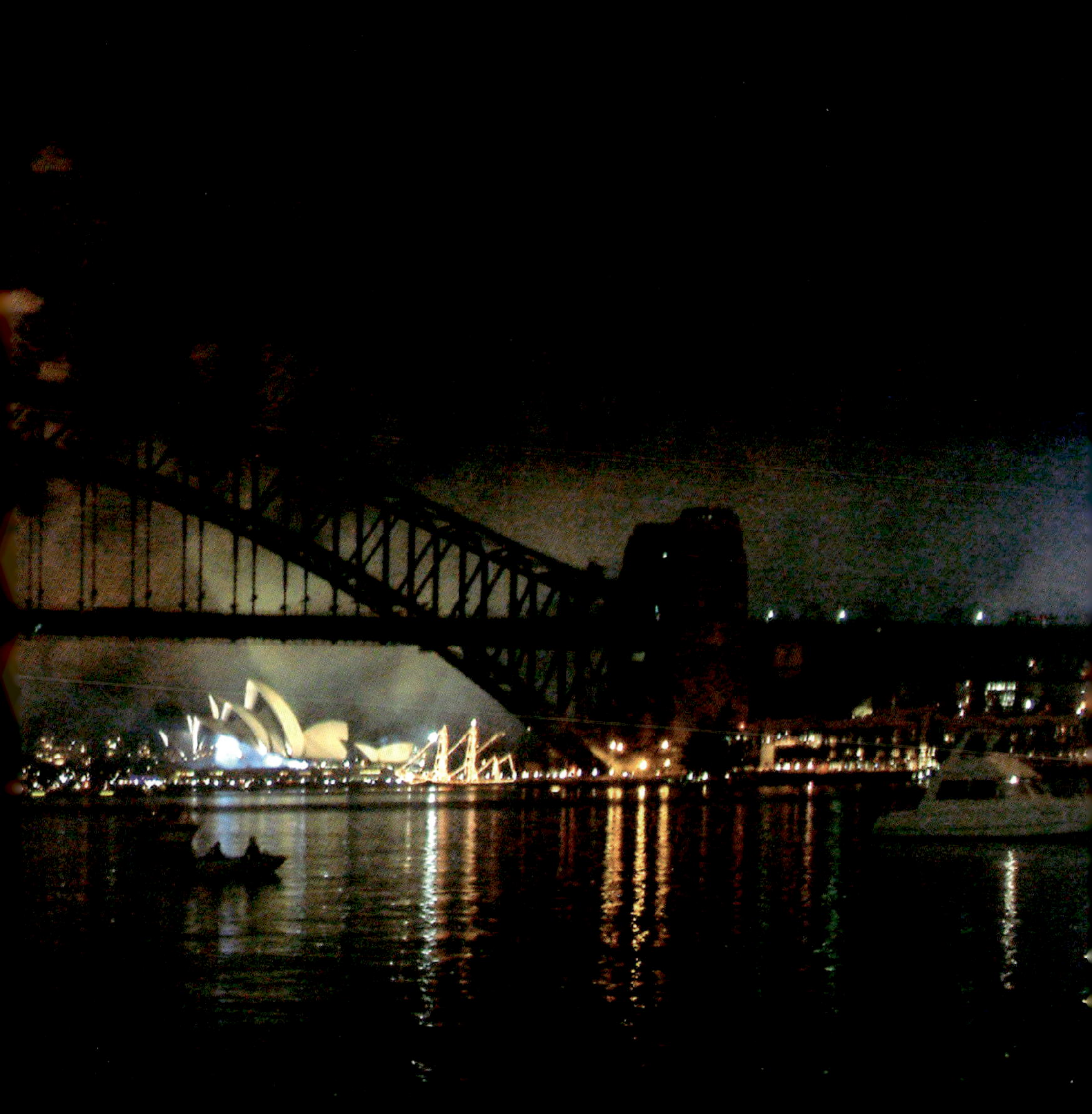

previous page. new year's eve sydney harbour

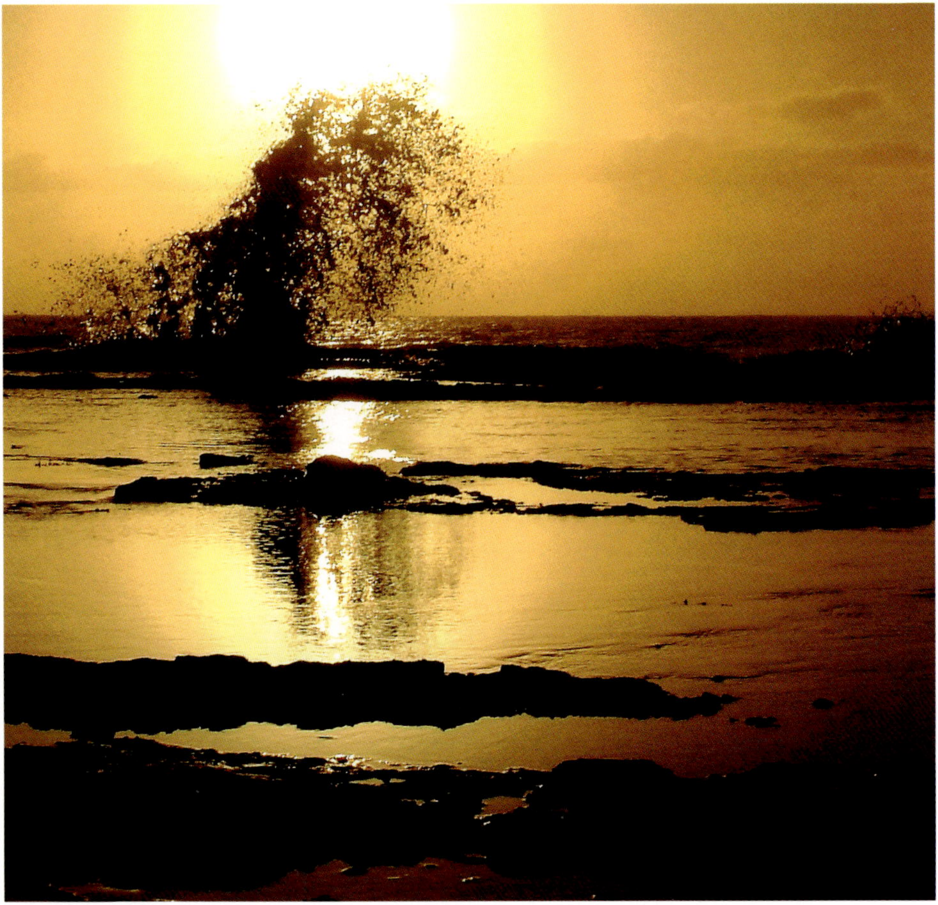

narrabeen head

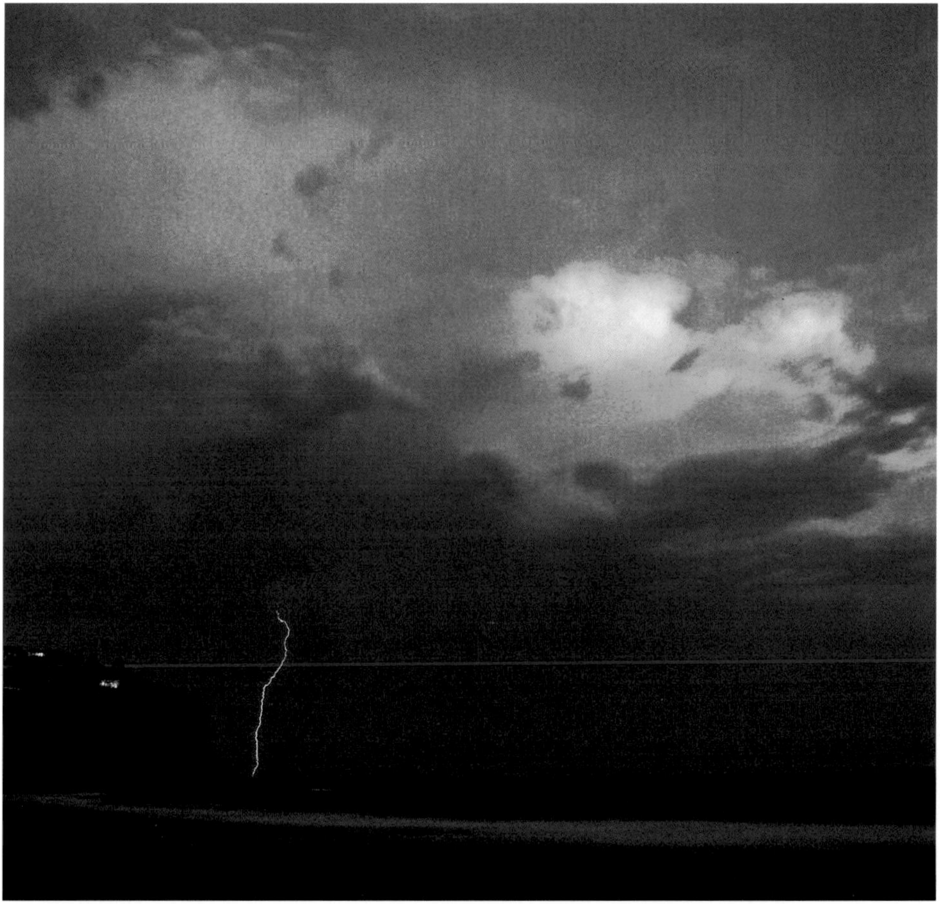

next page. newport beach

bilgola beach

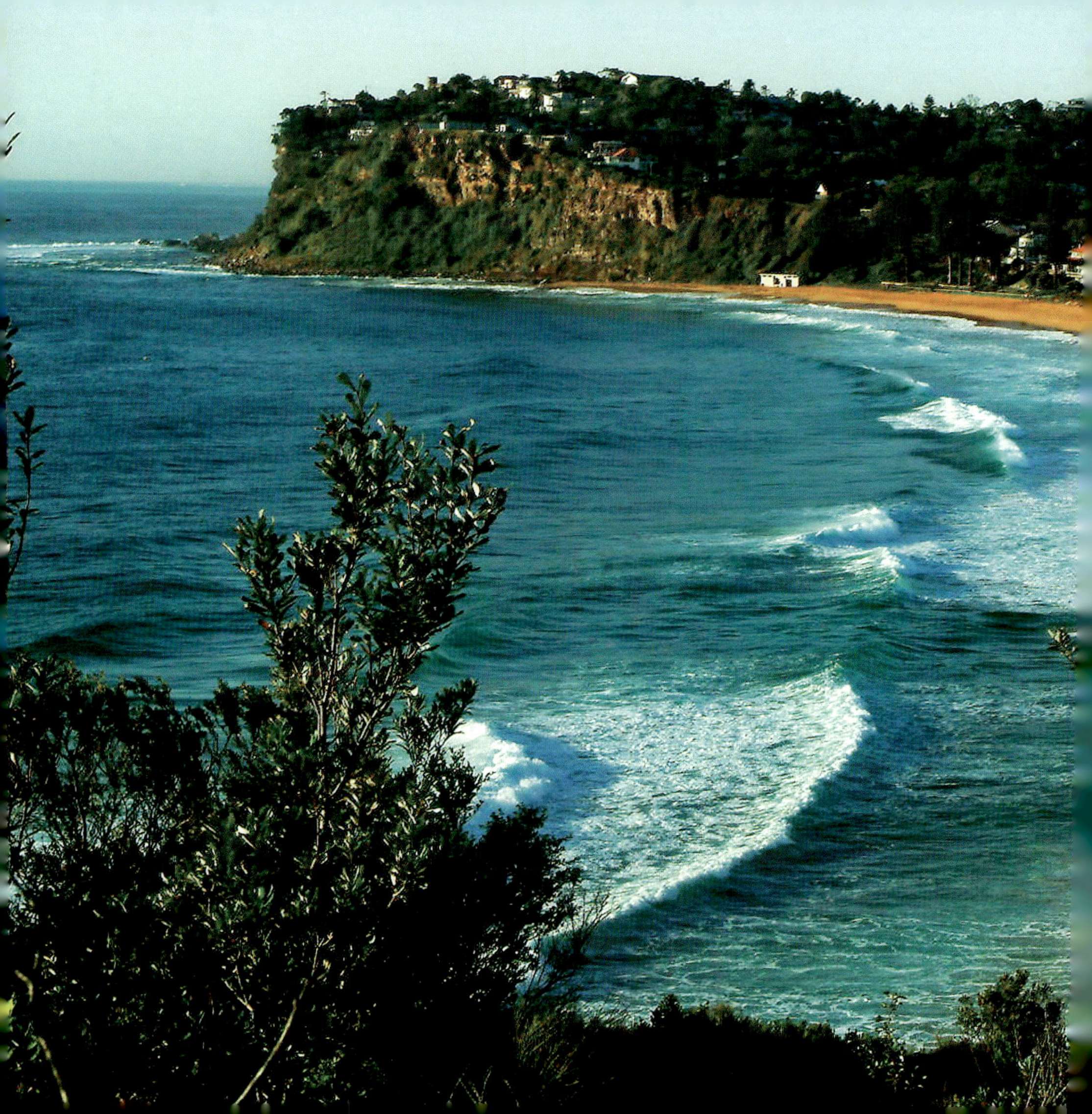

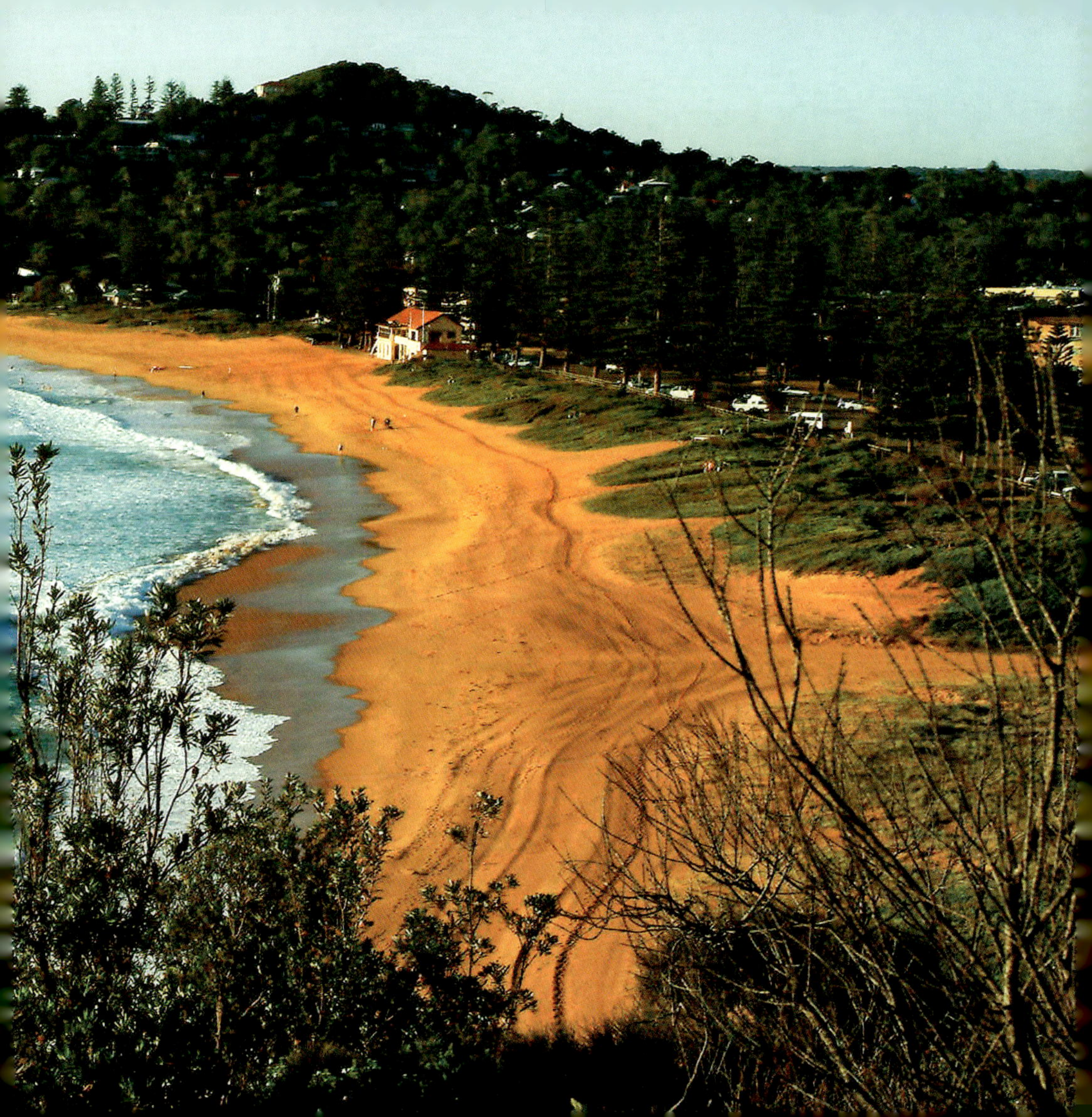

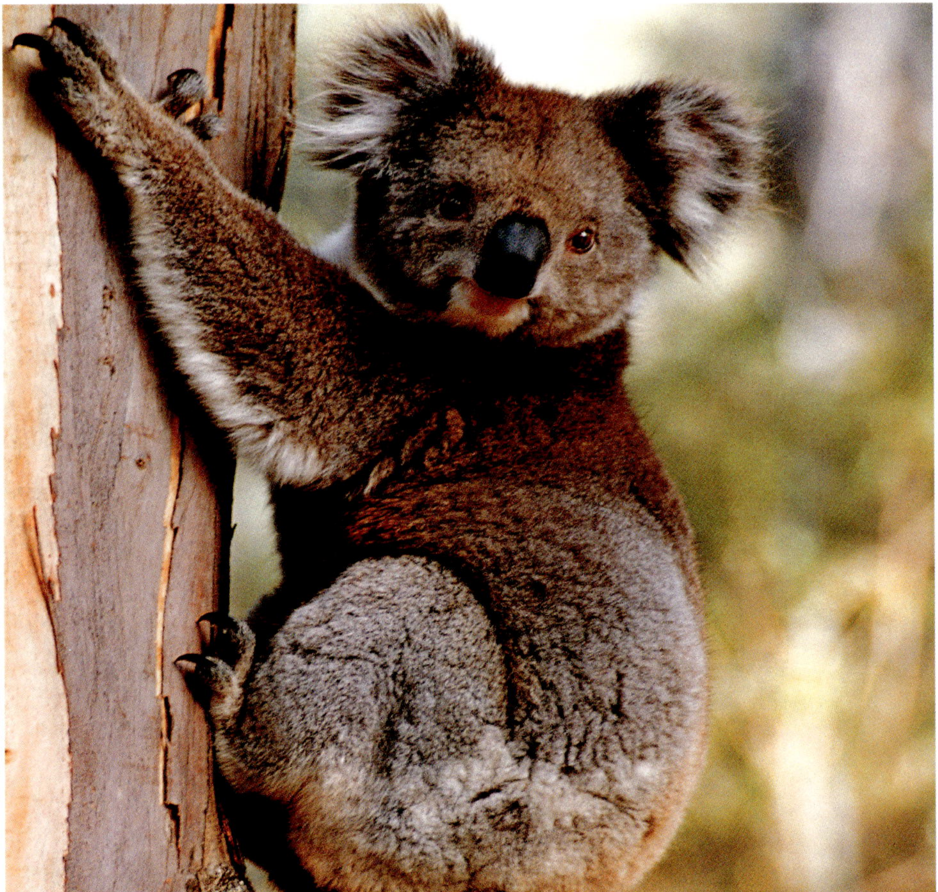

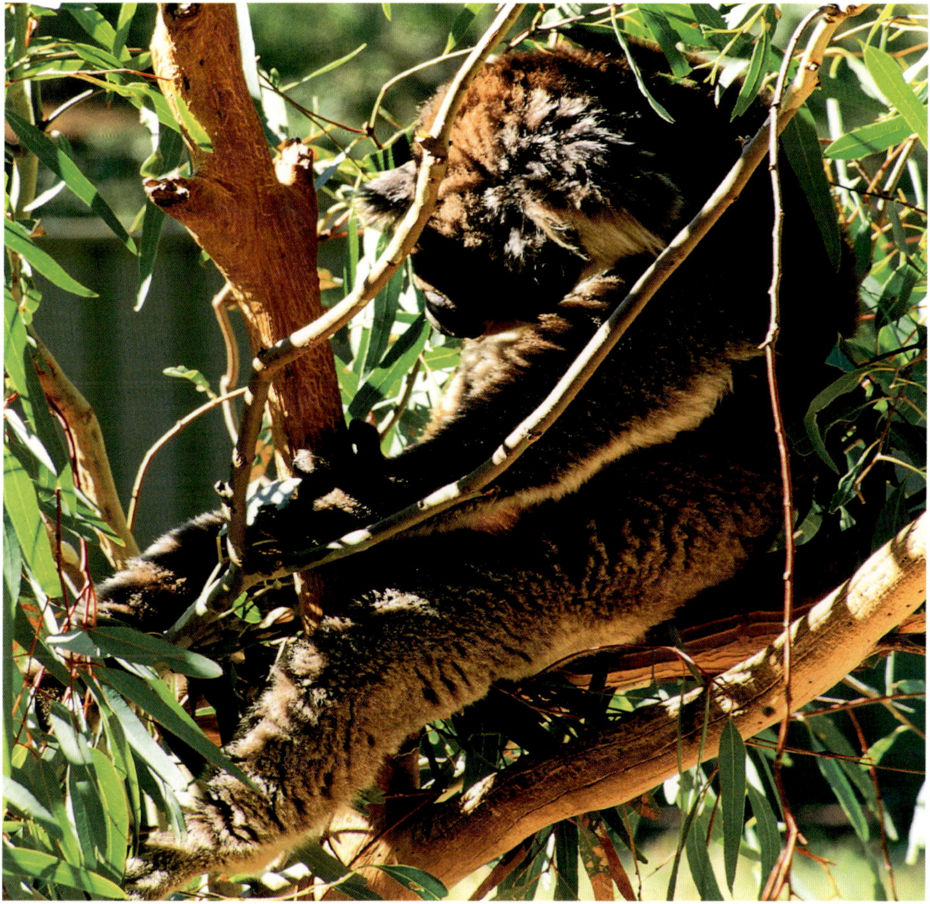

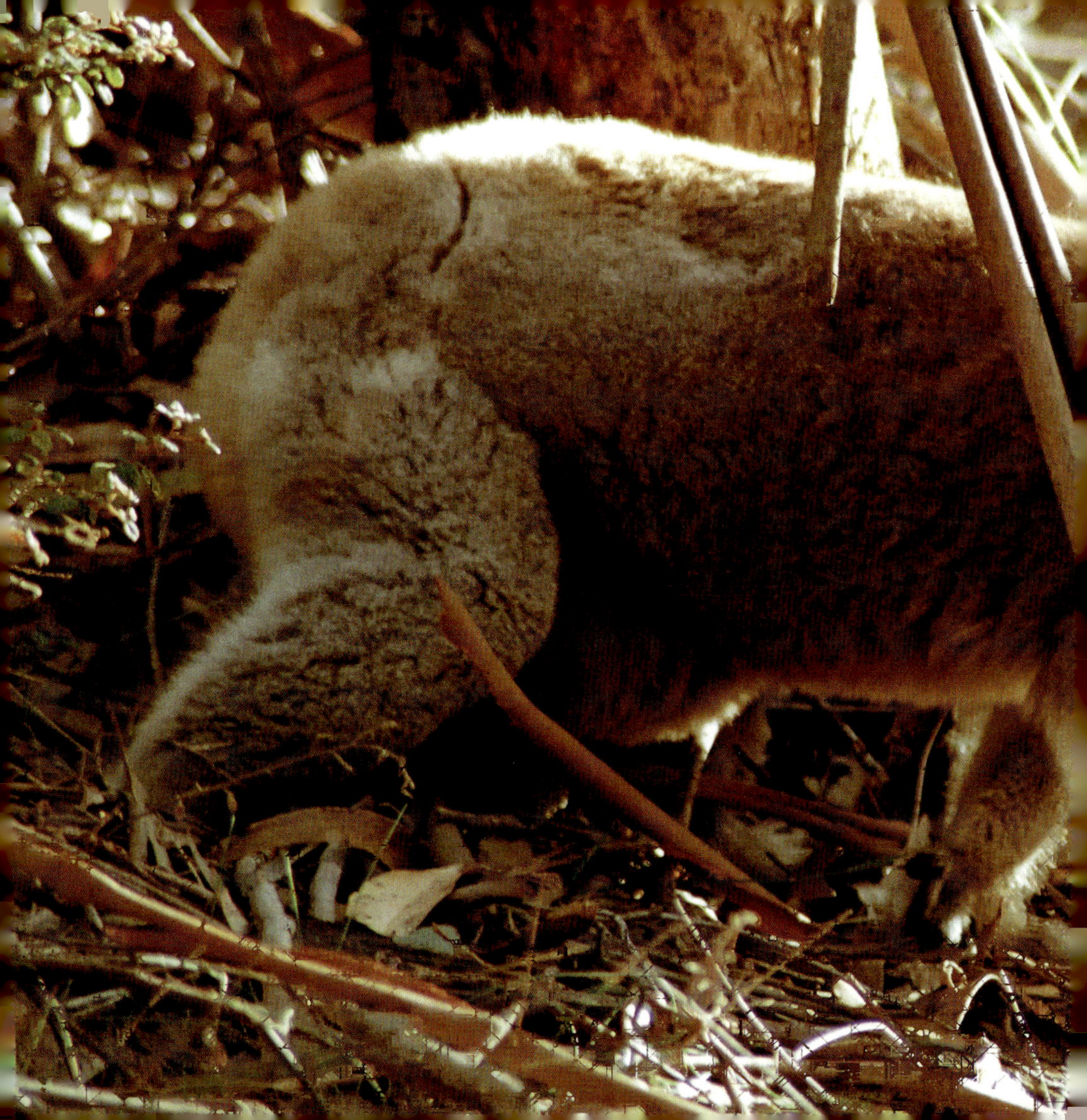

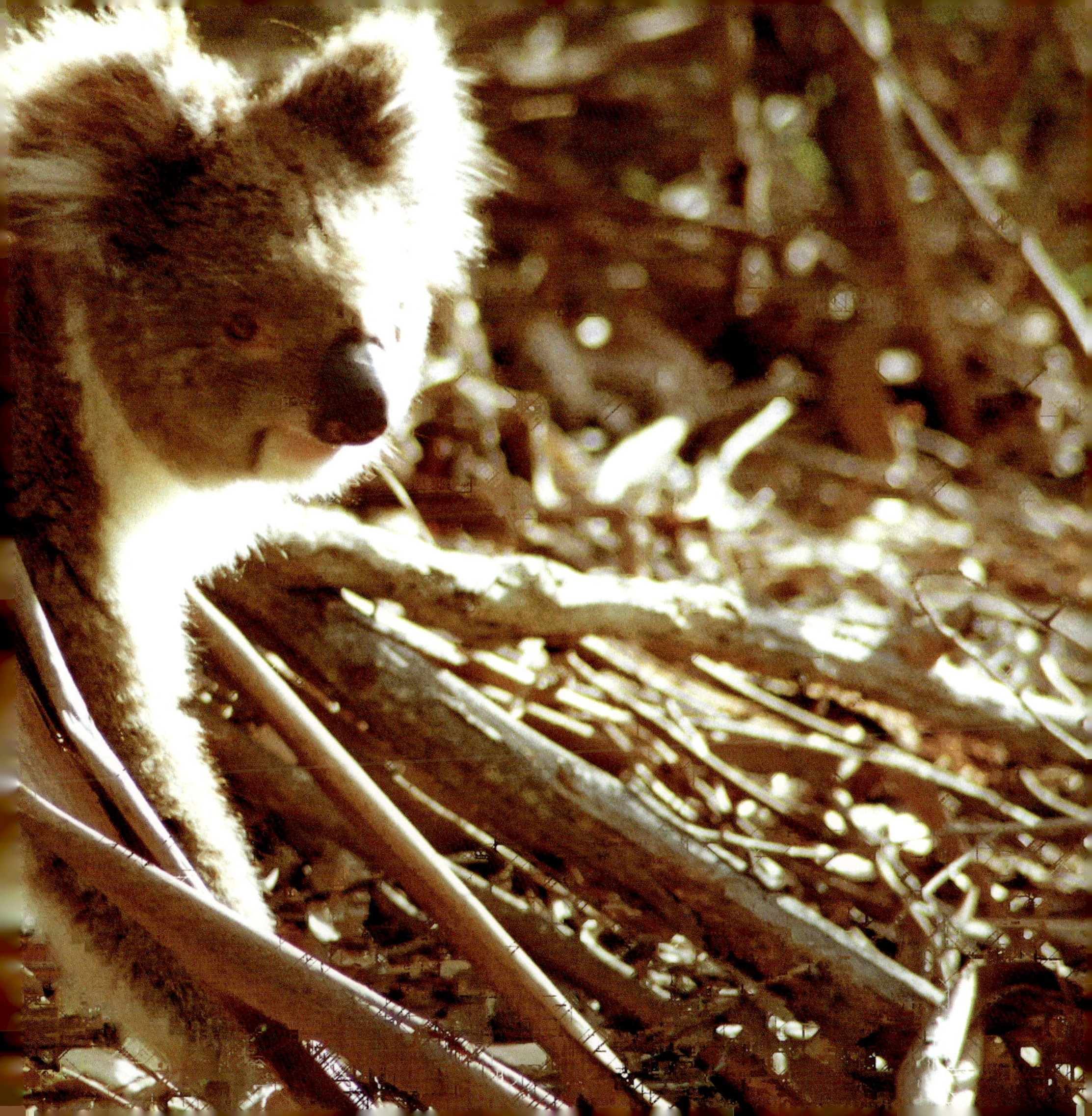

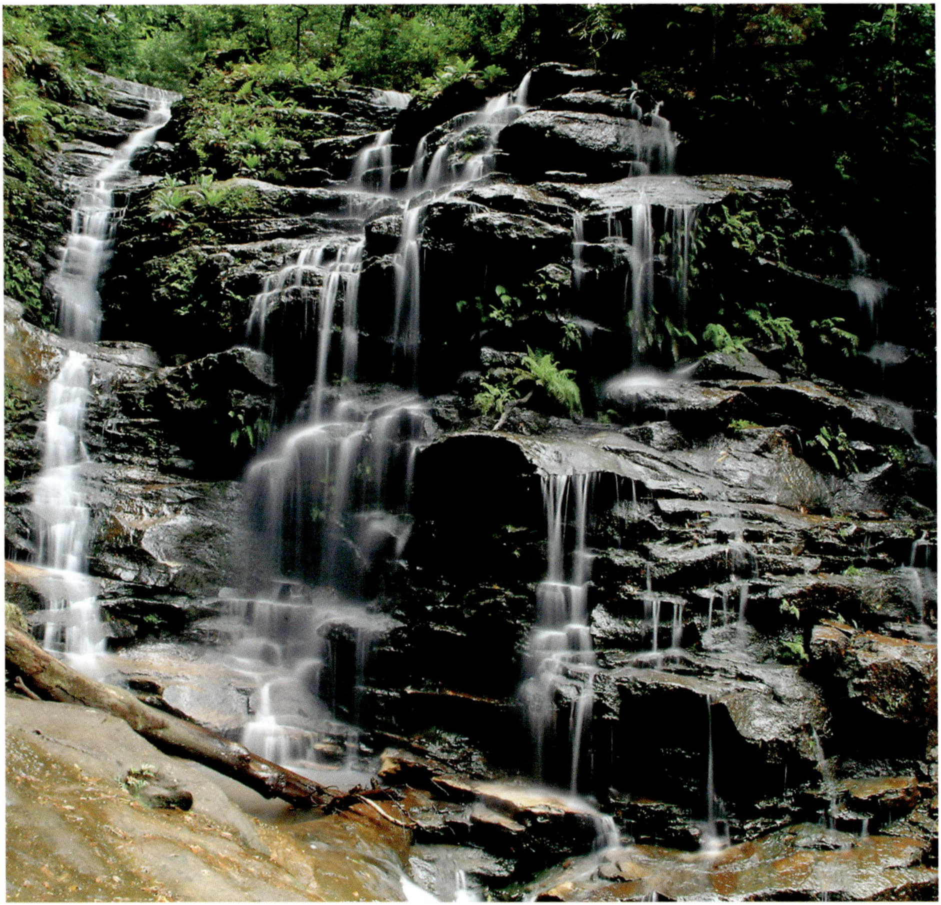

 valley of the waterfalls, katoomba

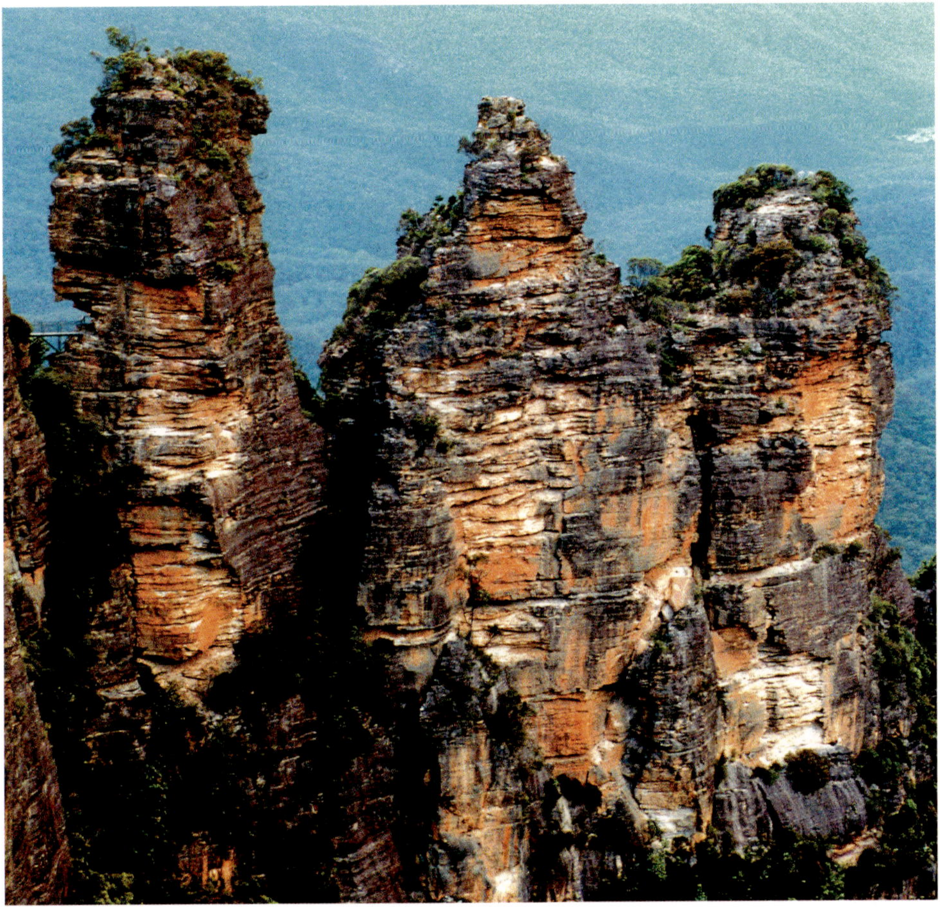

three sisters, katoomba

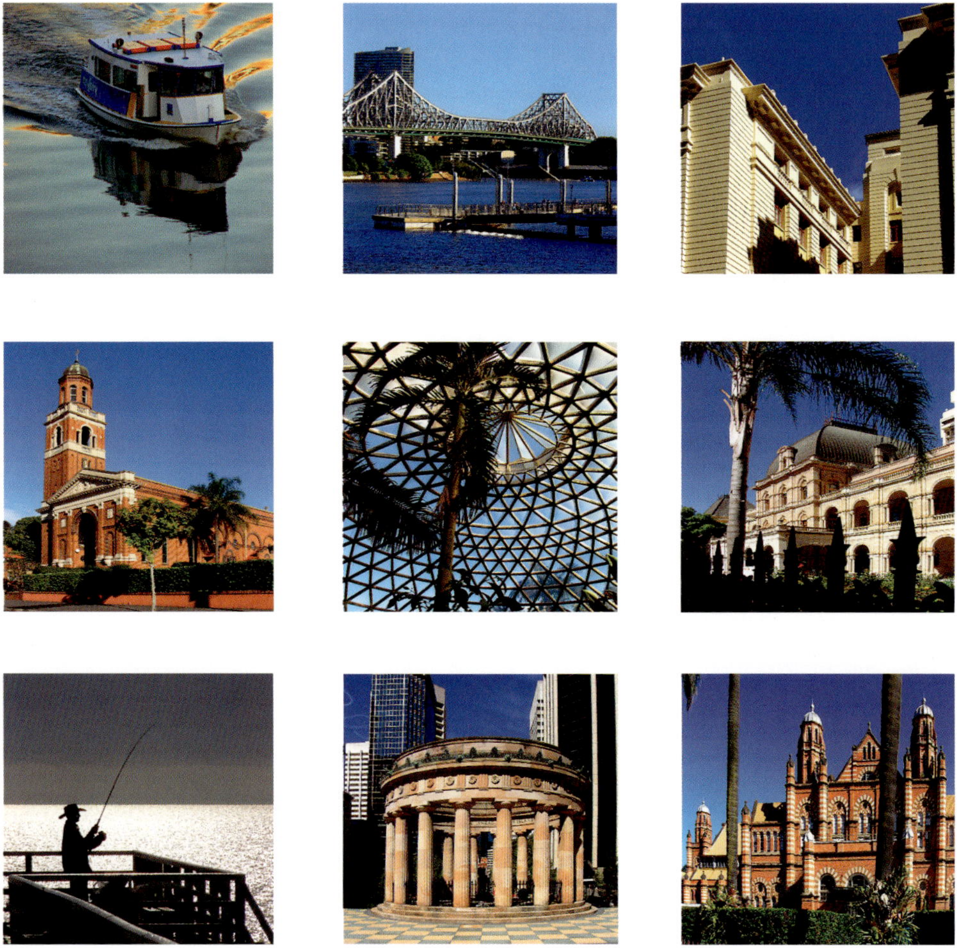

brisbane a.brisbane river b. storey bridge c. anzac square d. new farm church e. botanic gardens f. conrad treasury casino g. sandgate pier h. war memorial i. old museum

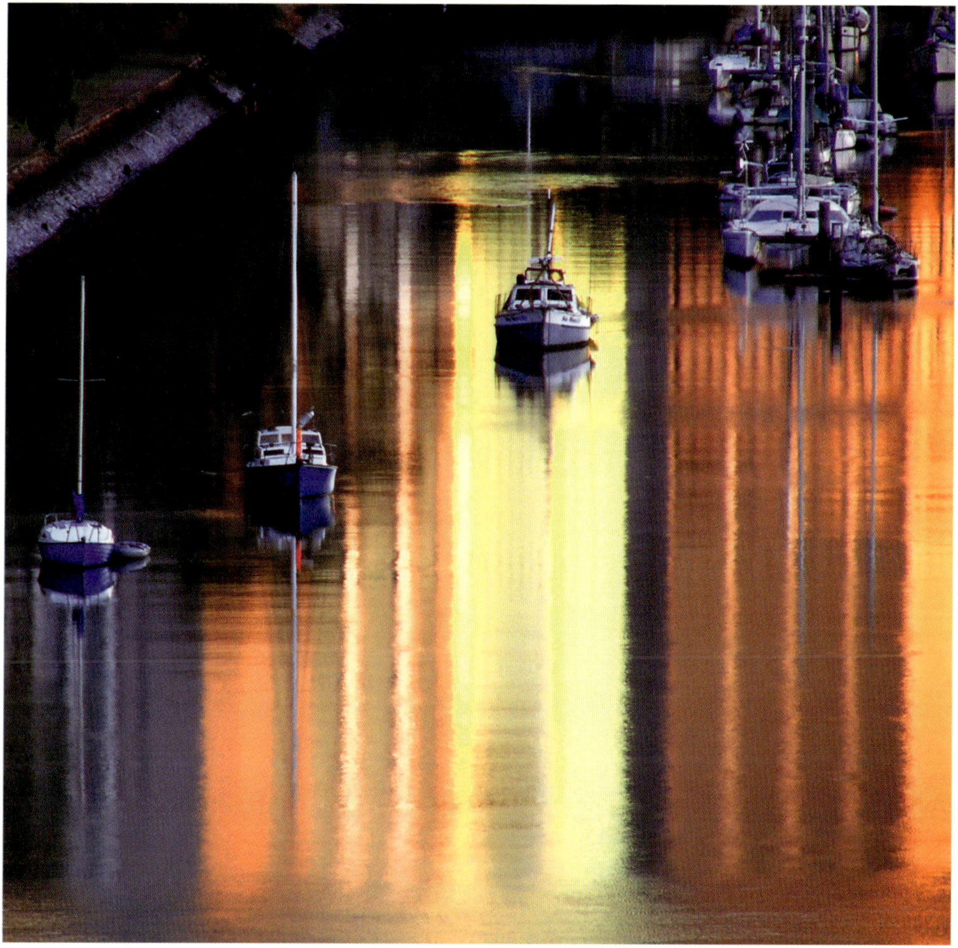

next page. brisbane river from kangaroo point cliffes

brisbane river

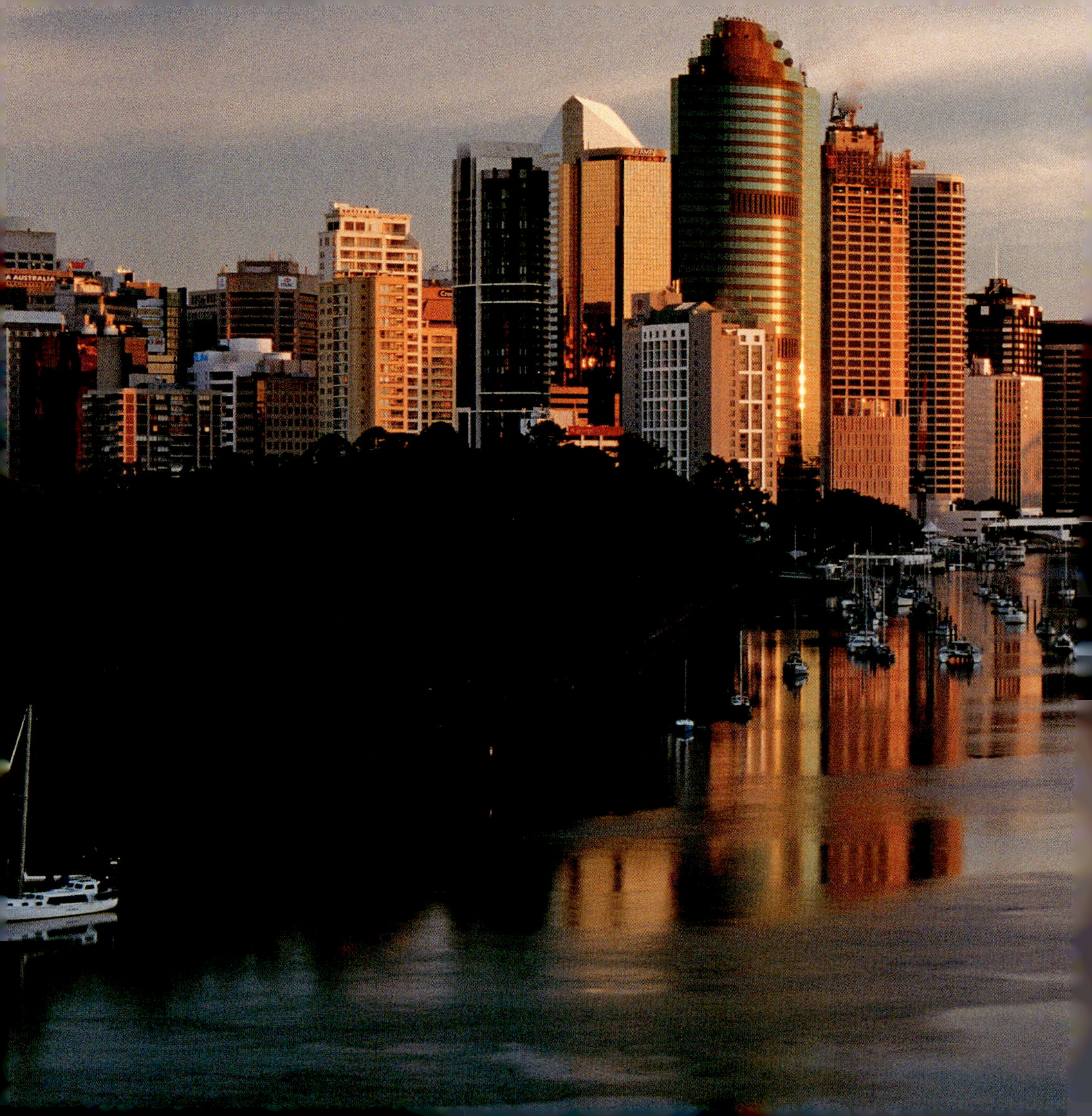

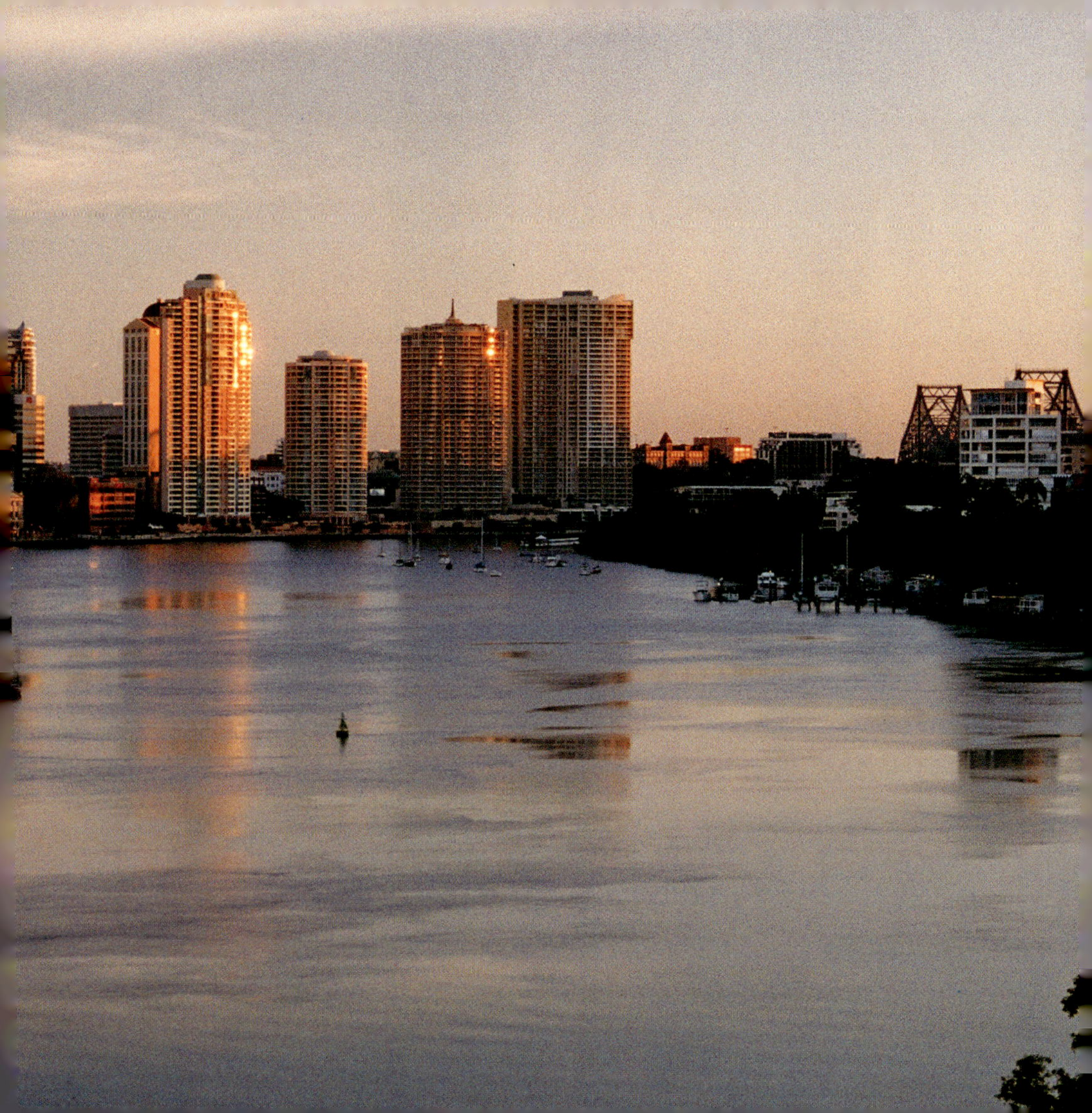

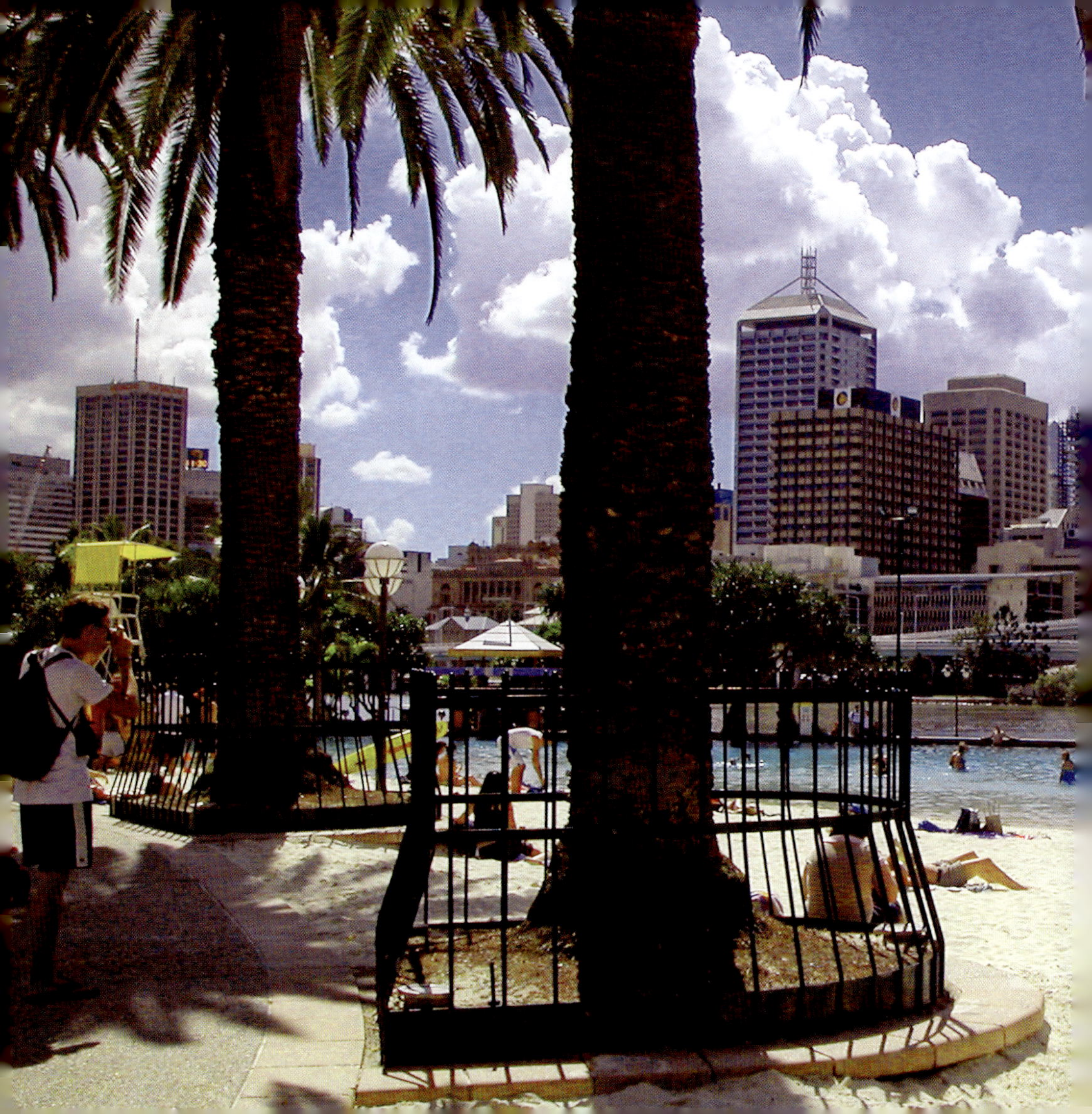

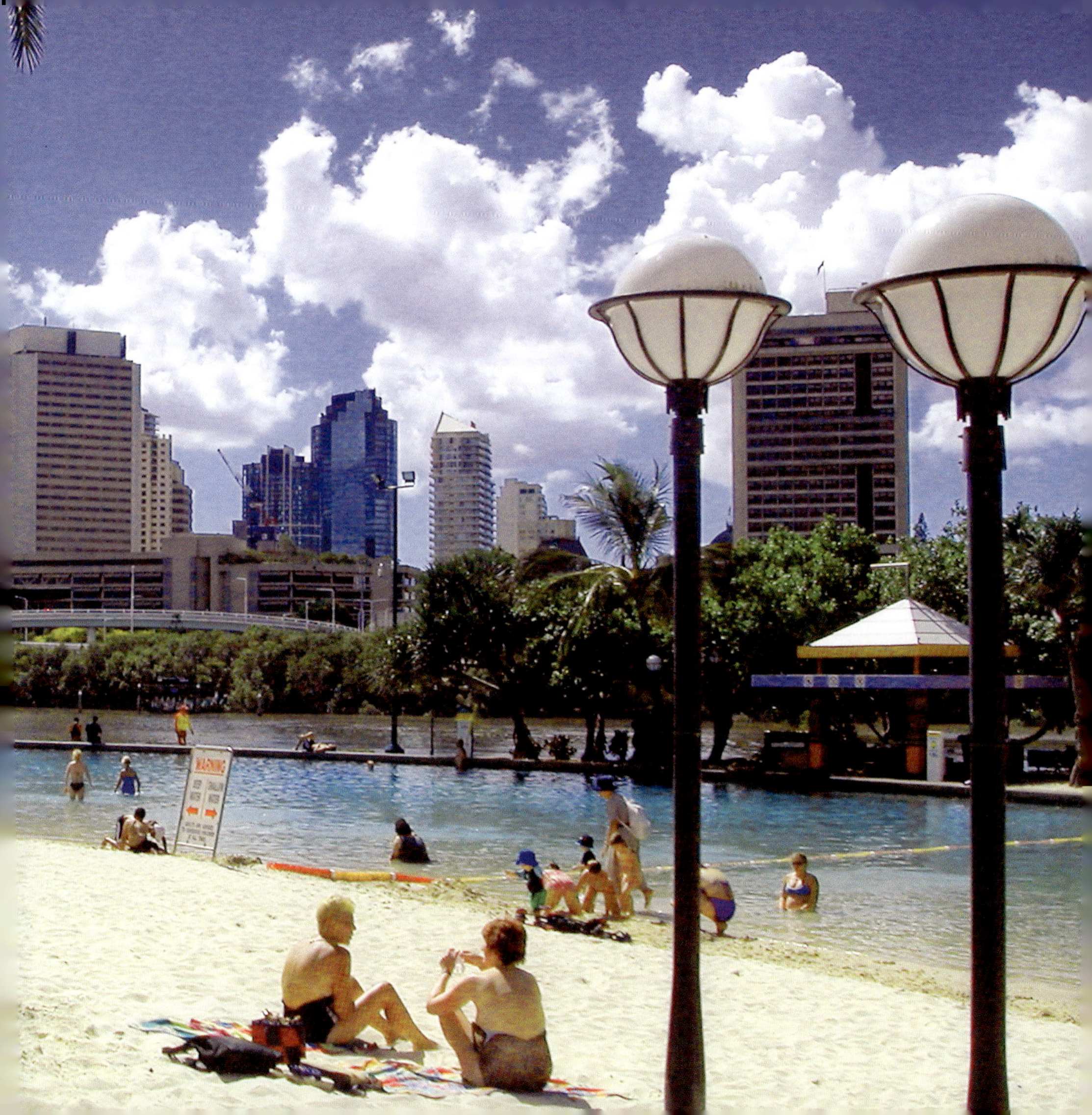

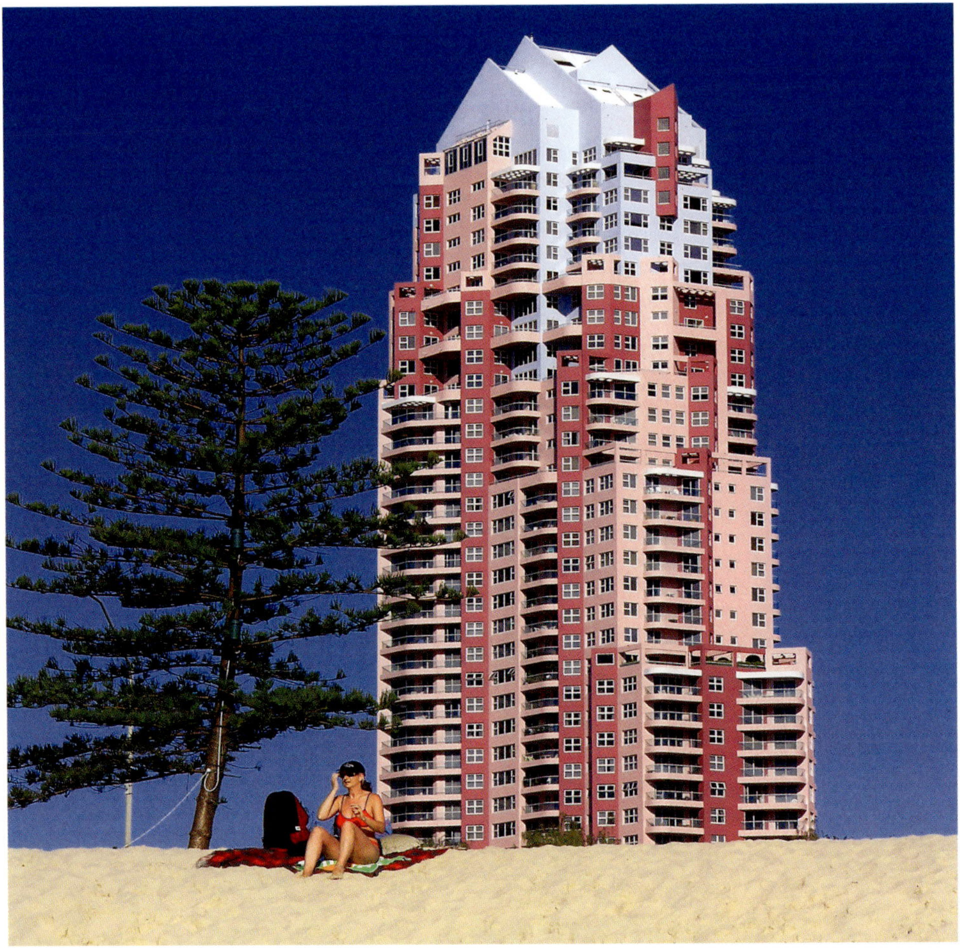

previous page. south bank, brisbane

next page. sunshine coast

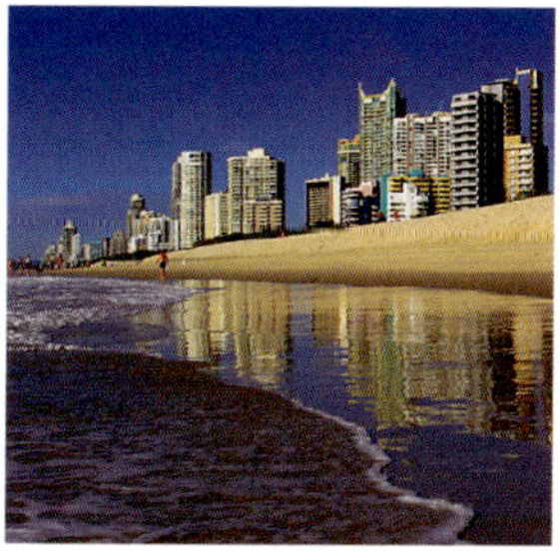
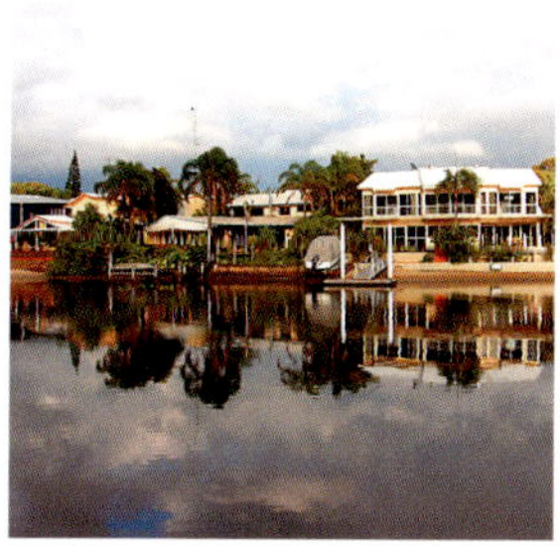
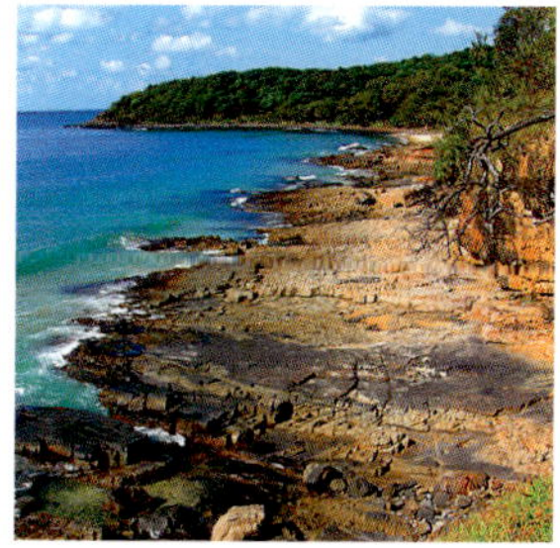
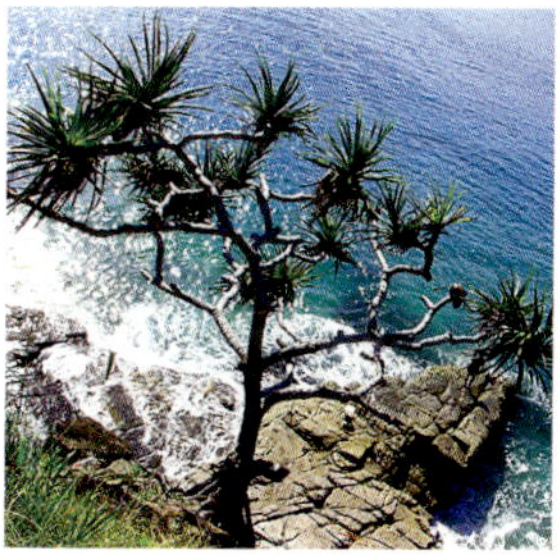
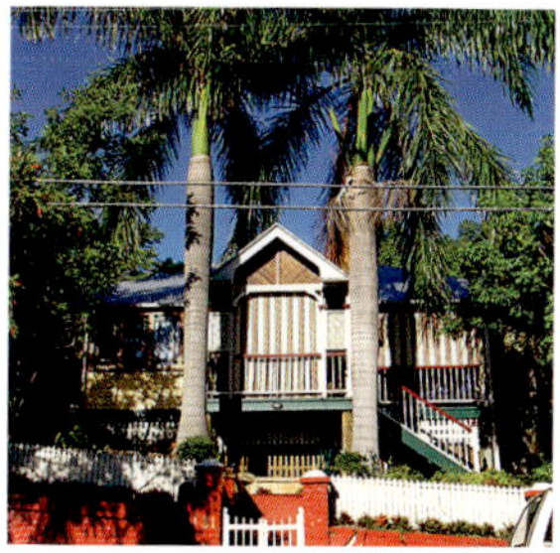
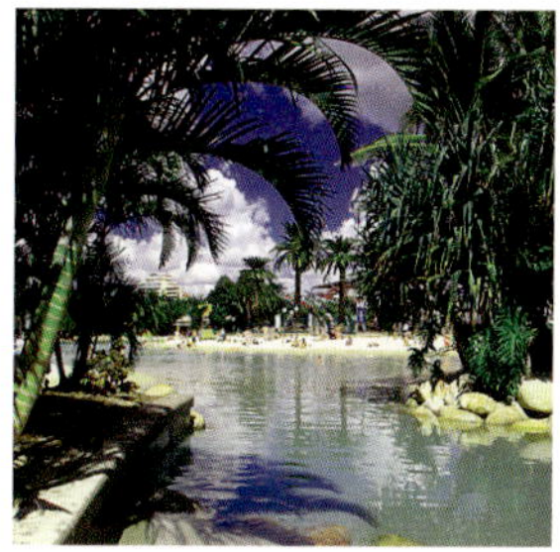
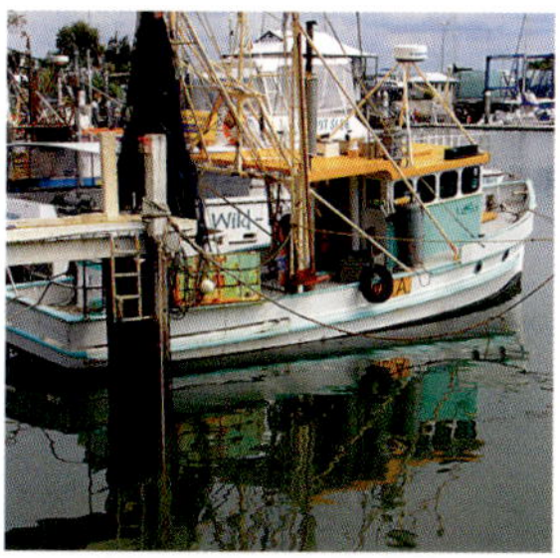
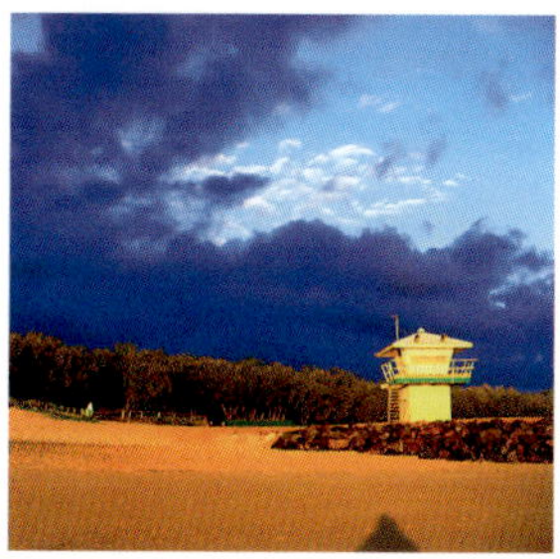
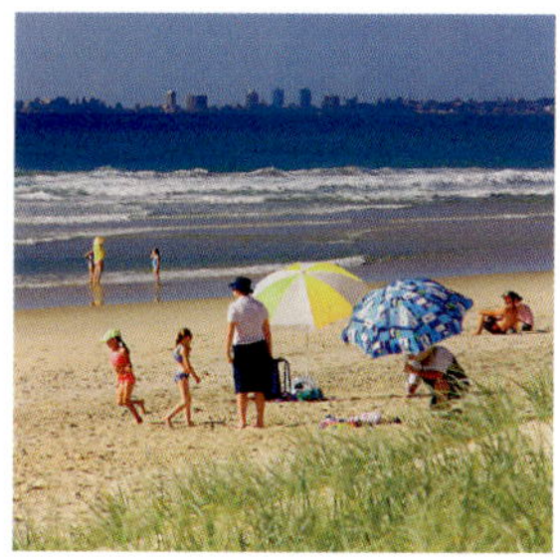

a. gold coast b. noosaville c&d. noosa national park e. queensland house f. brisbane southbank
g.deception bay h. noosa beach i. palm beach

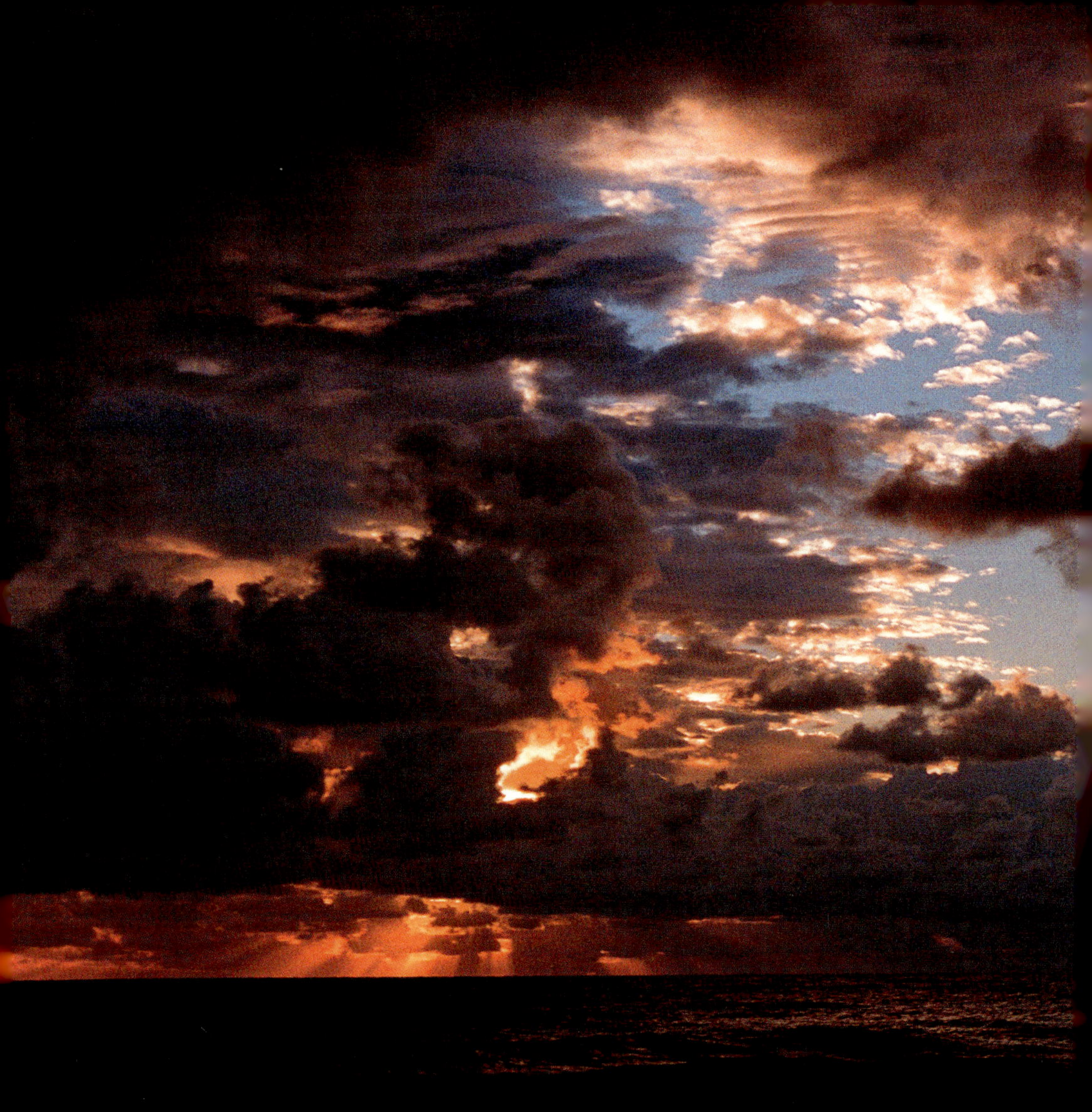

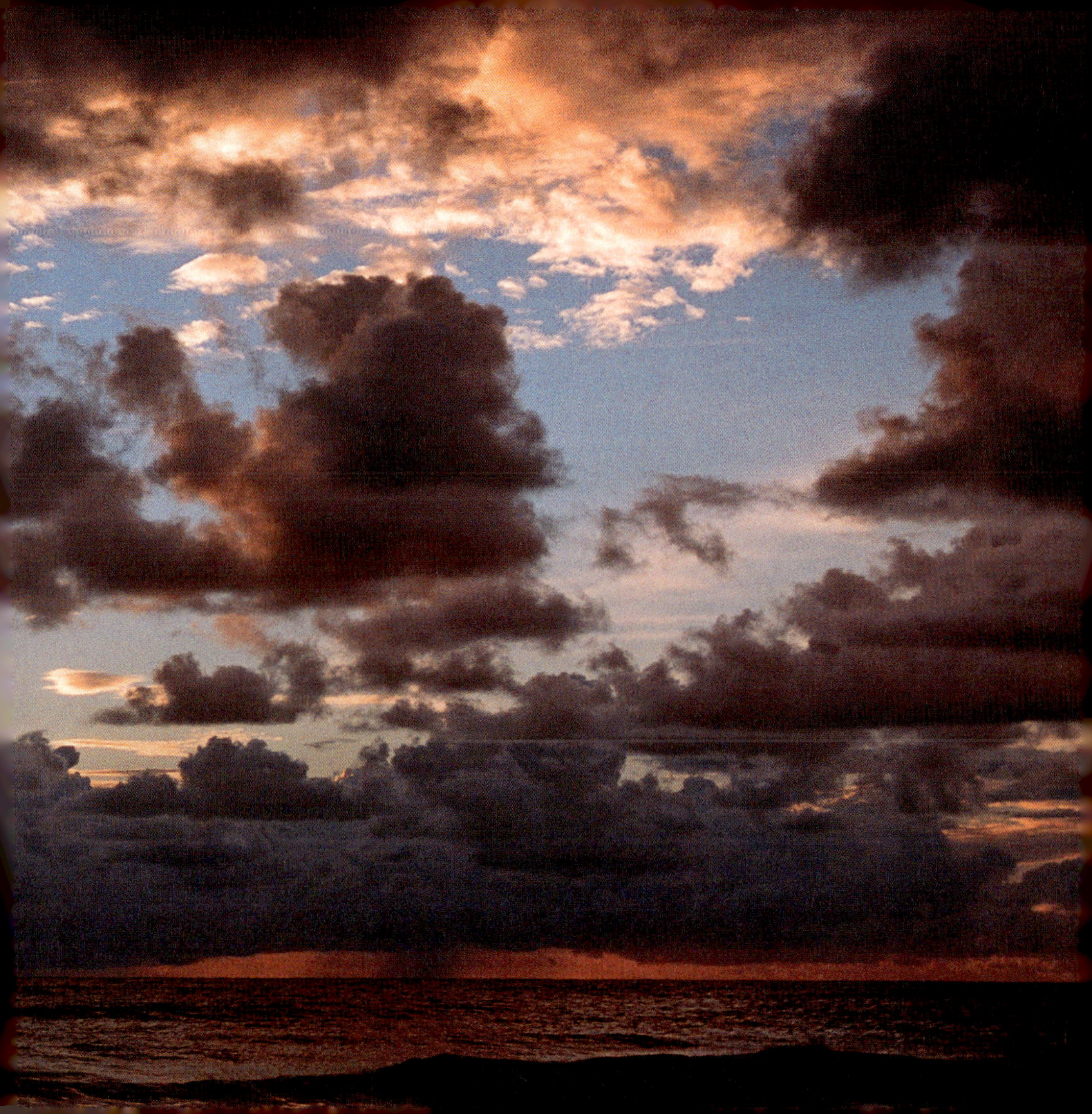

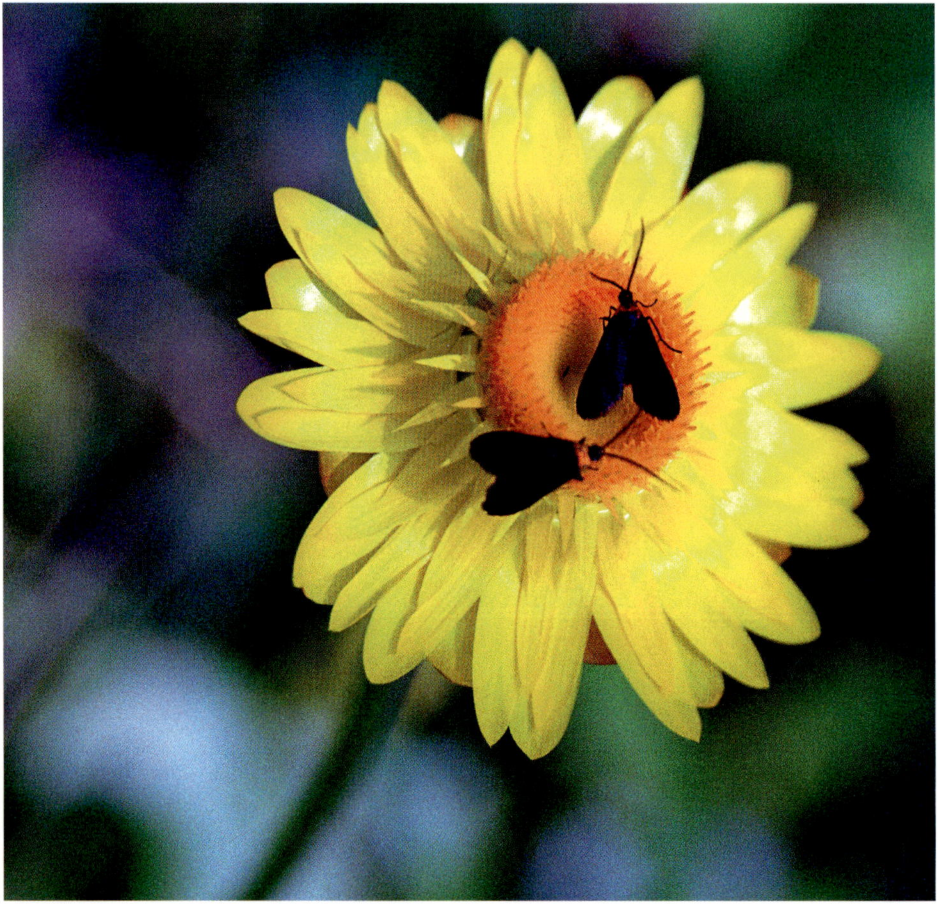

 daisy, fraser island

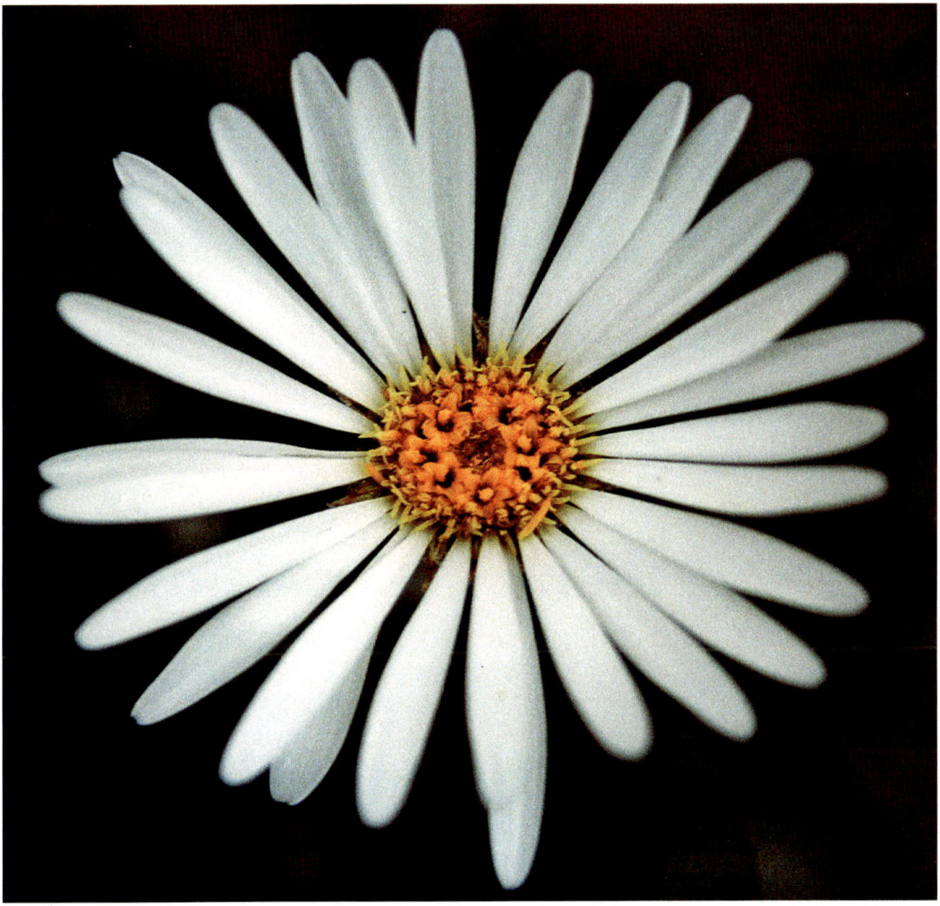

daisy, victorian highlands

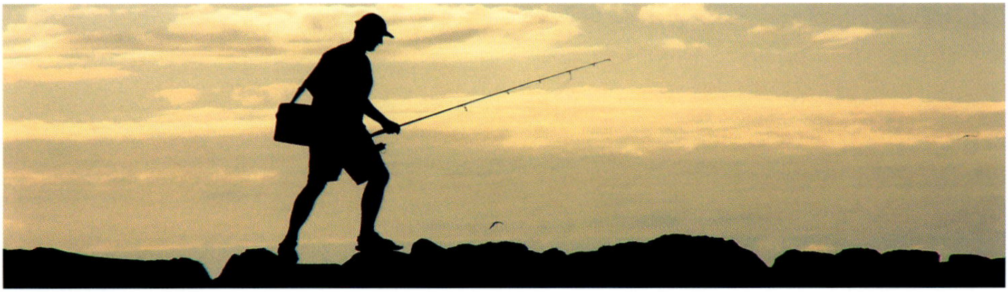

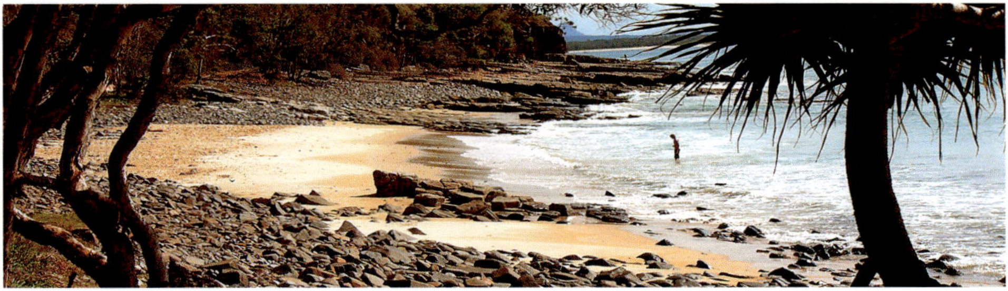

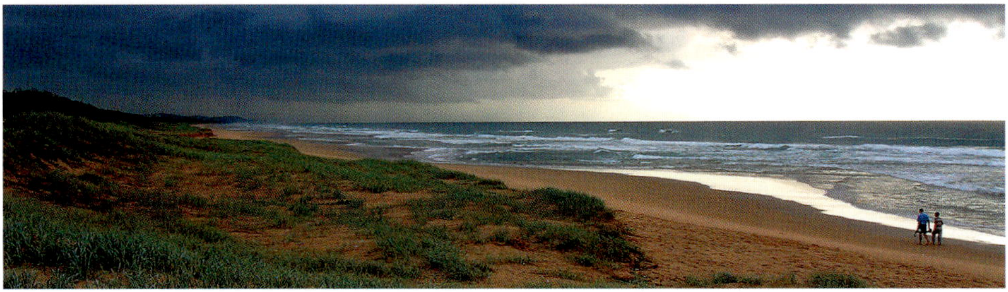

 sunshine coast a. noosa beach b. noosa national park c. peregian beach

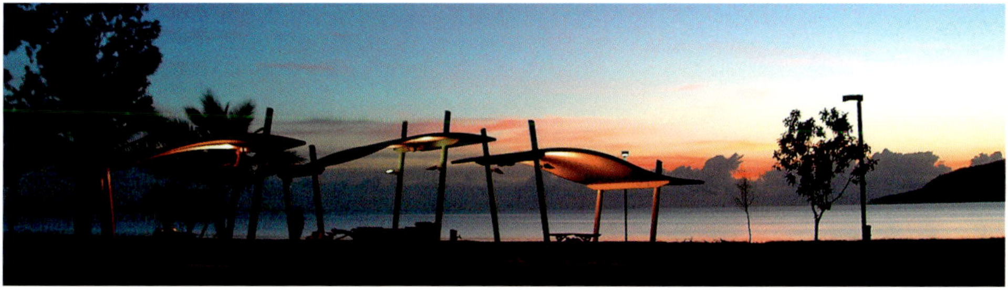

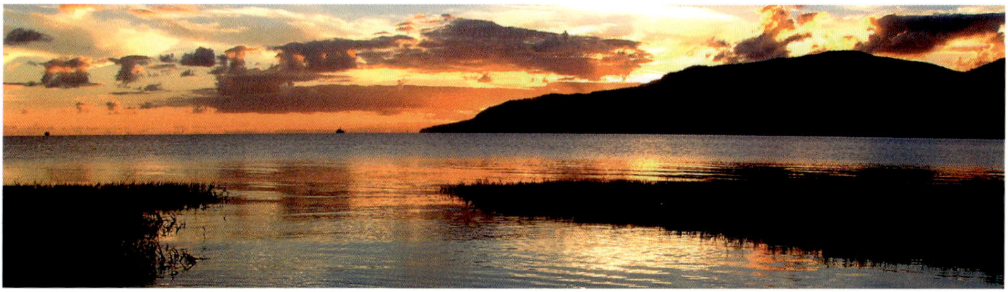

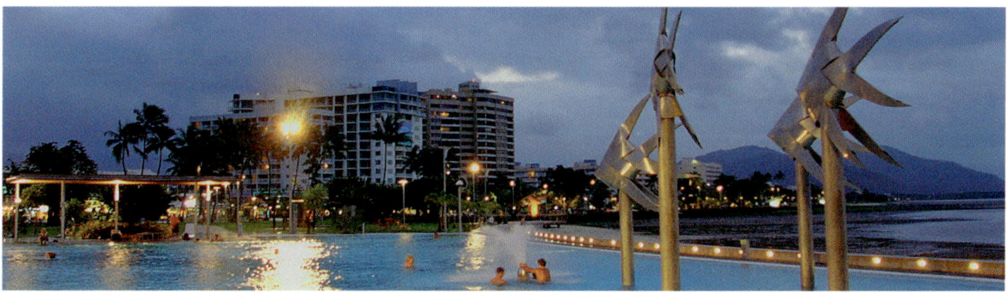

cairns foreshore

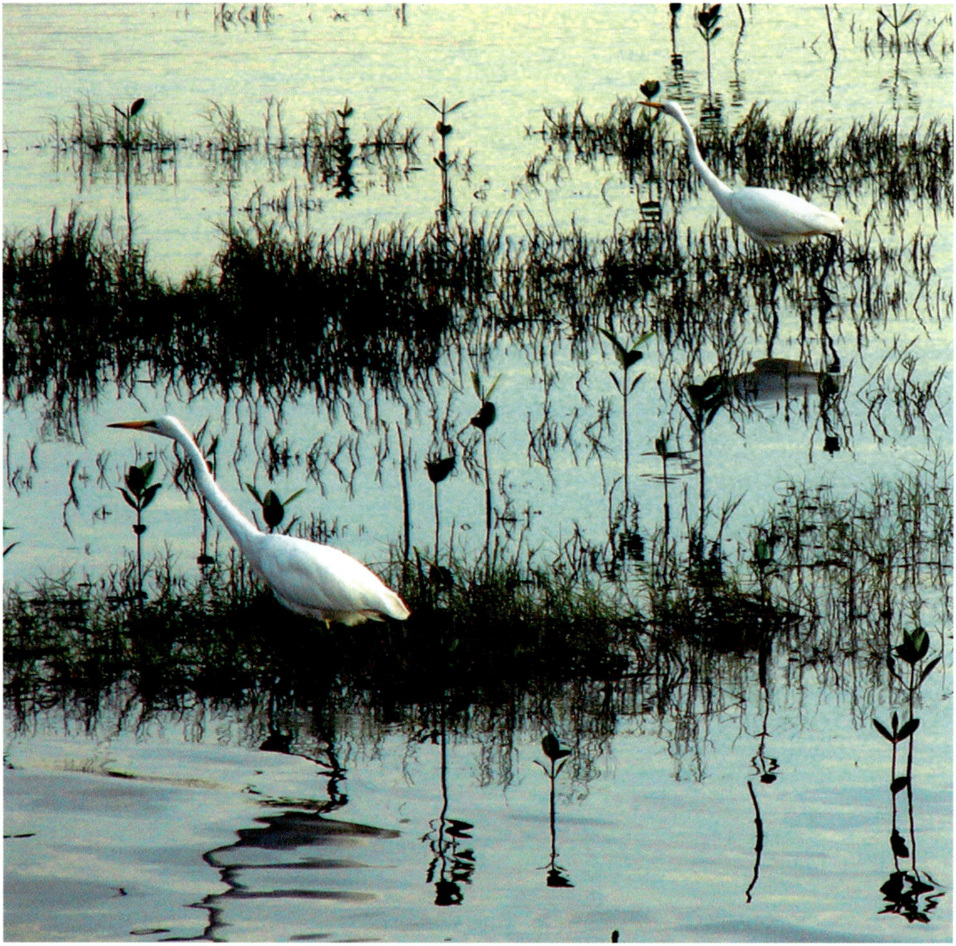

 birds fishing, cairns foreshore

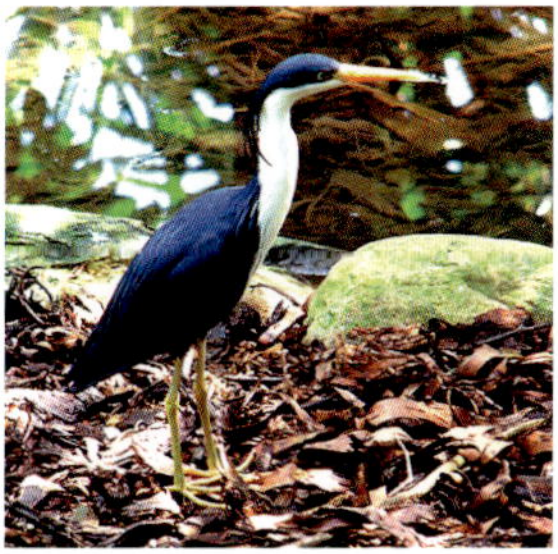

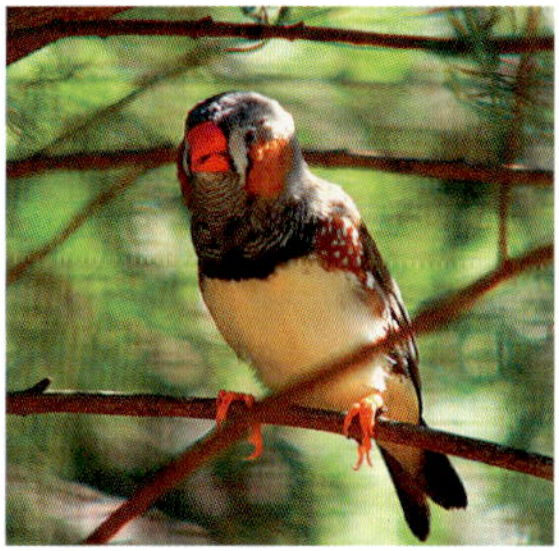

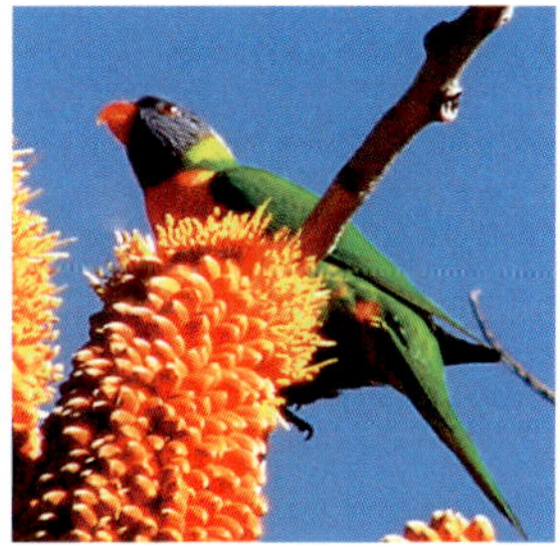

next pages. port douglas

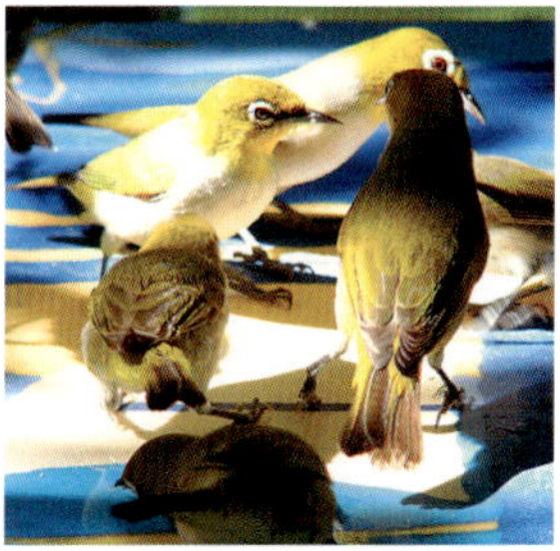

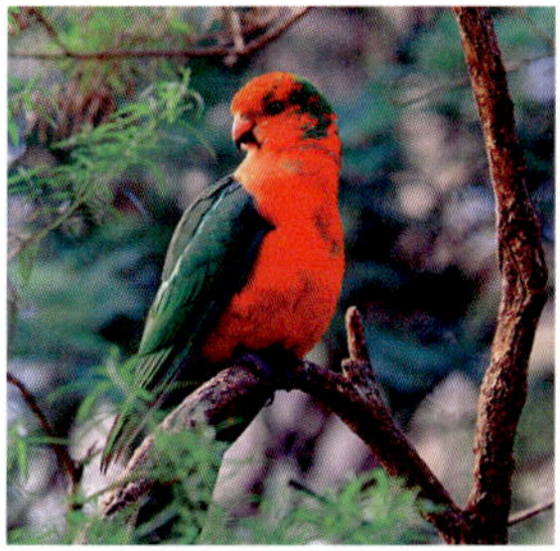

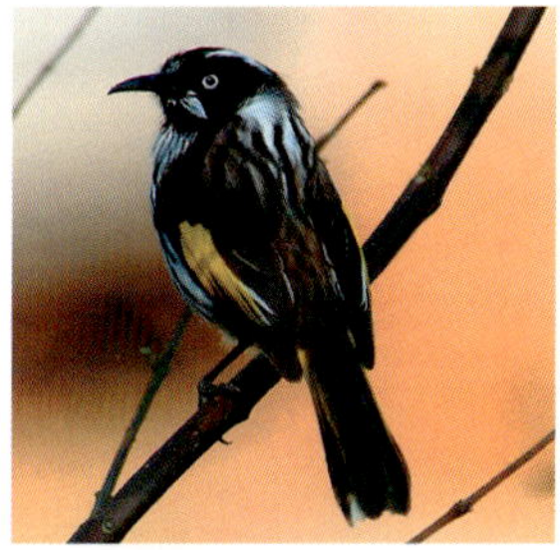

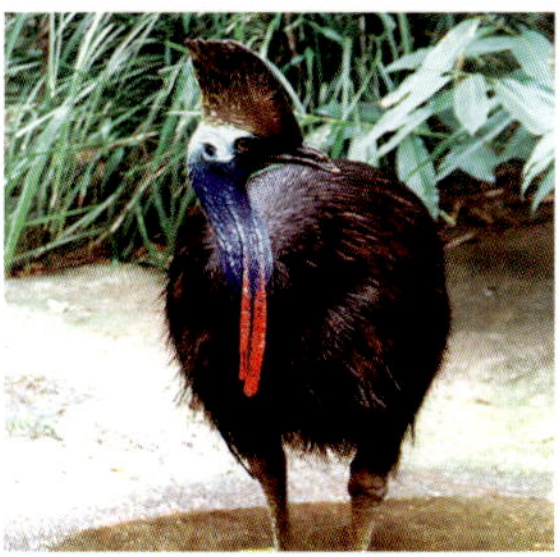

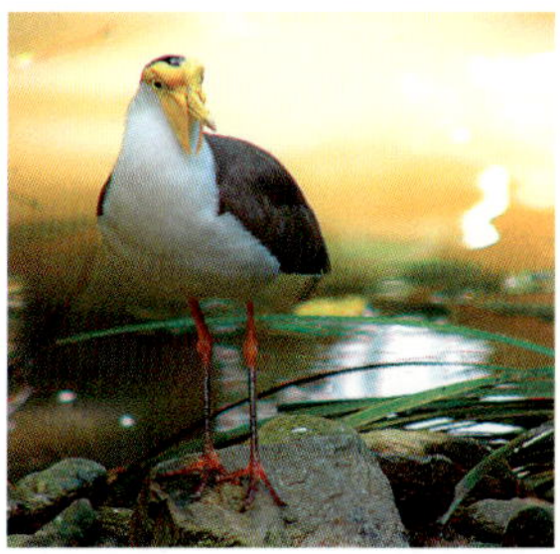

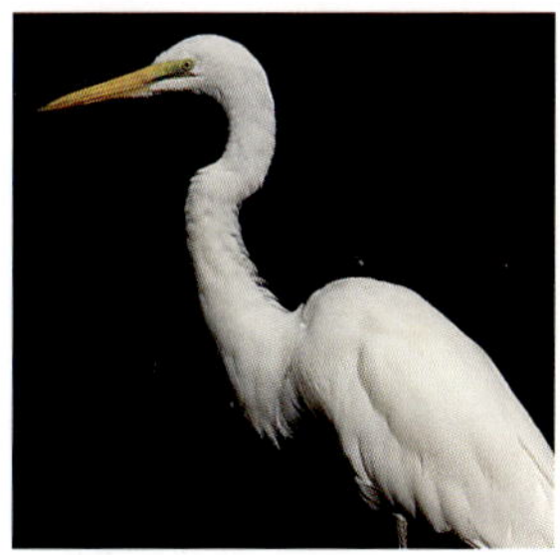

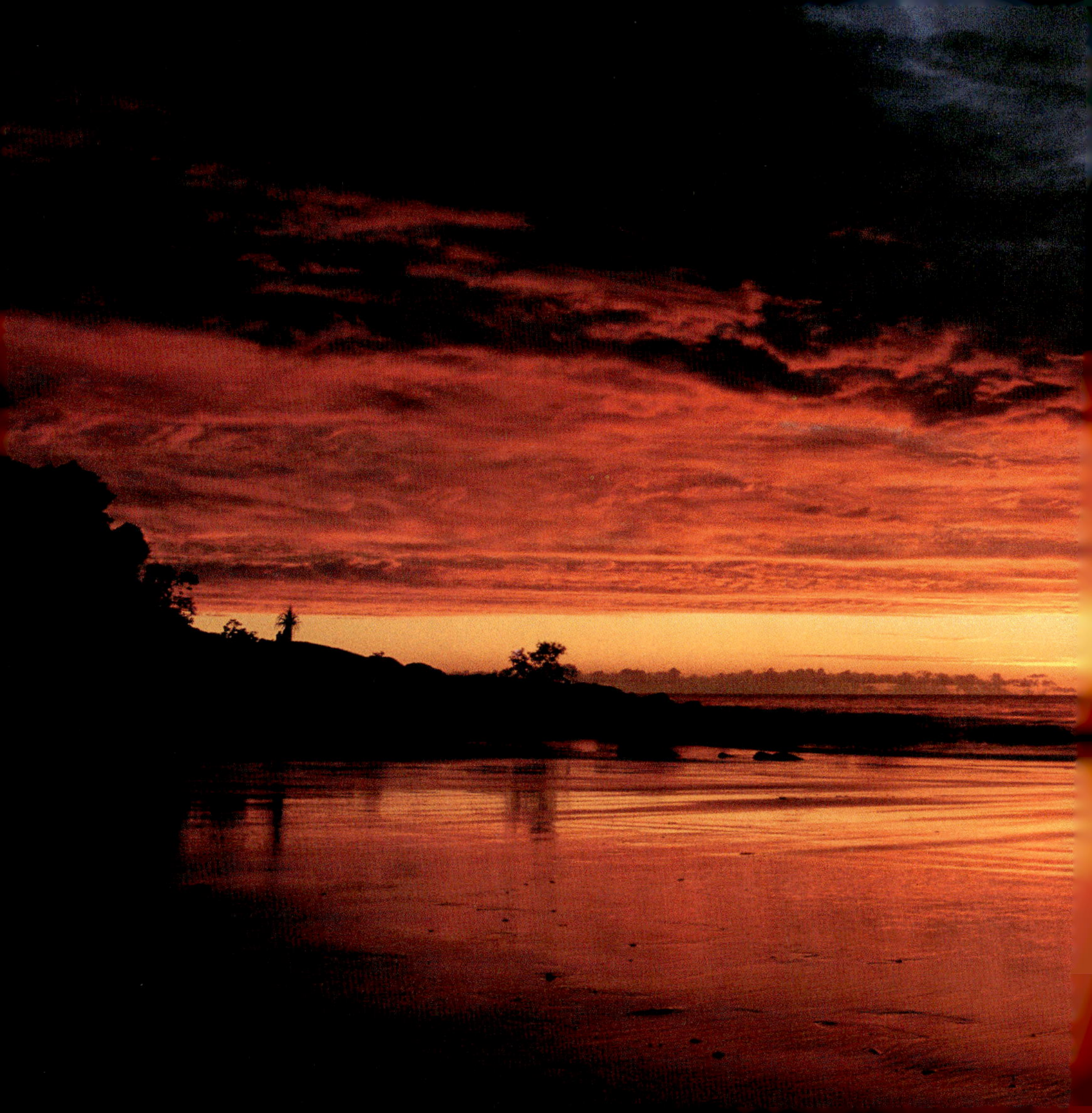

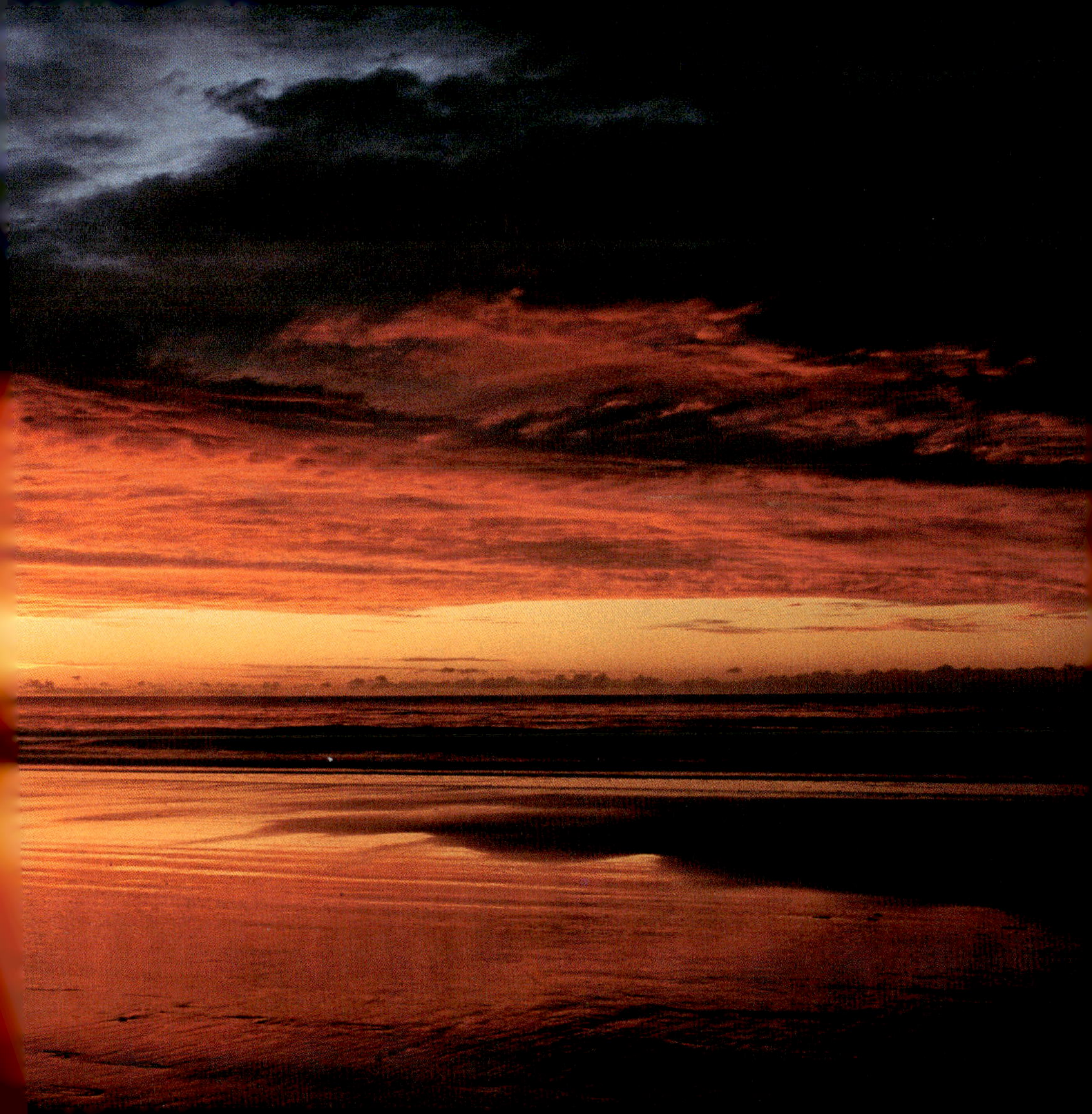

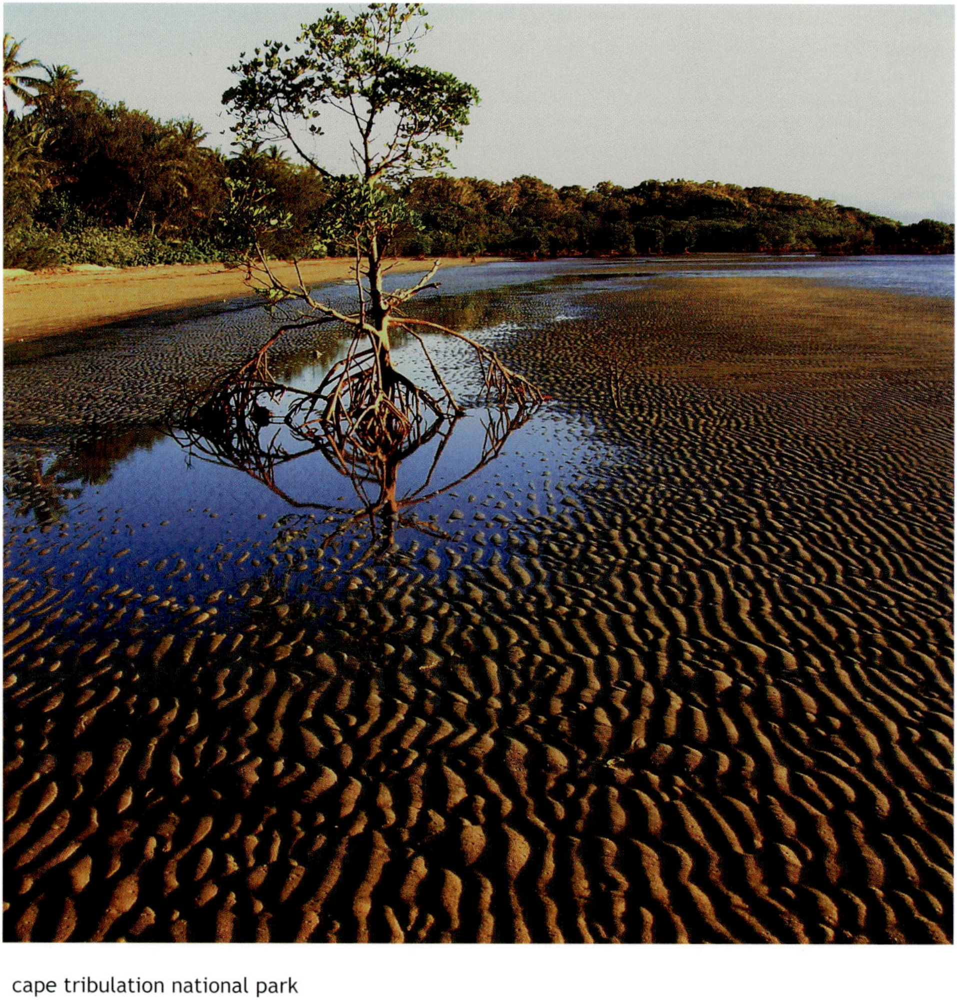

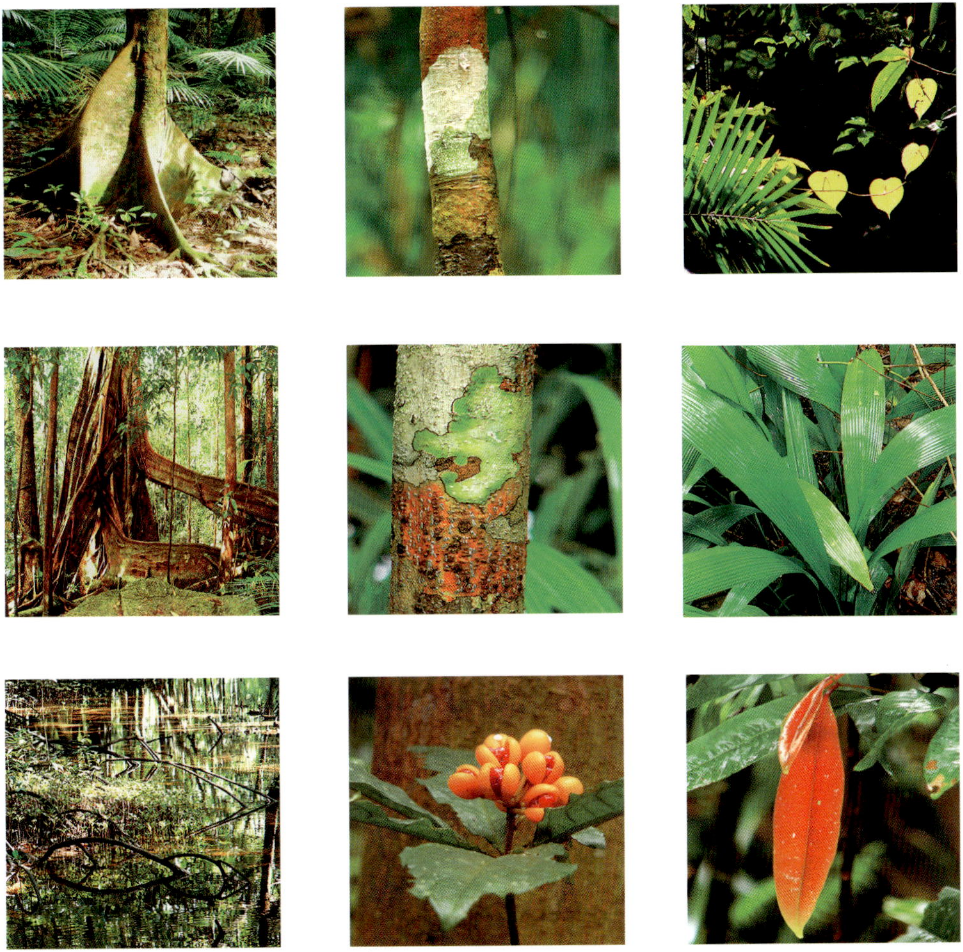

rainforest, mossman gorge

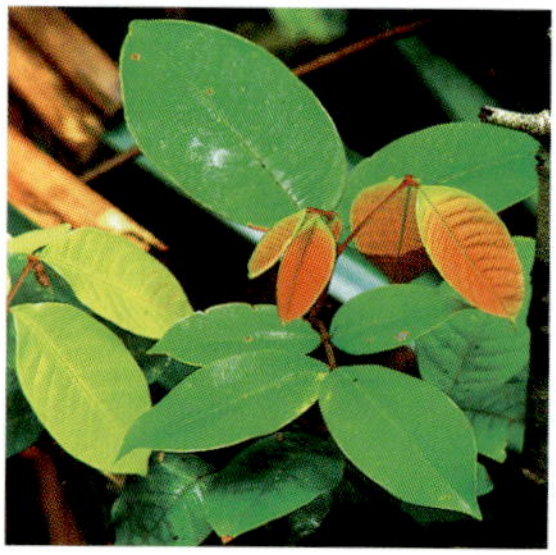
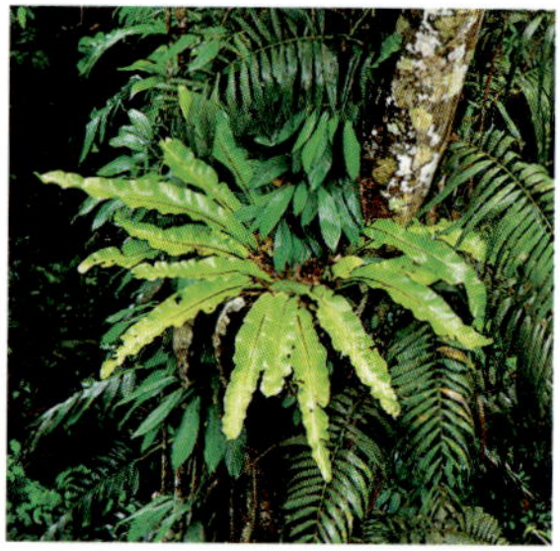
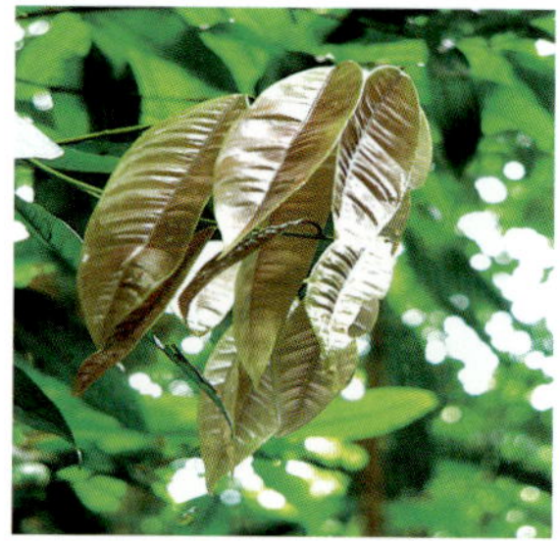
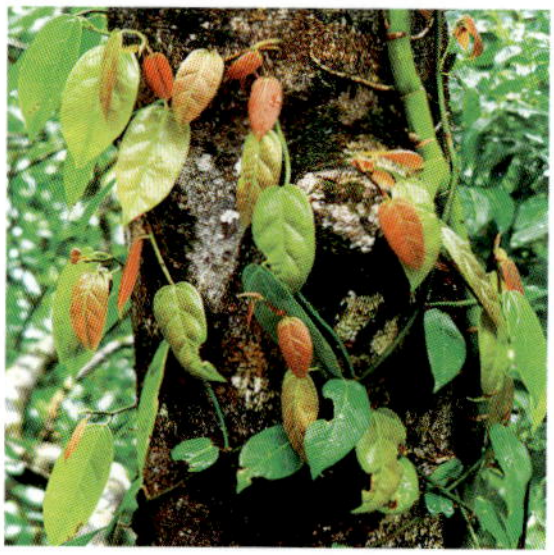
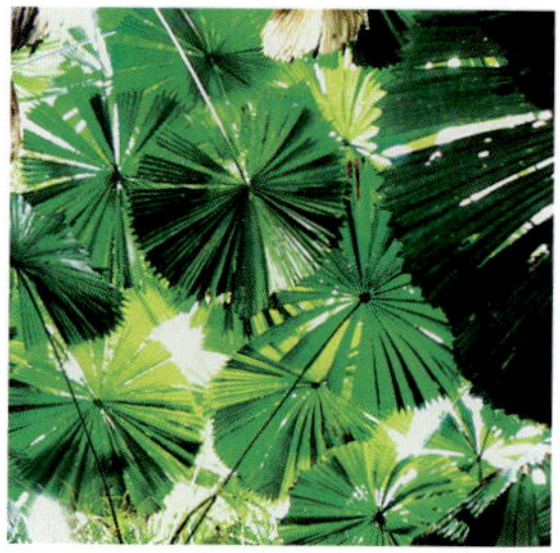
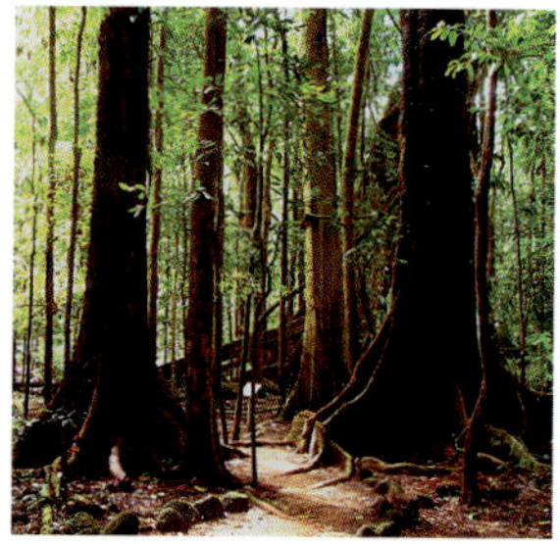
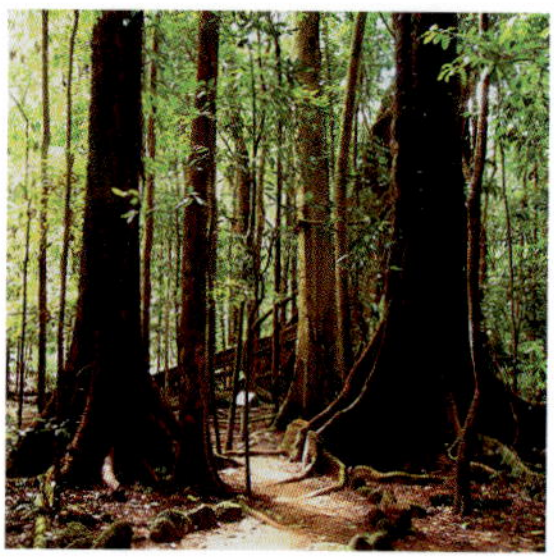
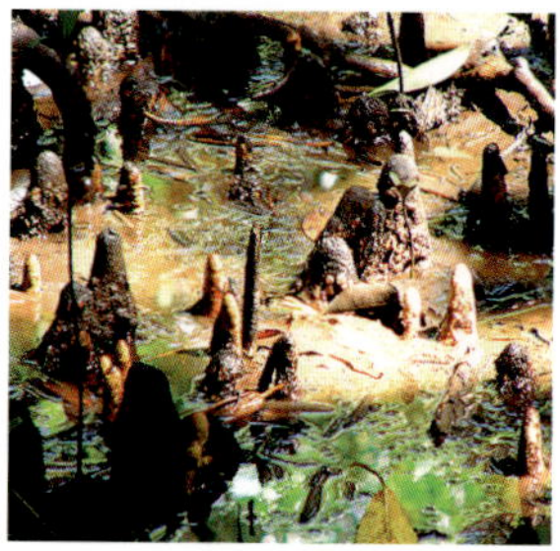
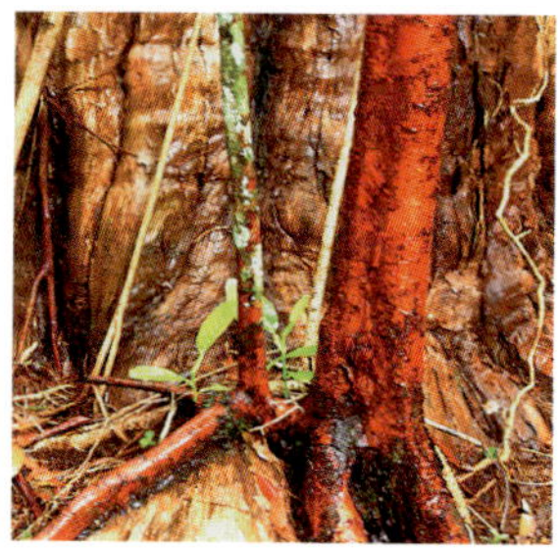

 rainforest, cape tribulation

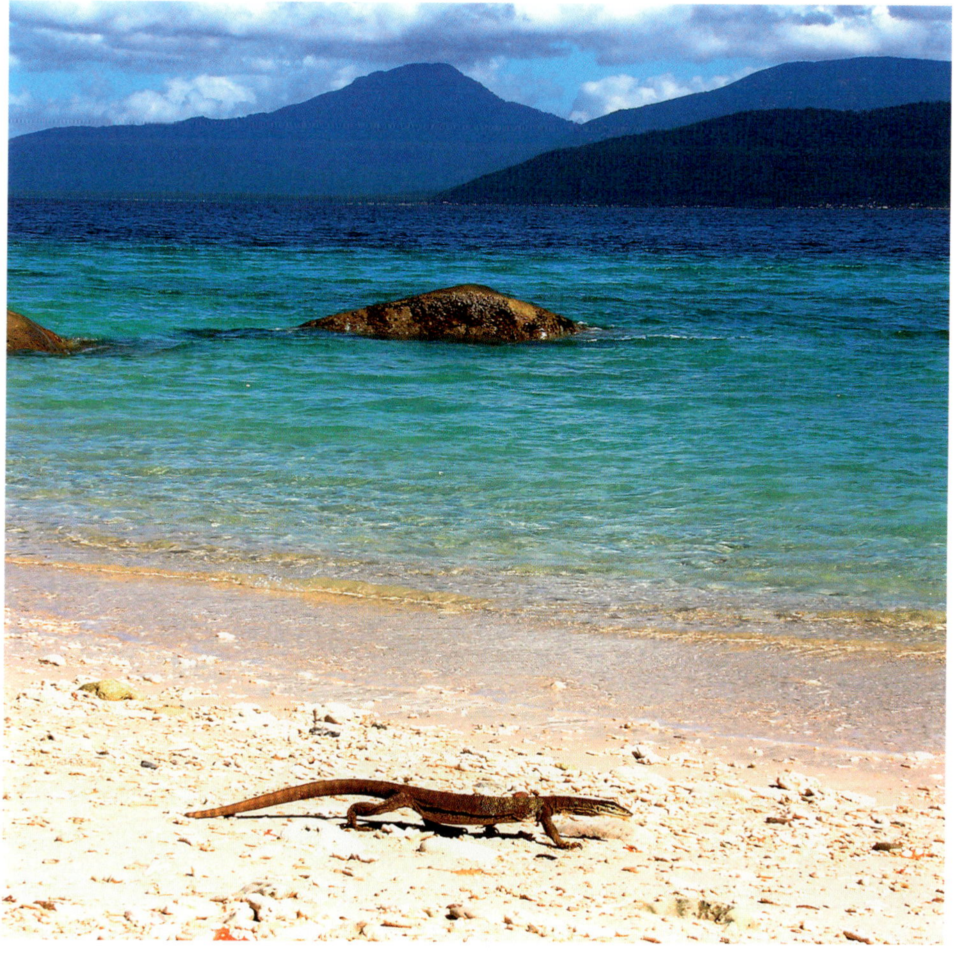

fitzroy island

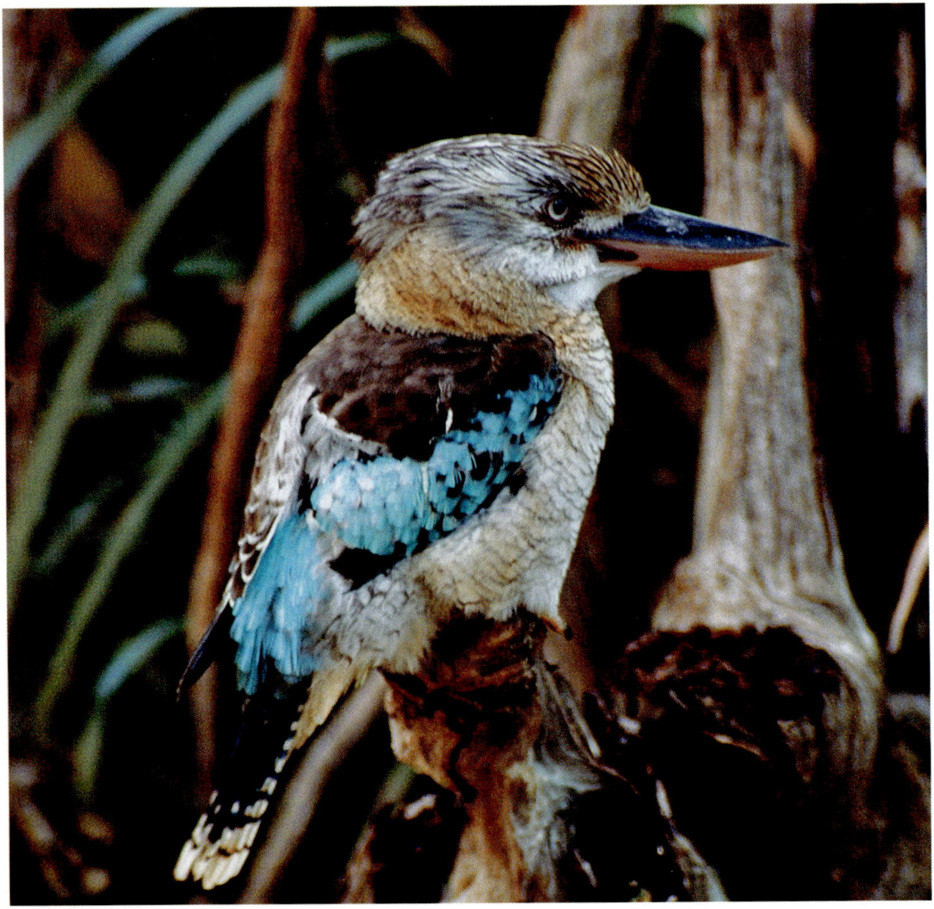

 blue winged kookaburra

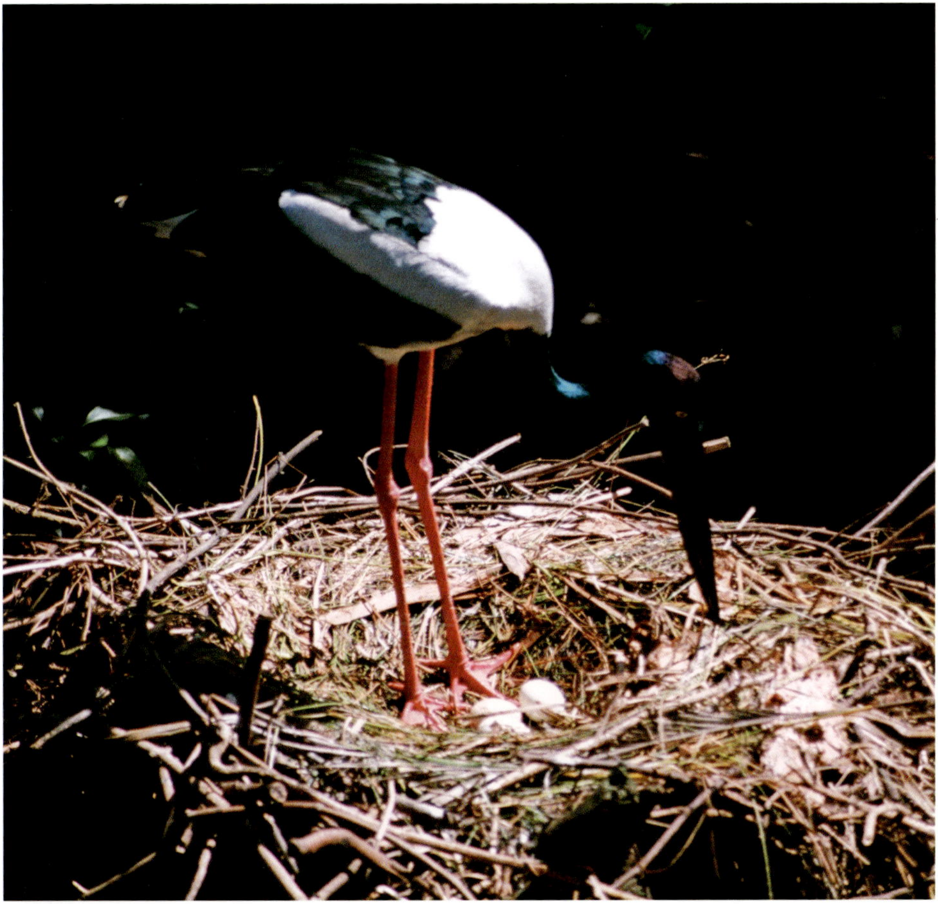

next page. nourlangie rock

black-necked stork

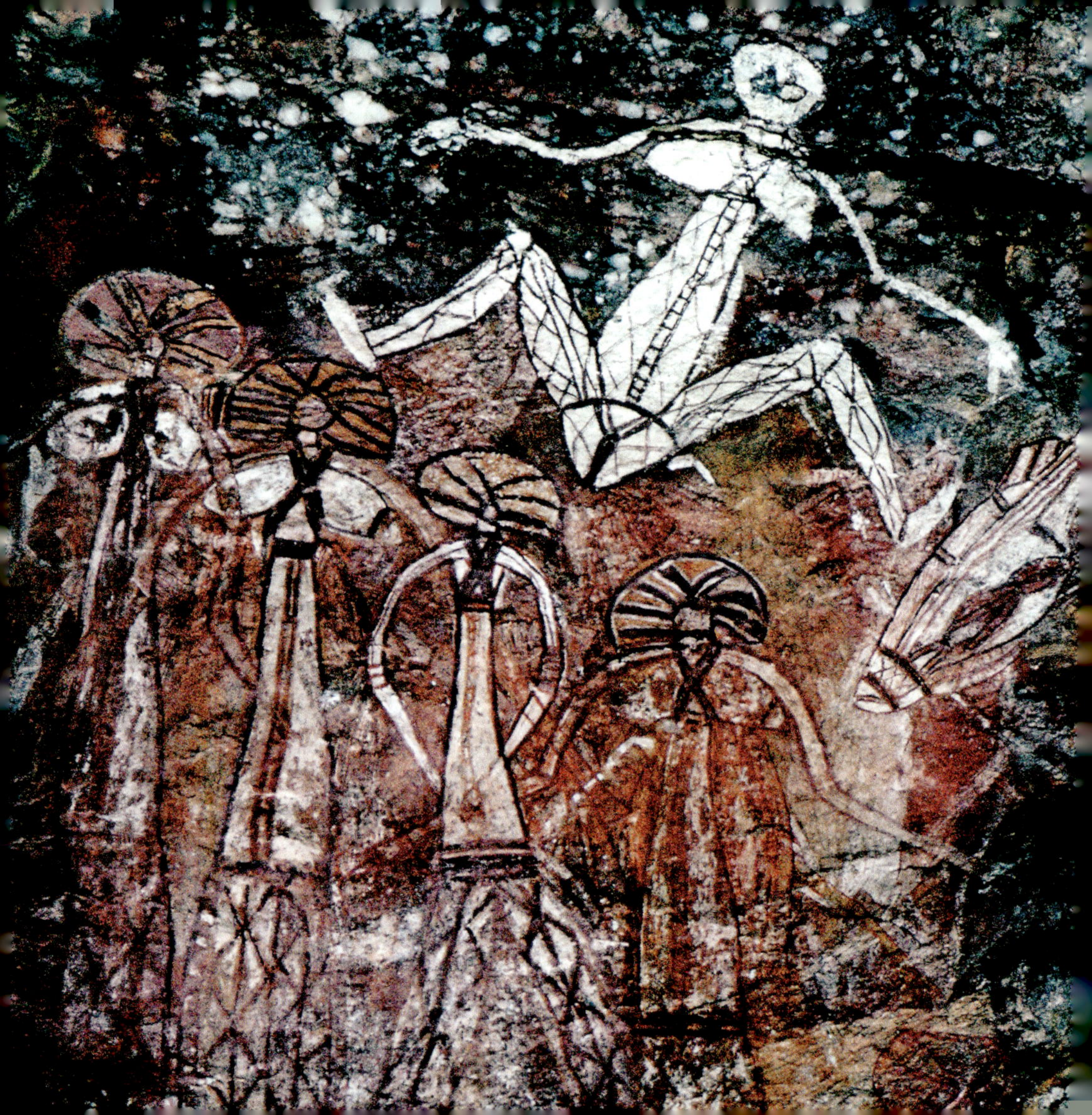

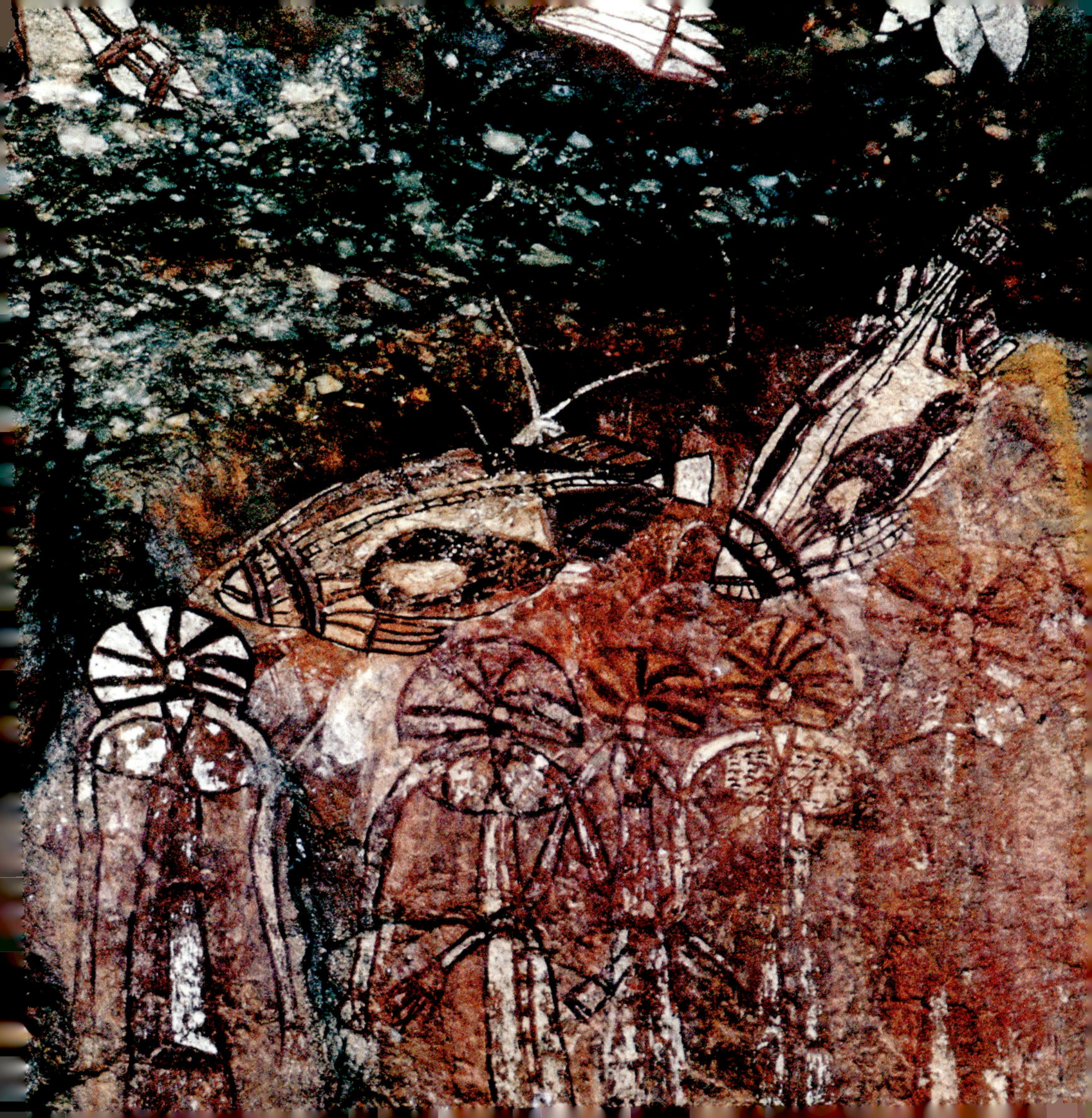

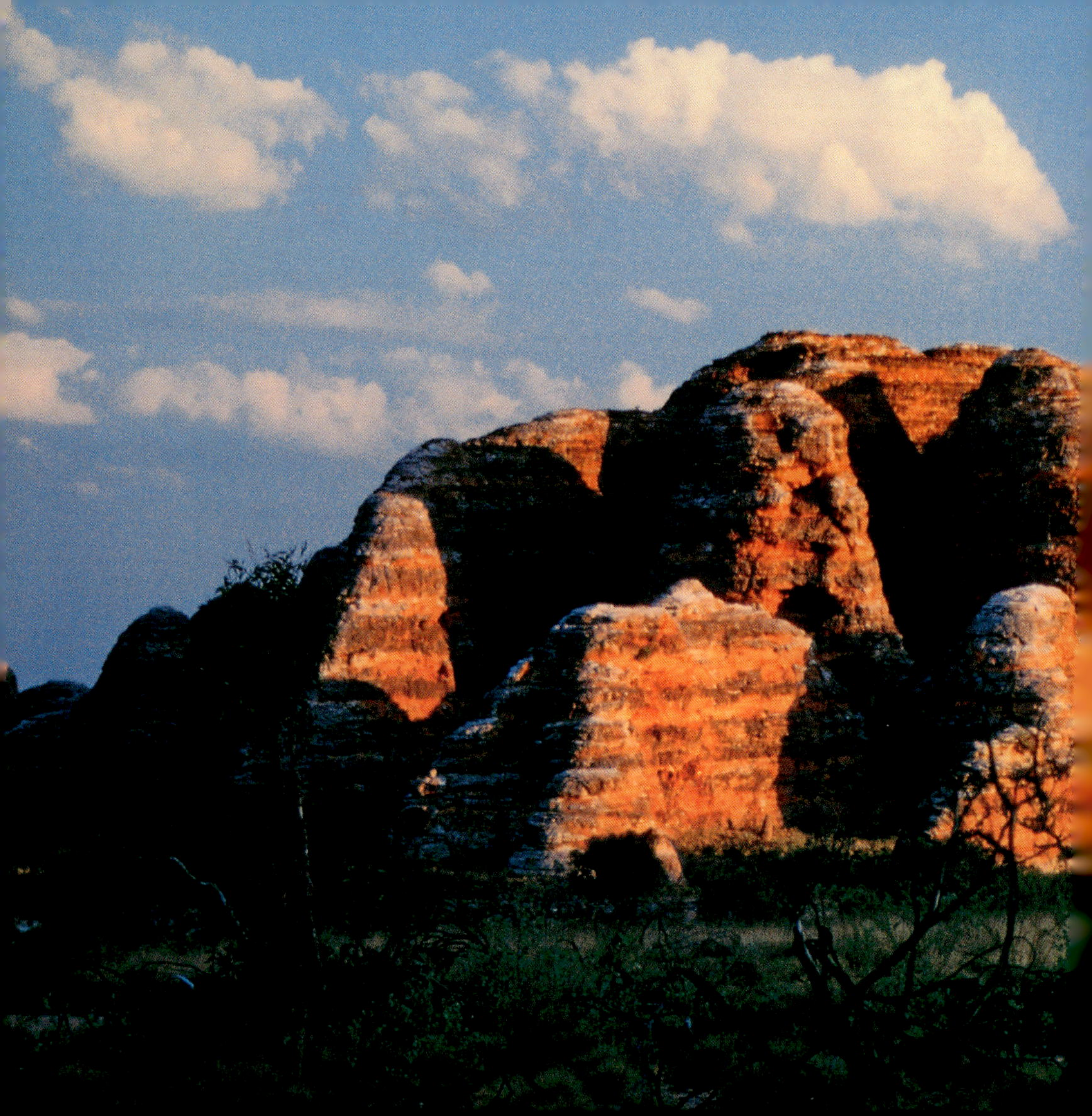

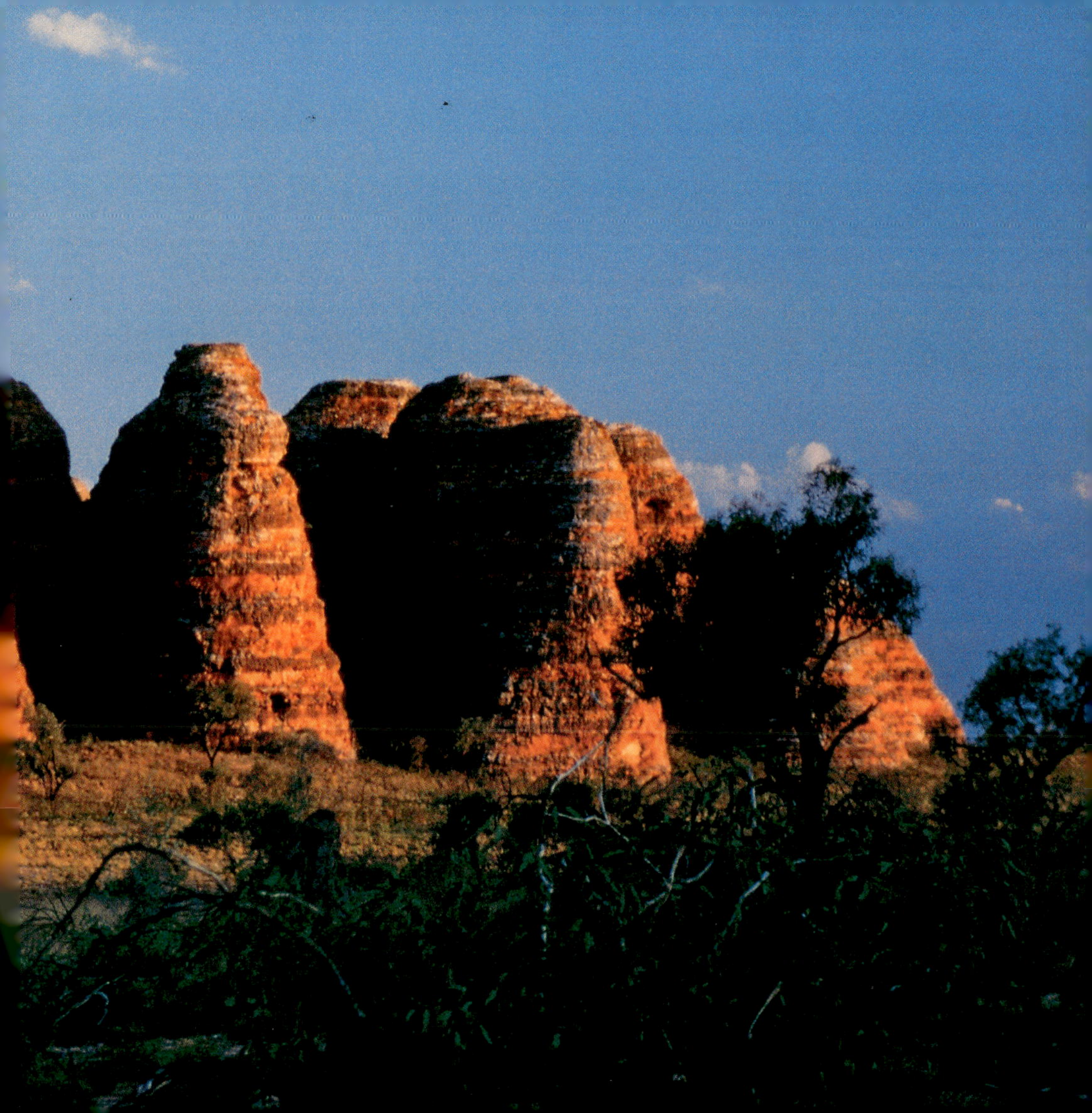

previous page. purnululu national park

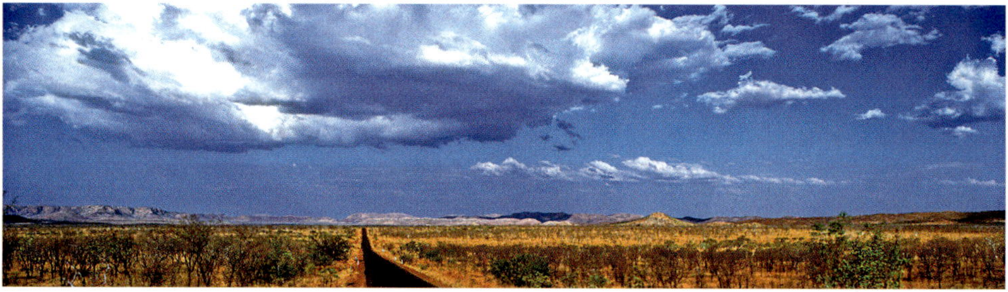

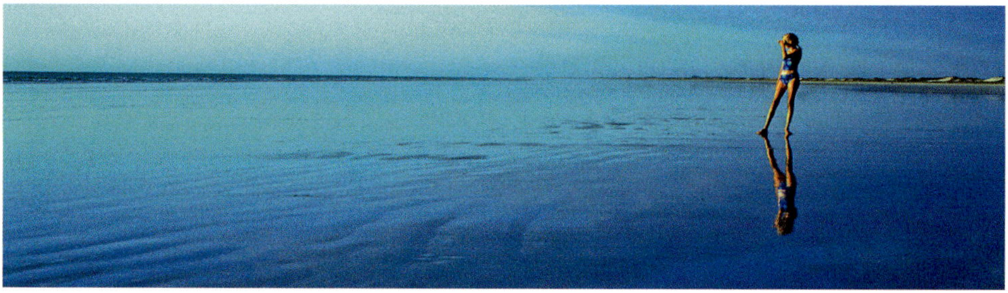

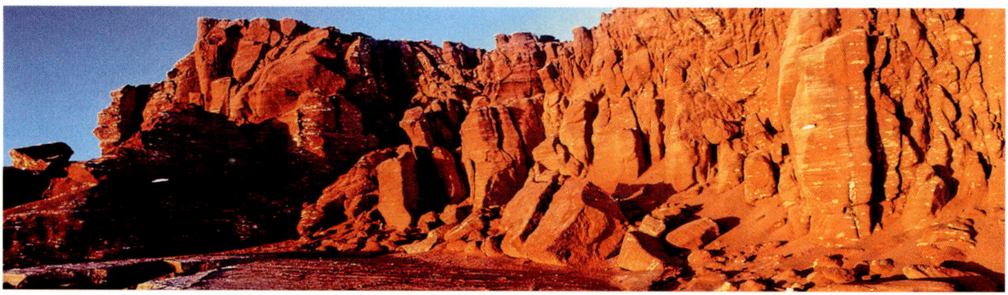

 a. kimberly b. cable beach c. cape leveque

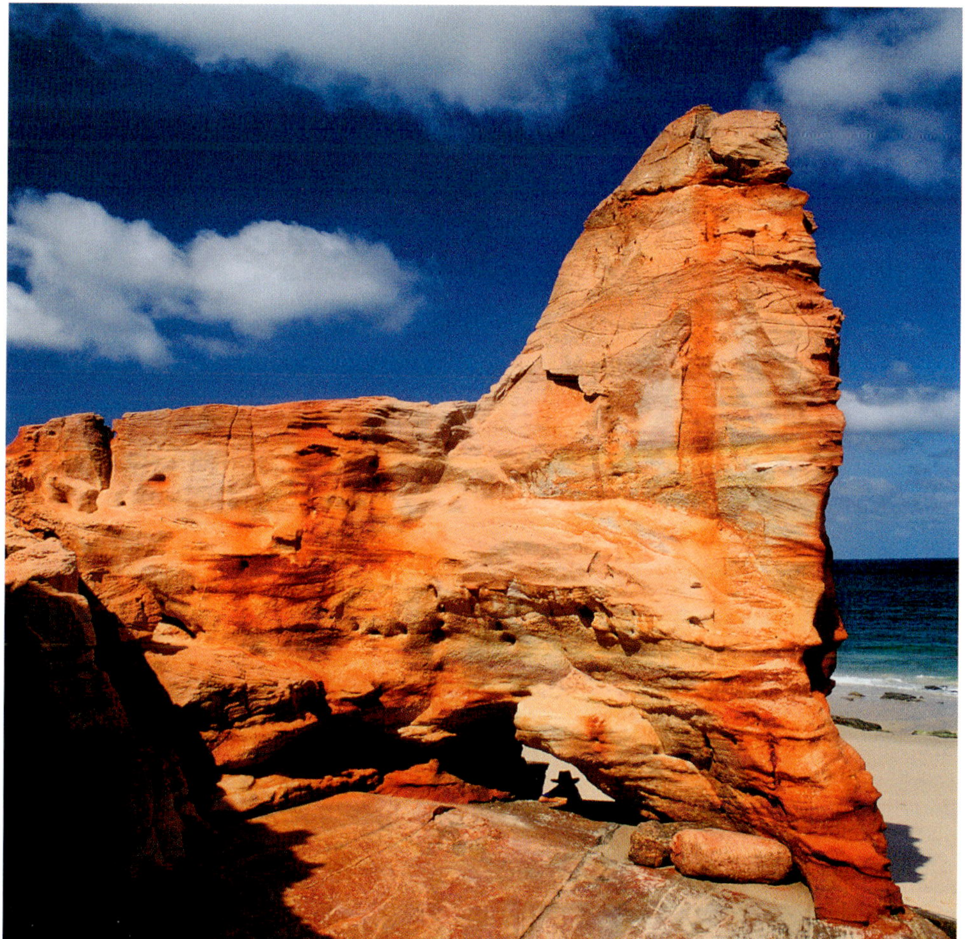

next page. hamersley range, pilbara

cape leveque

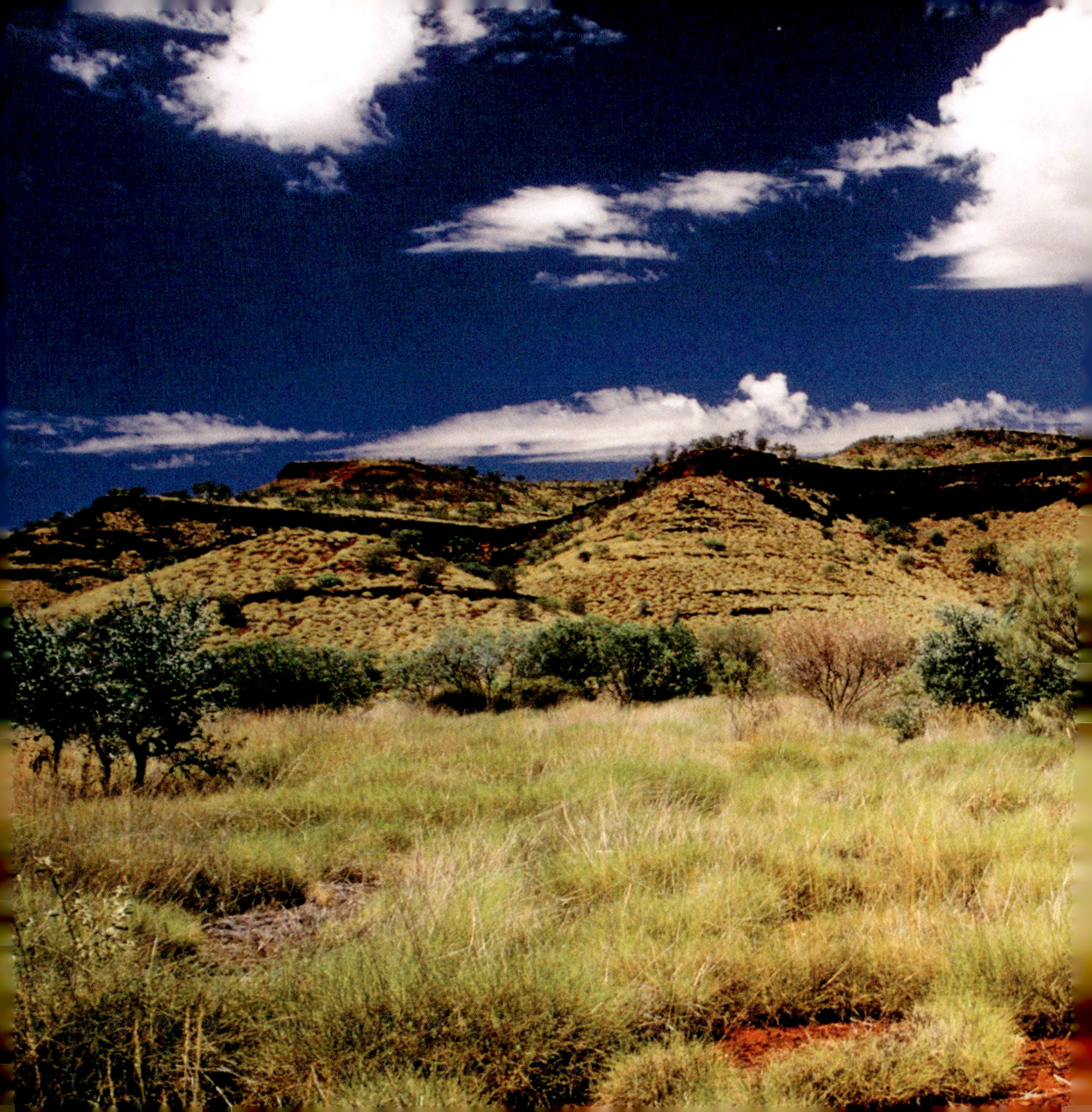

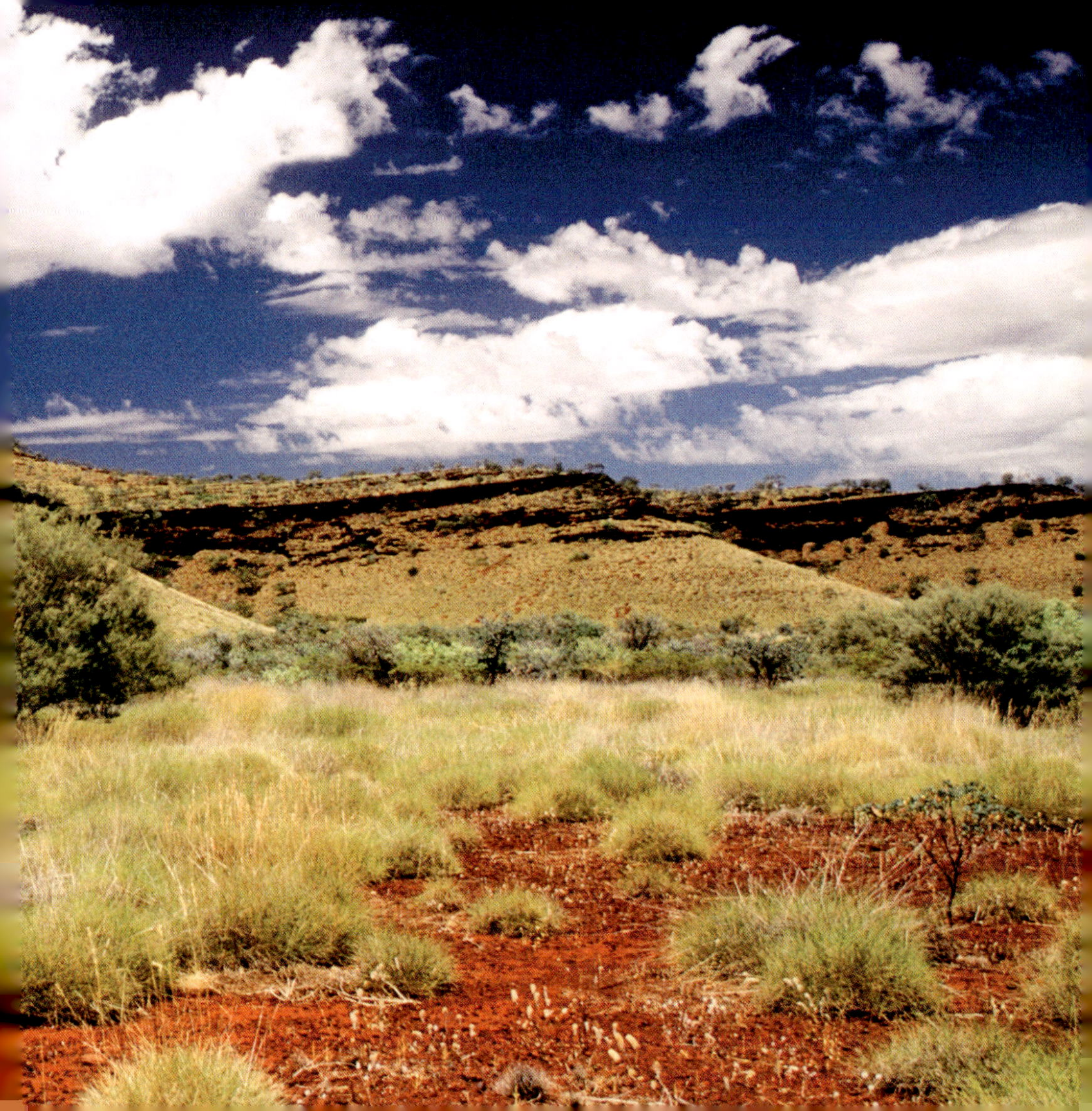

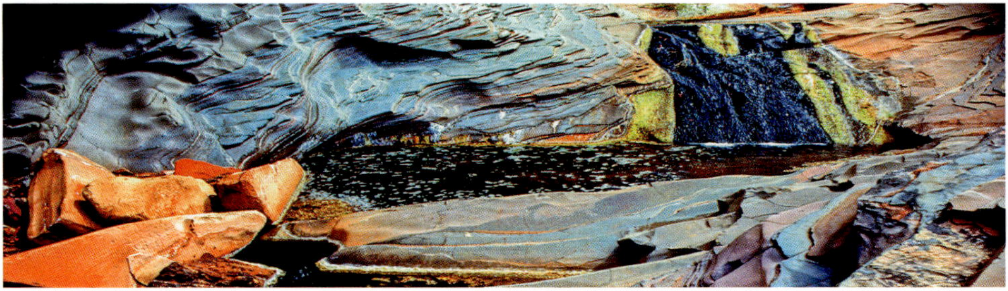

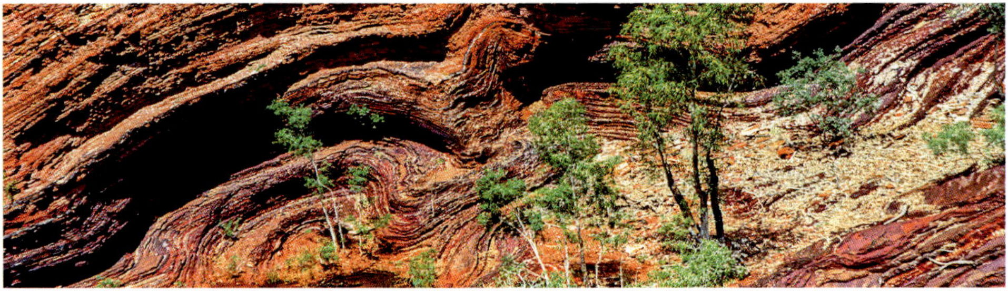

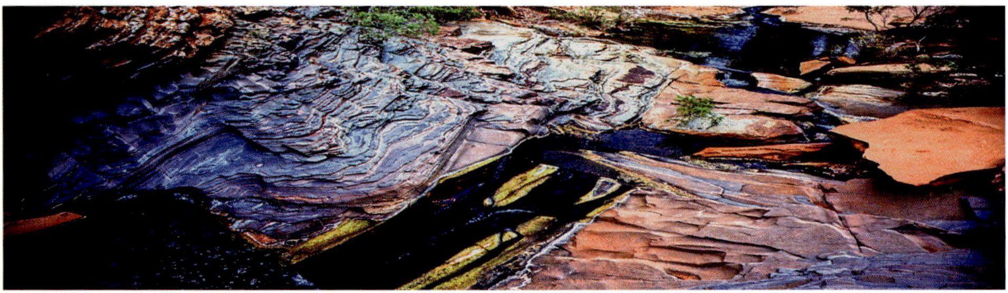

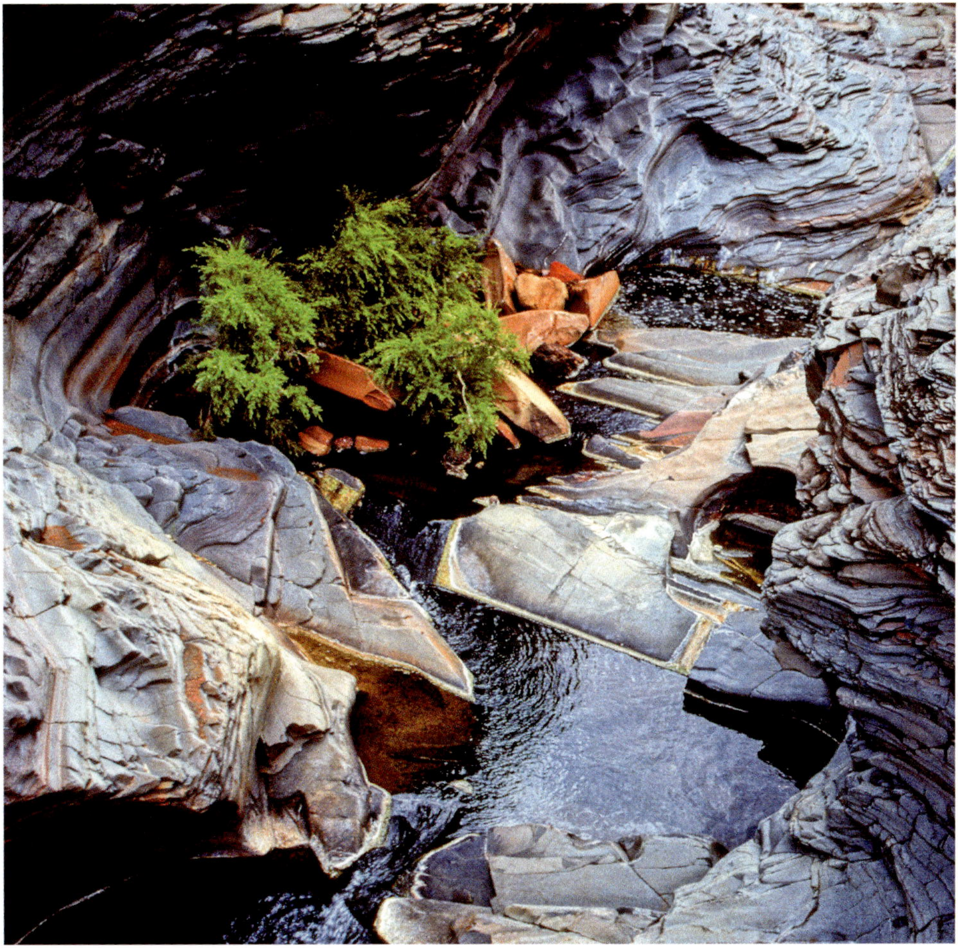

next page. karajini national park

karajini national park

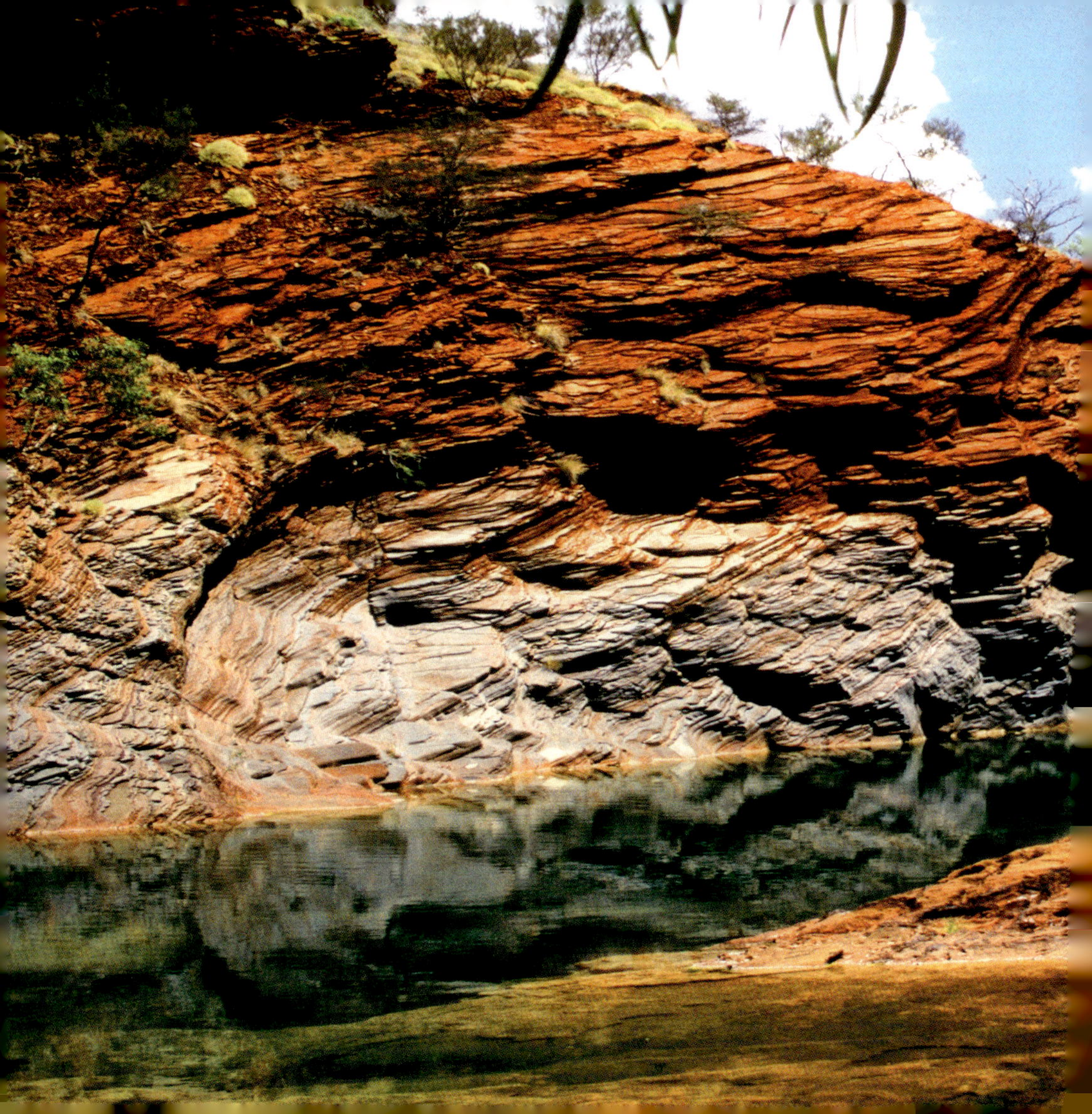

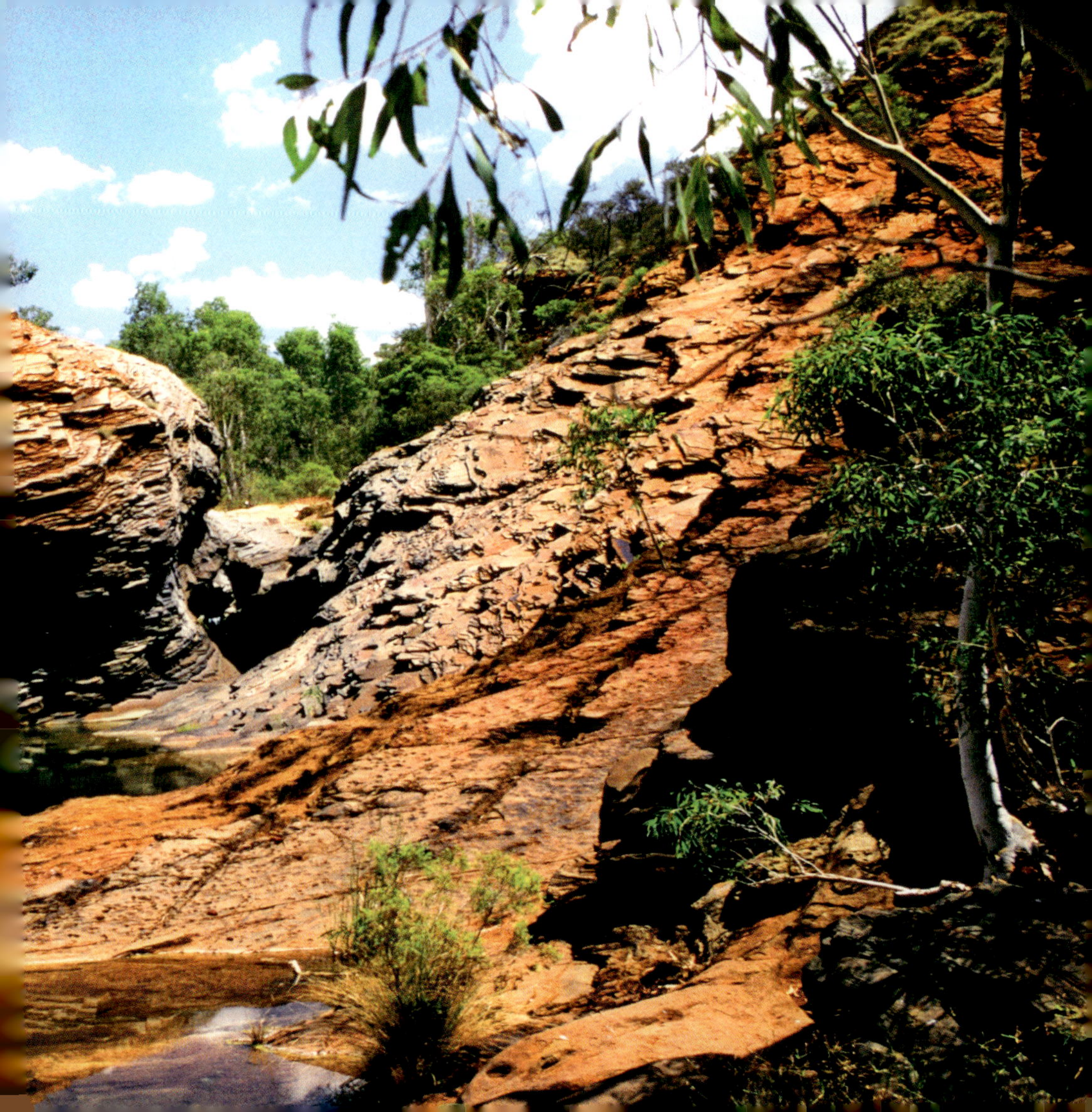

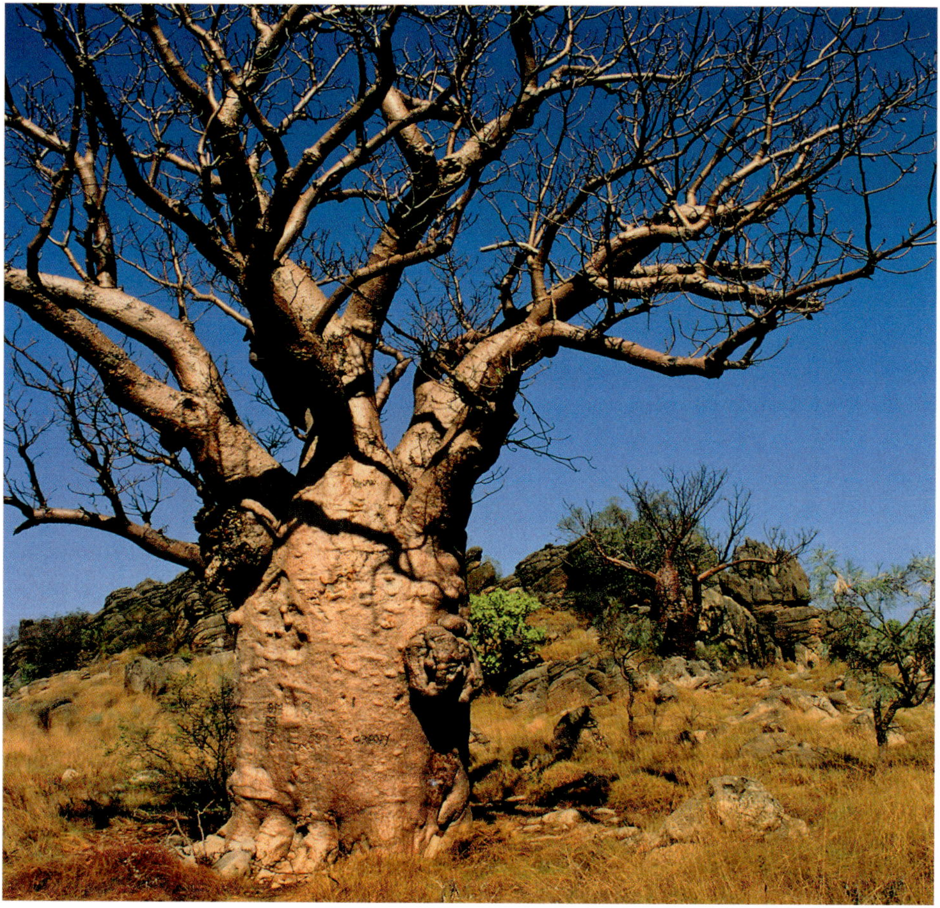

 boab tree, kimberley

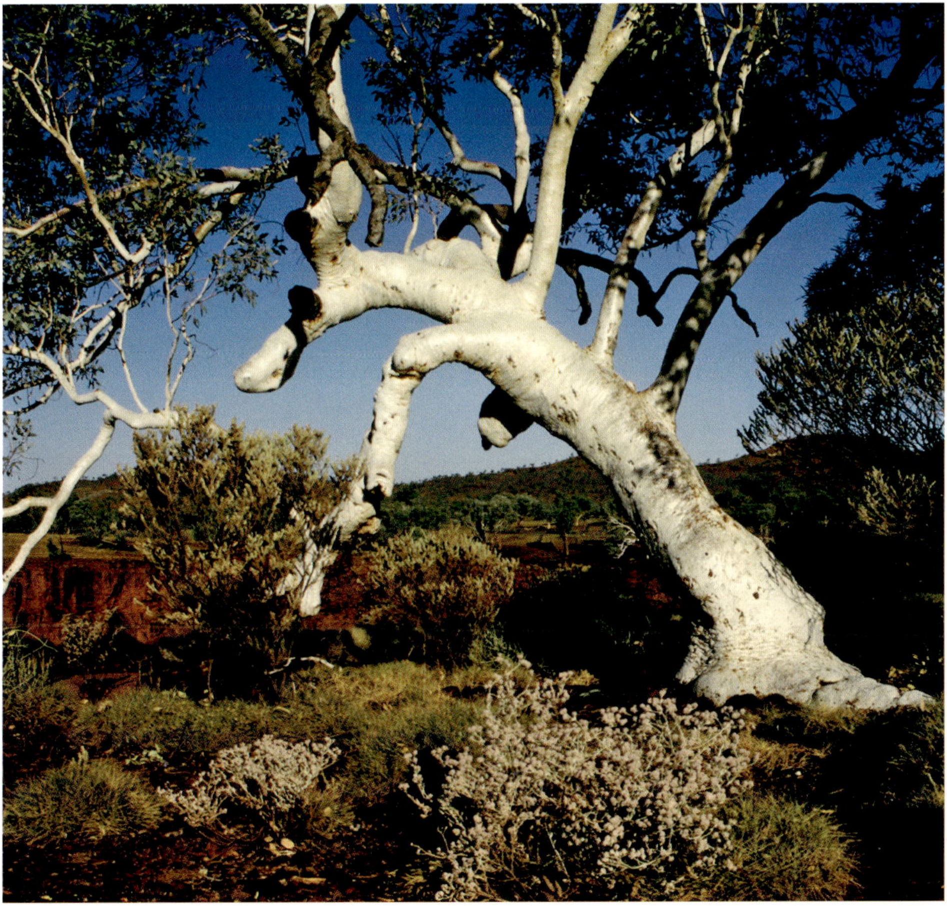

next page. cape leseur

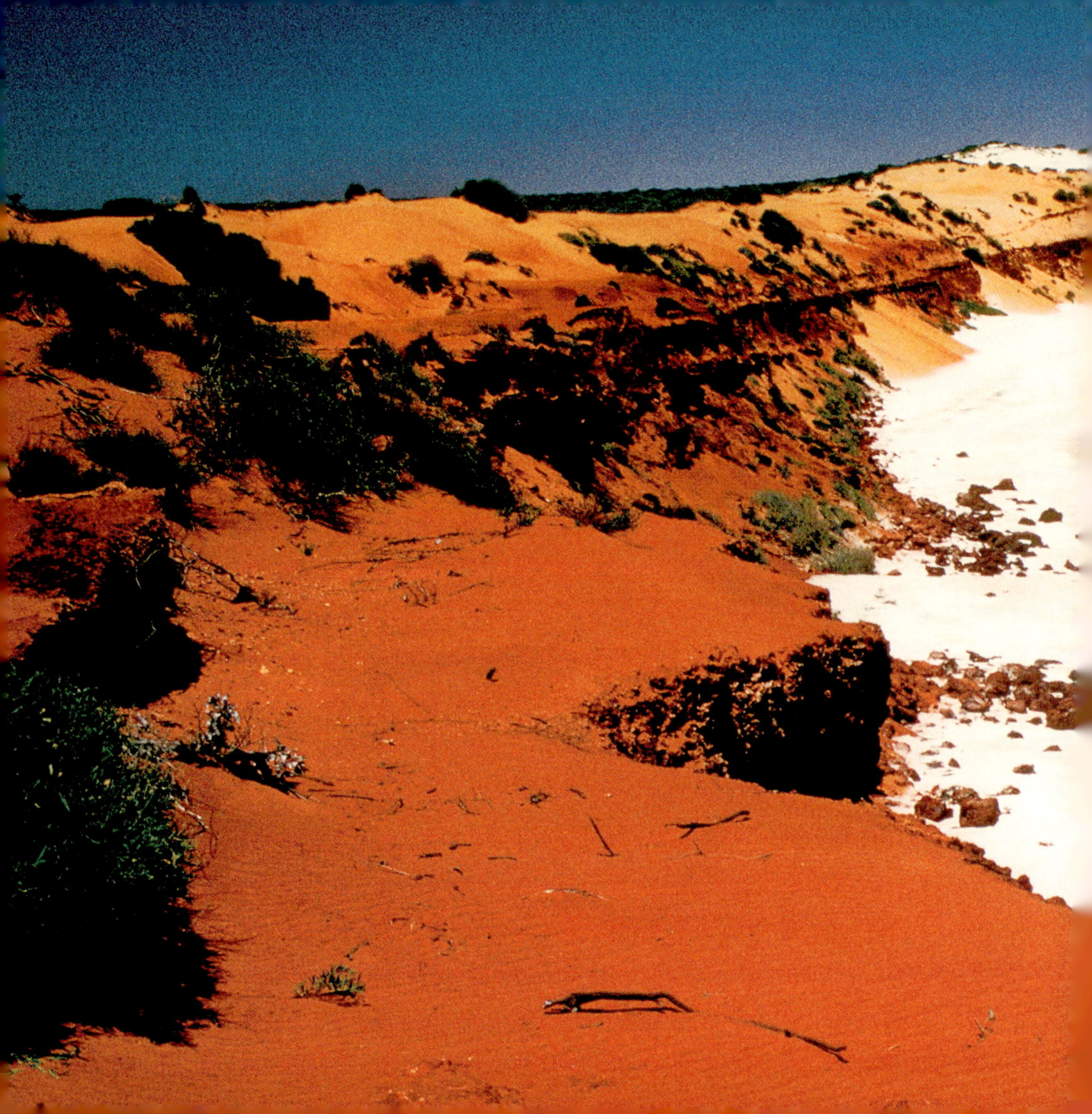

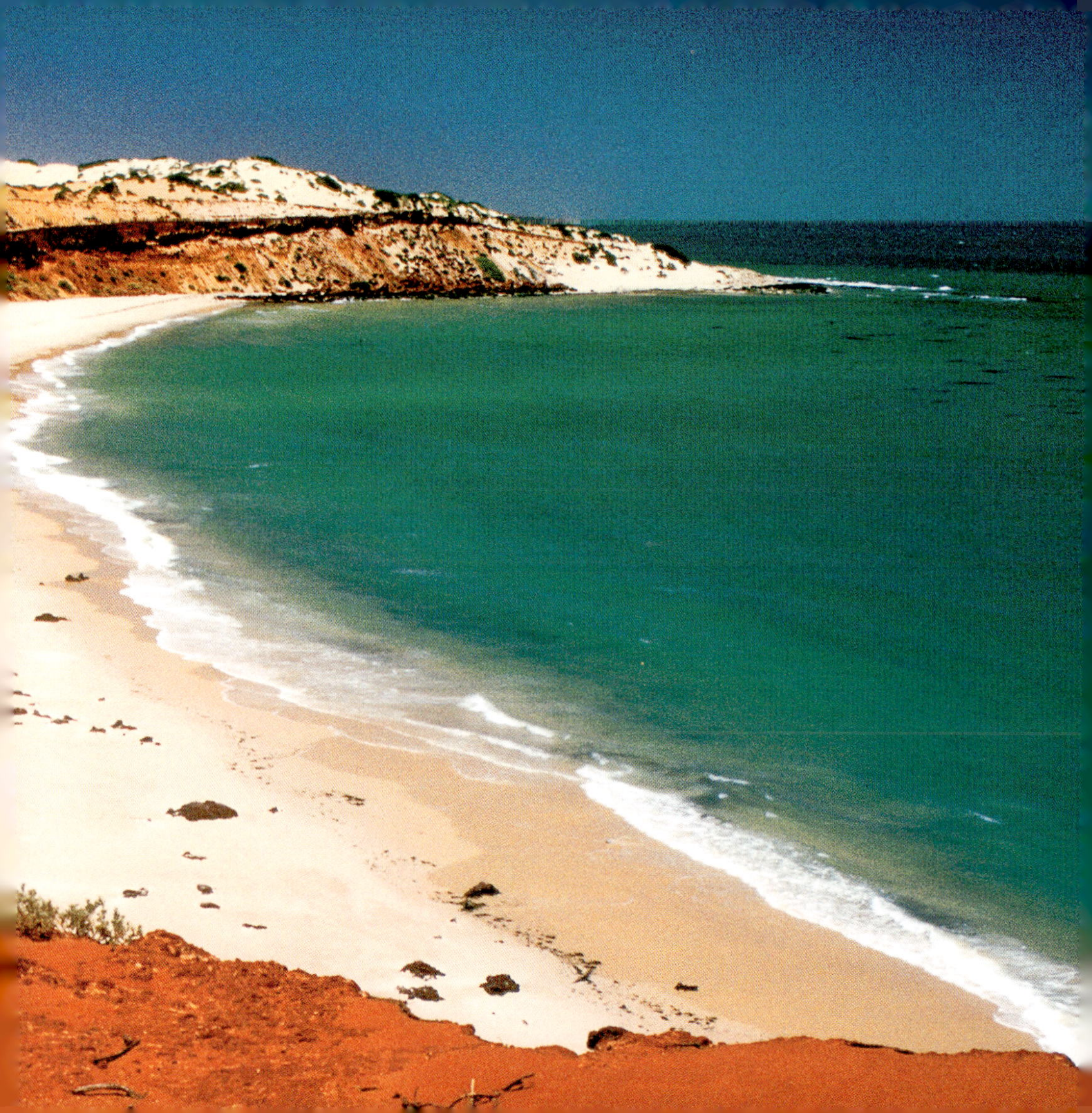

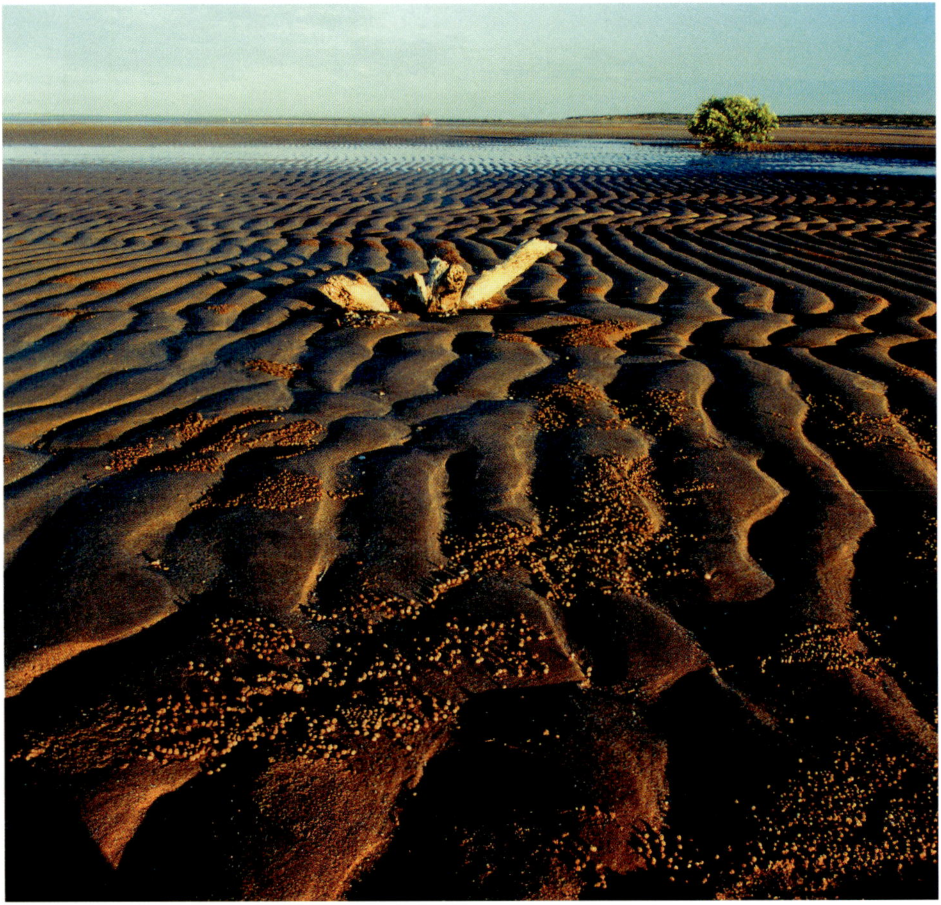

 mud flats, port hedland

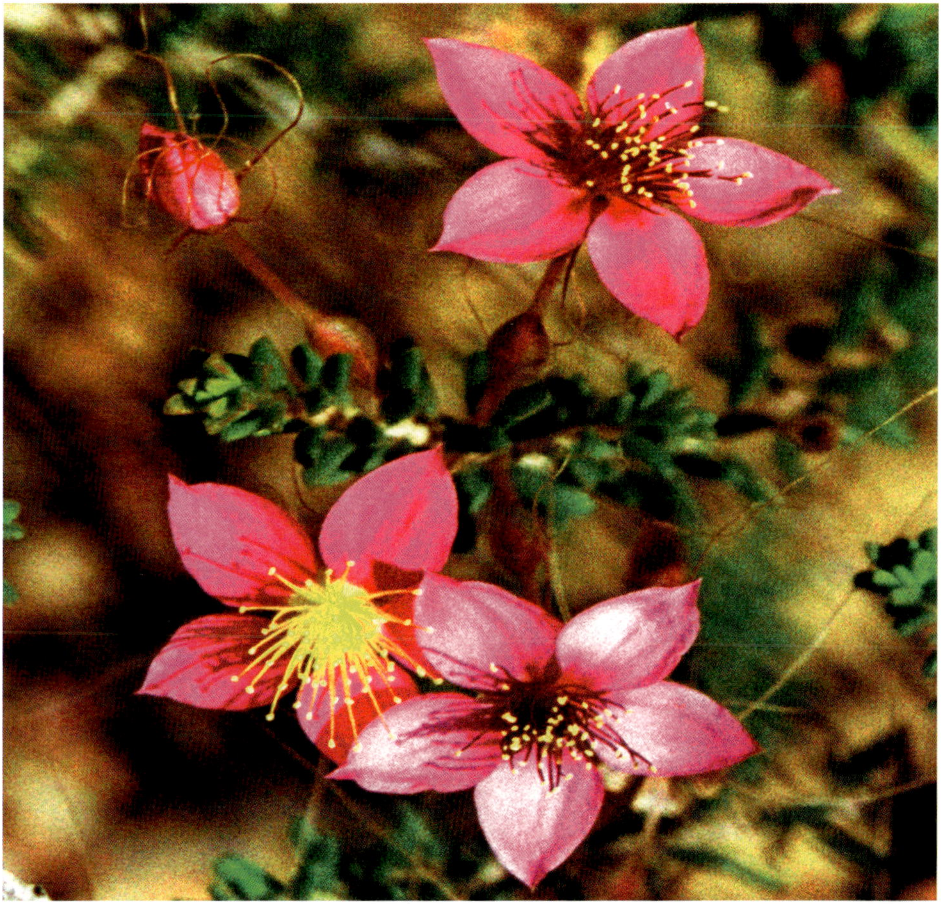

next page, pinnacles

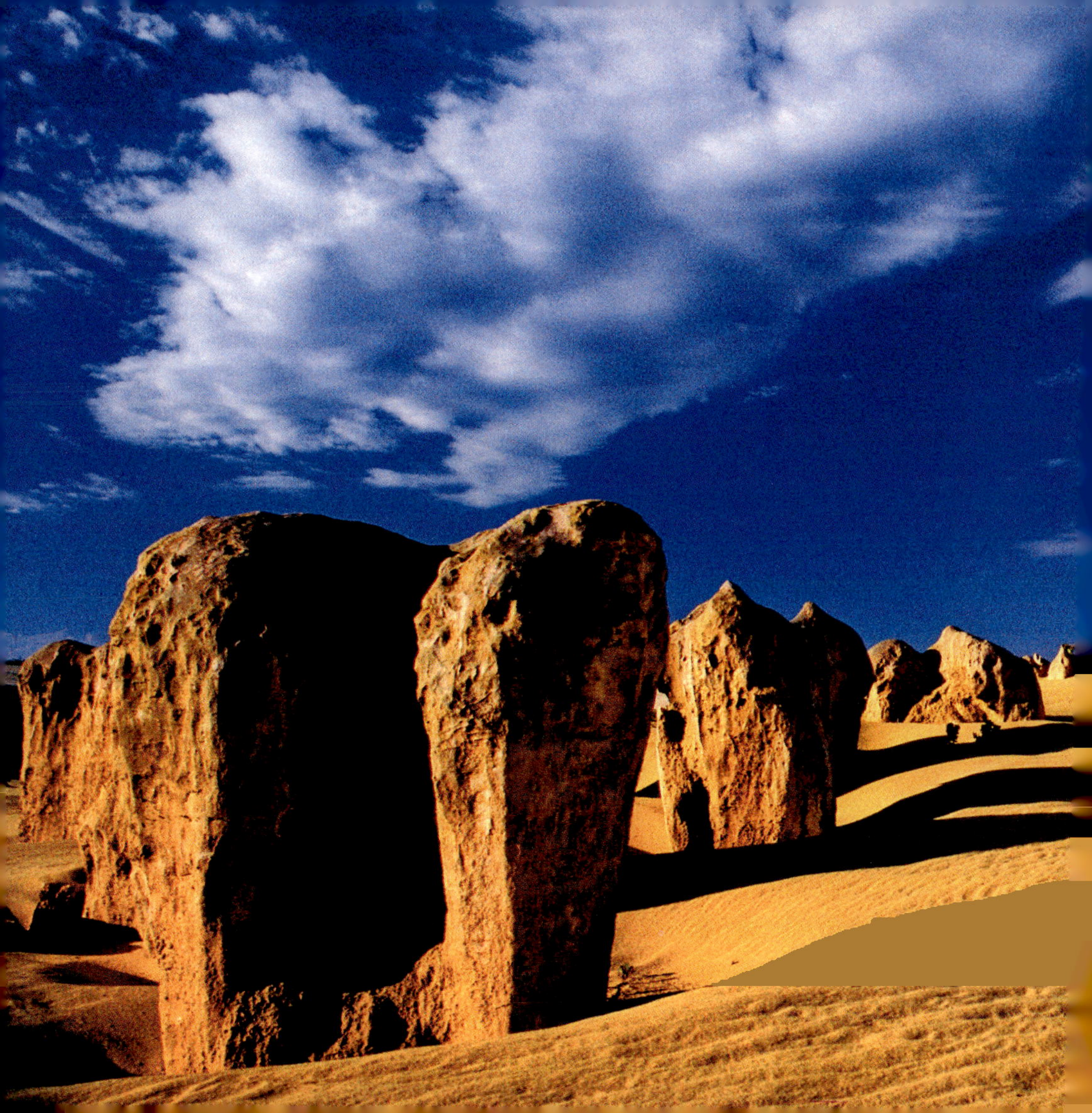

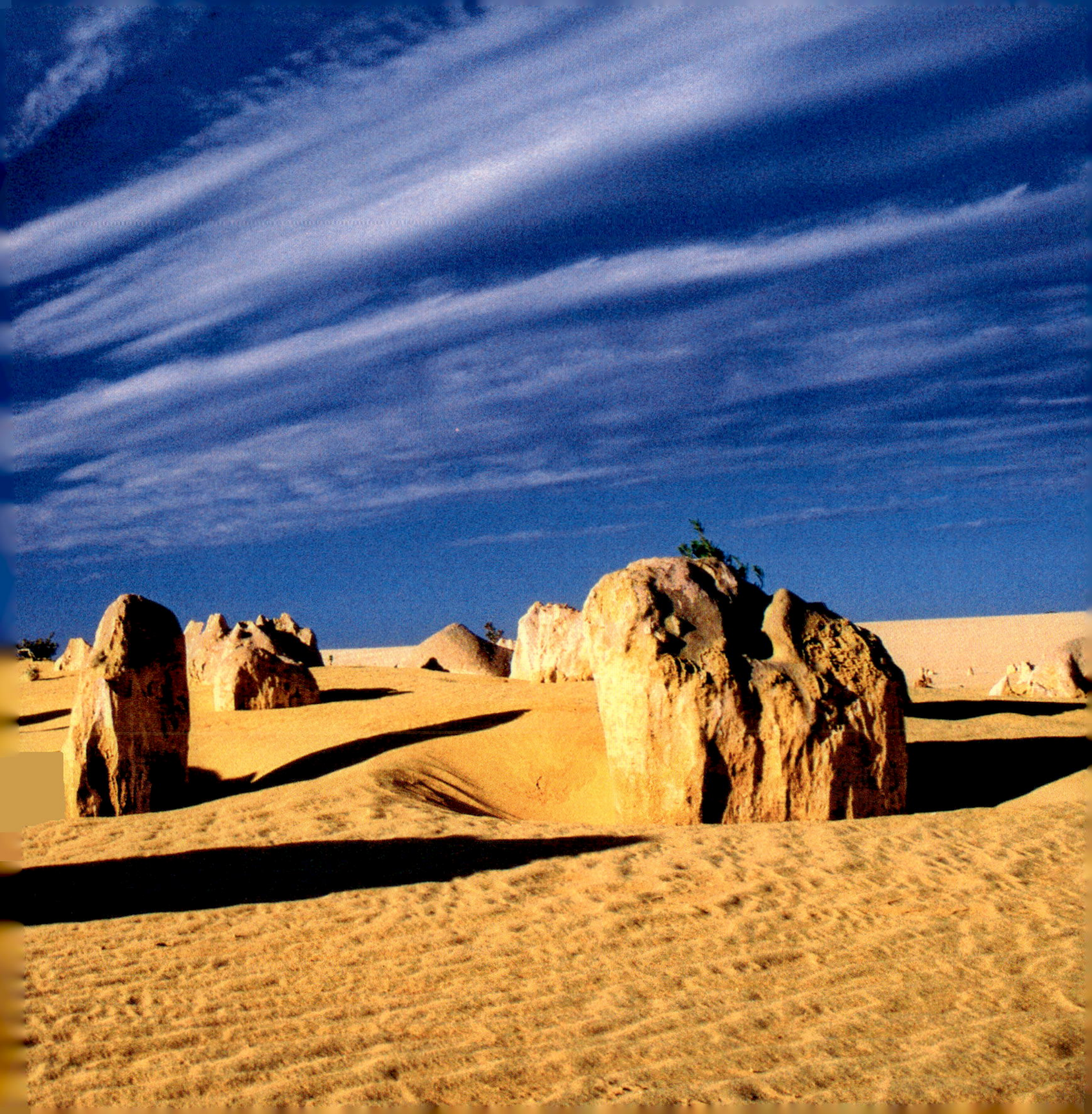

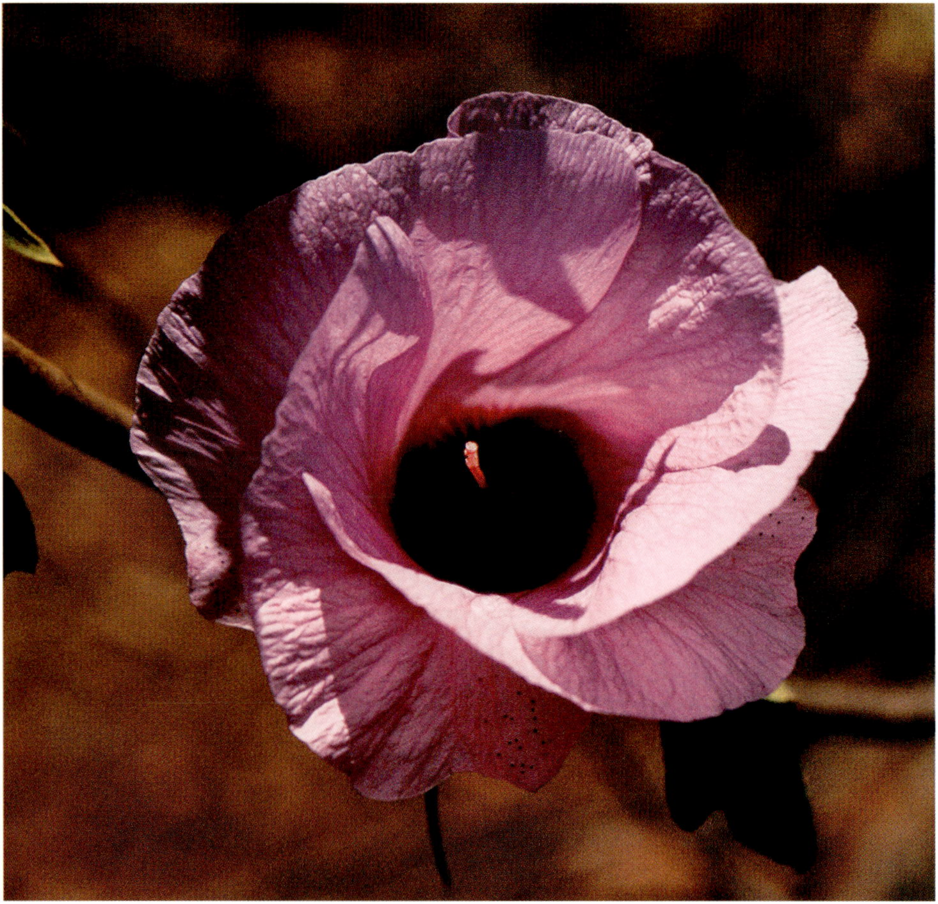

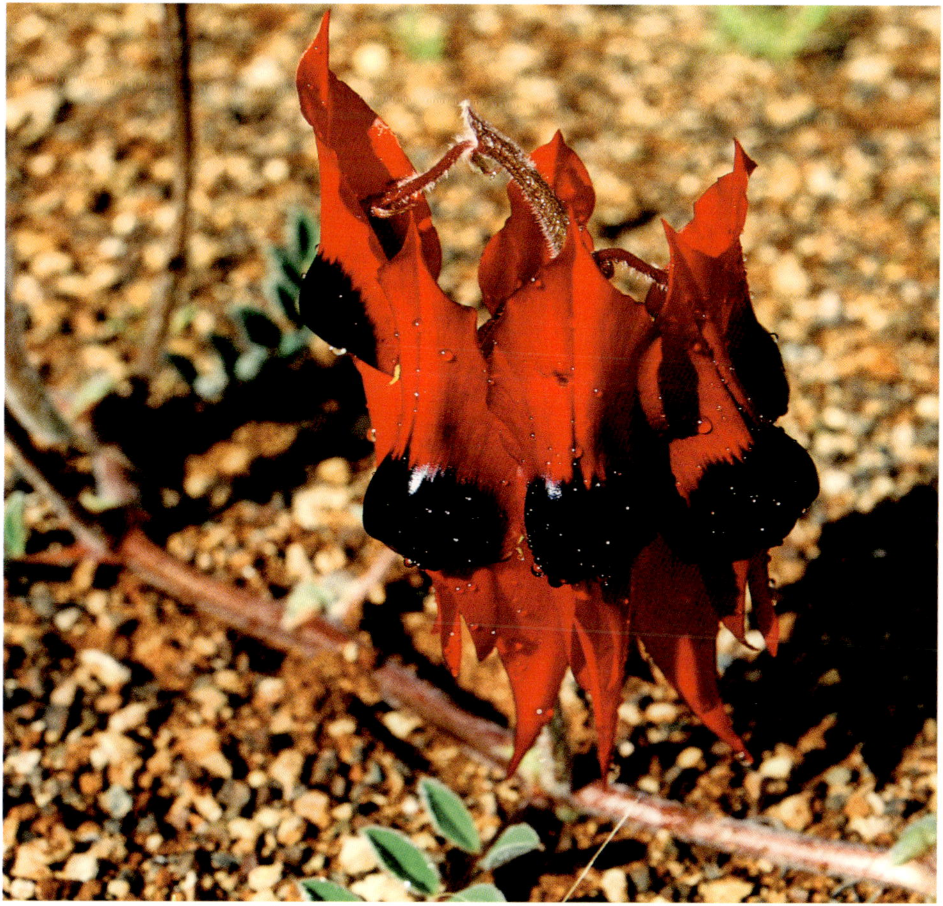

next page. swan river, perth

sturt desert pea

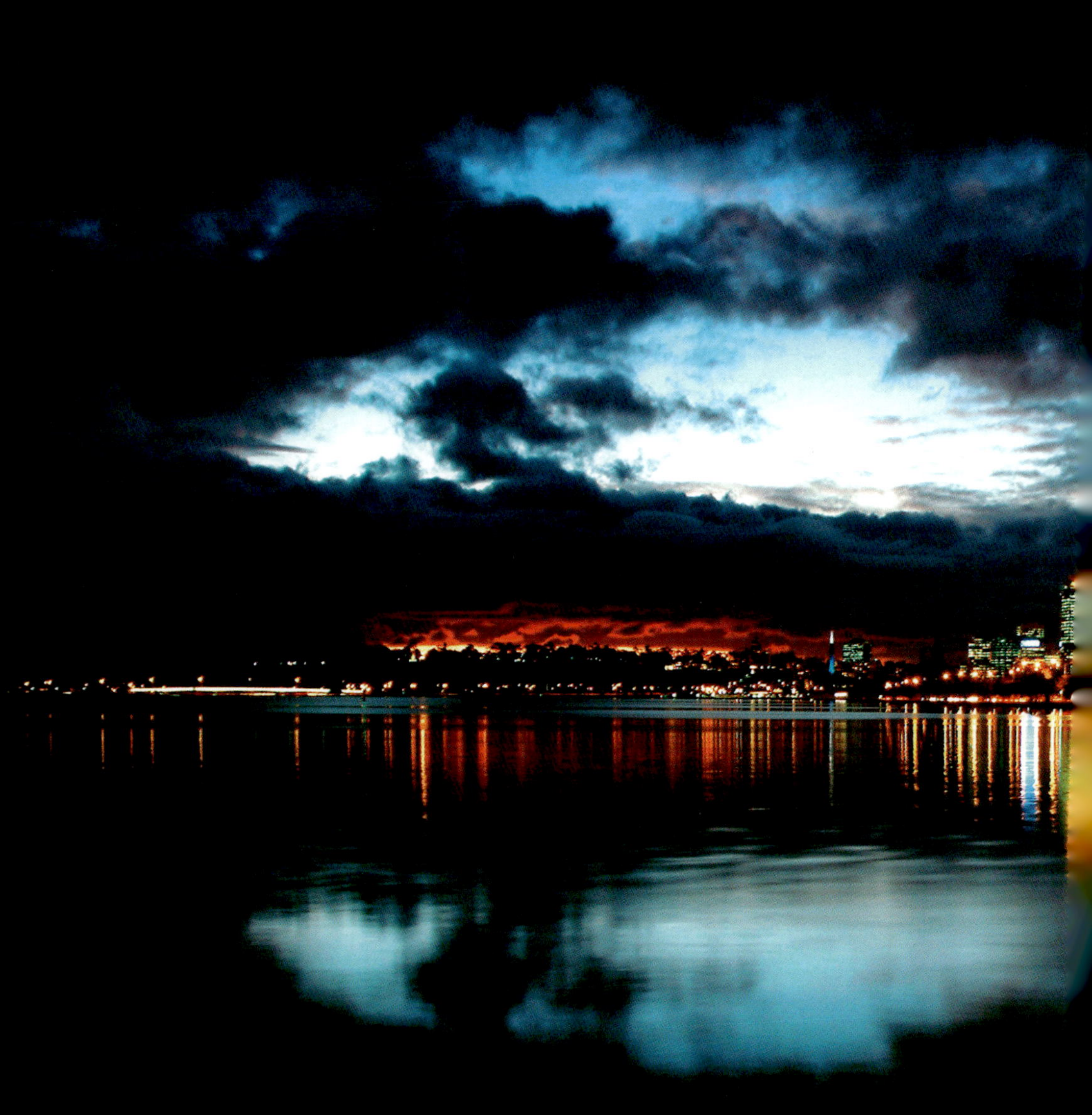

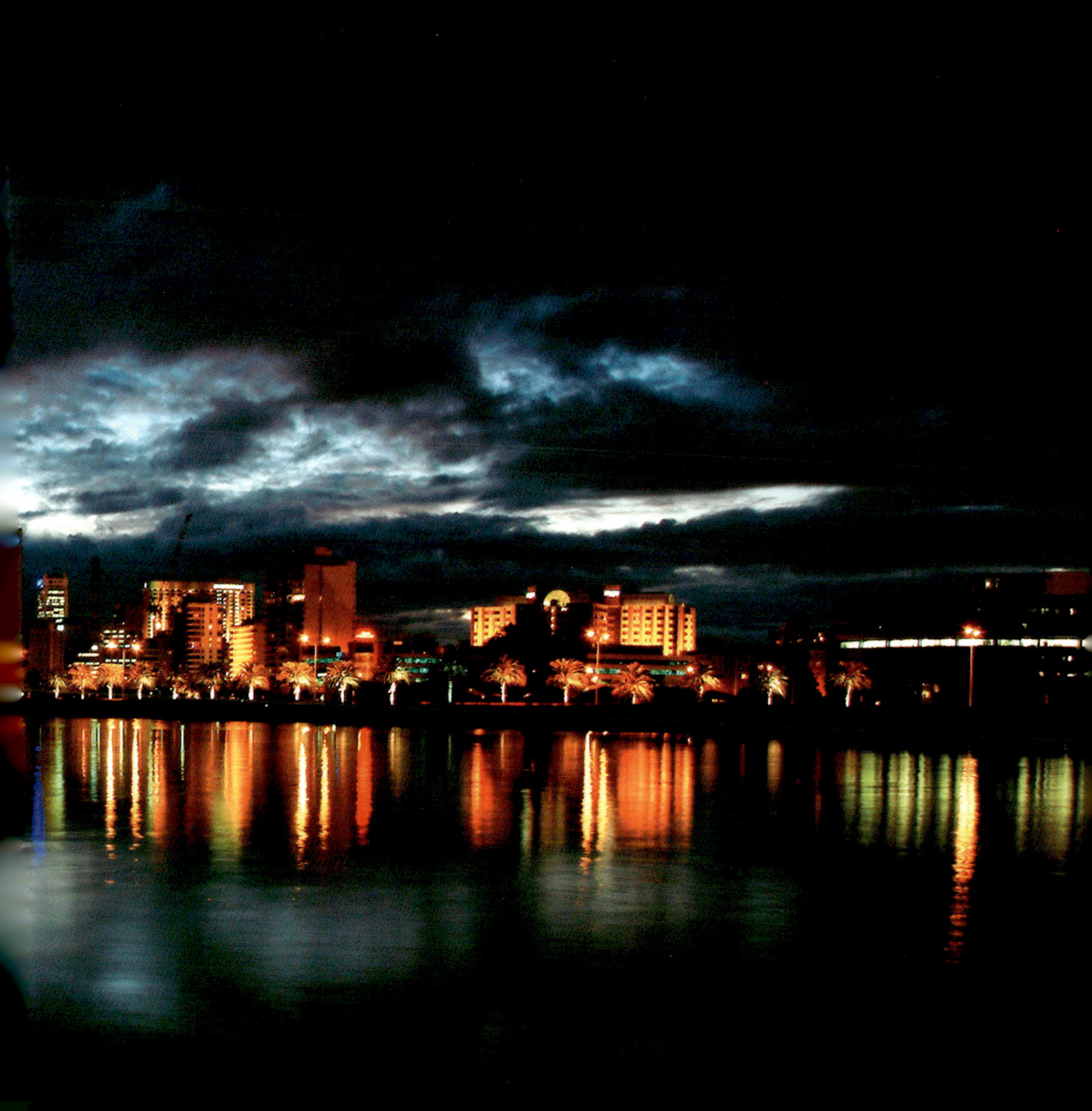

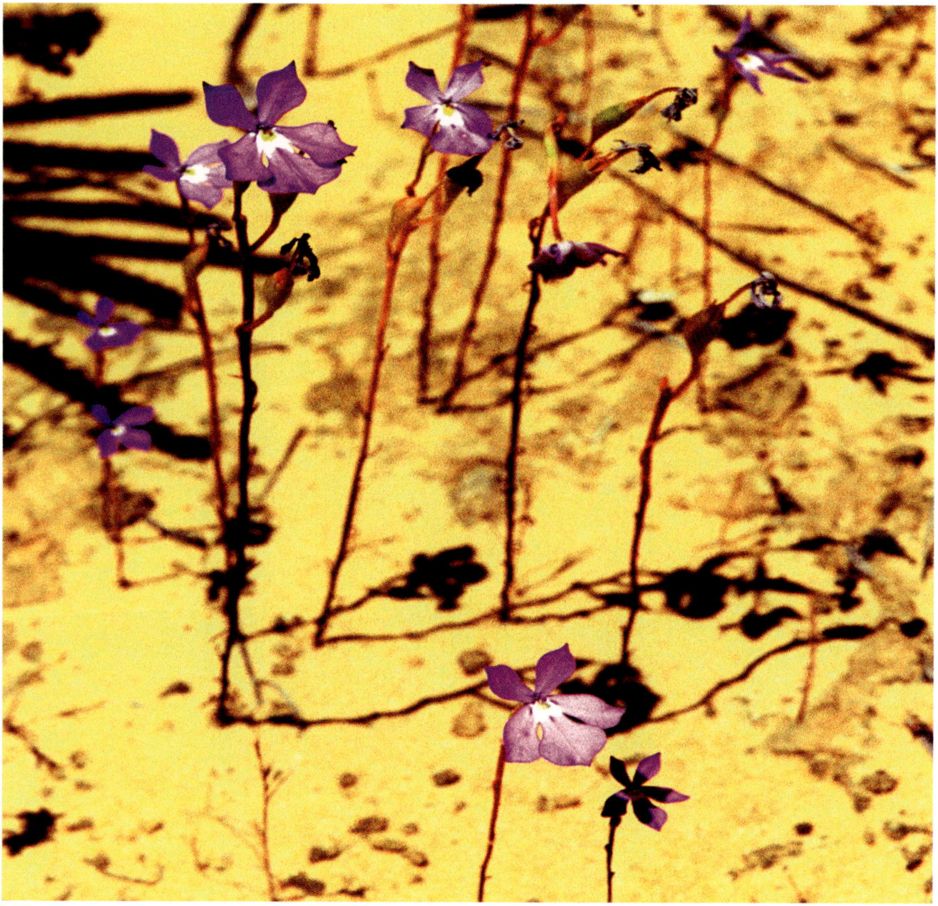

 desert flower, pinnacles

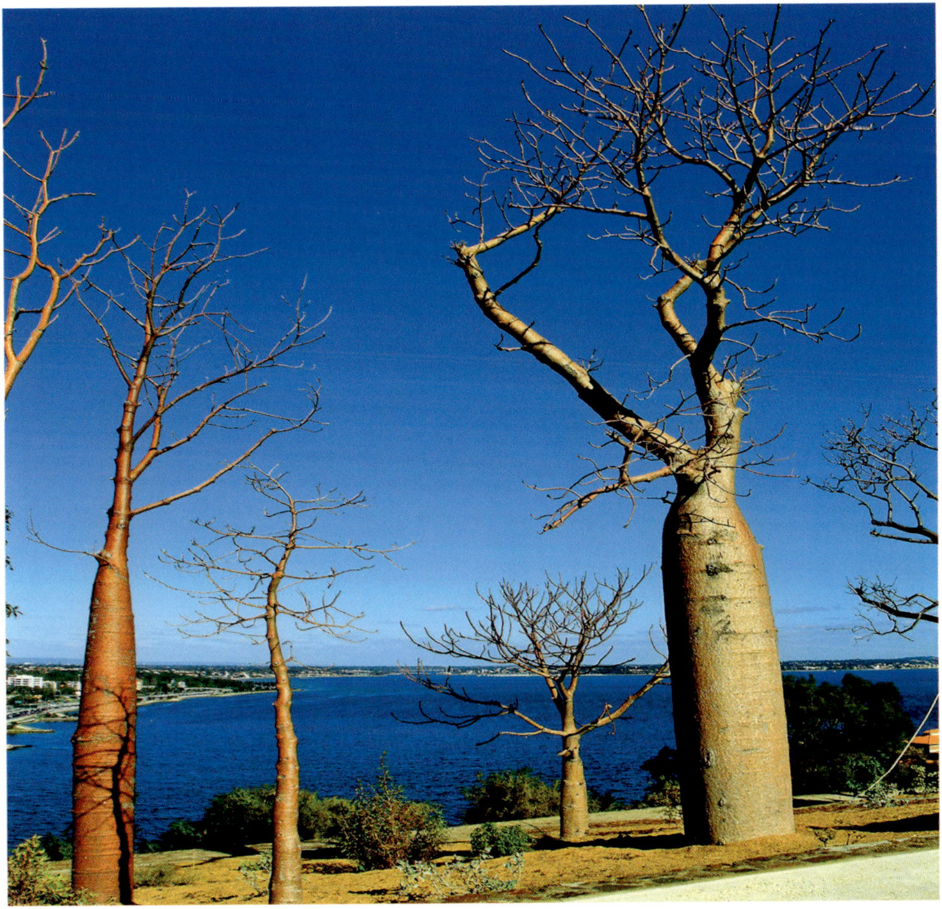

boab trees, kings park, perth

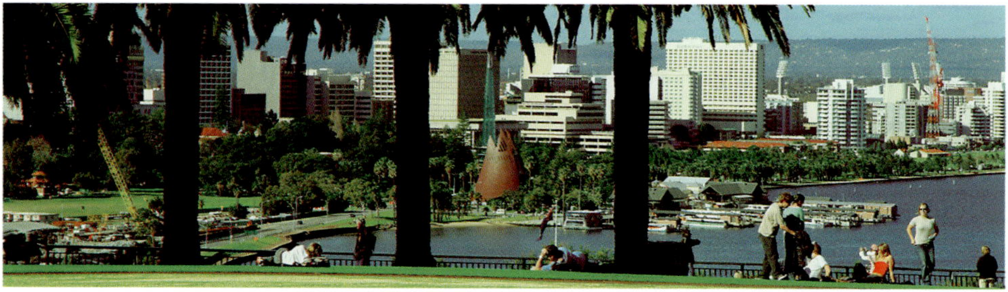

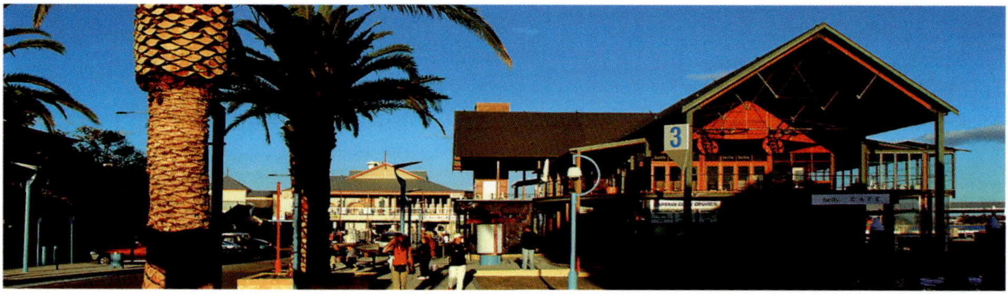

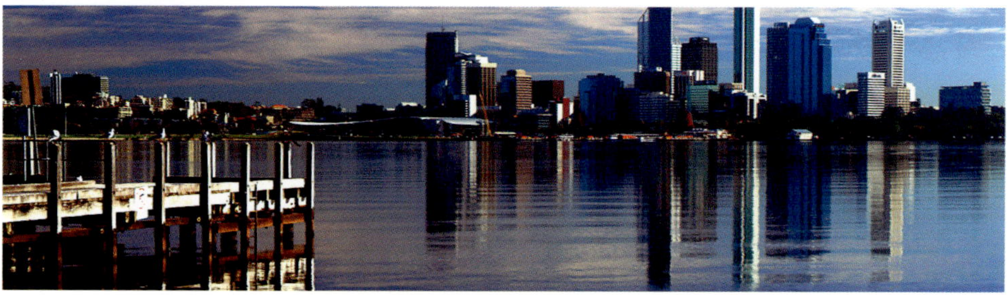

 a. view from kings park b. barrack square c. swan river

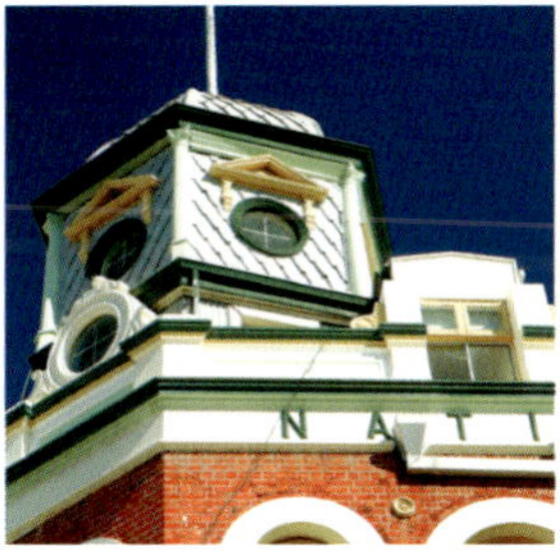
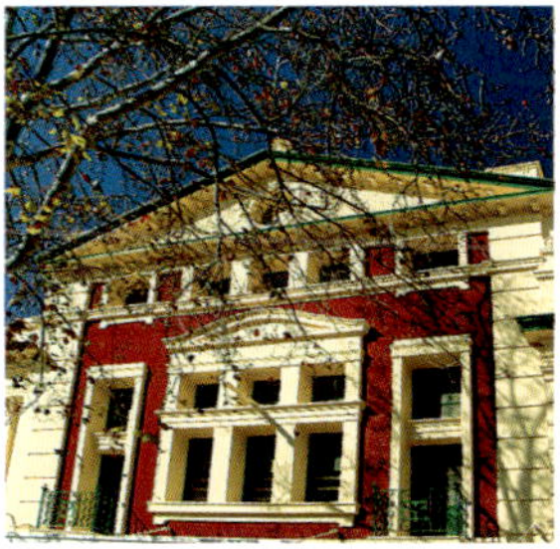
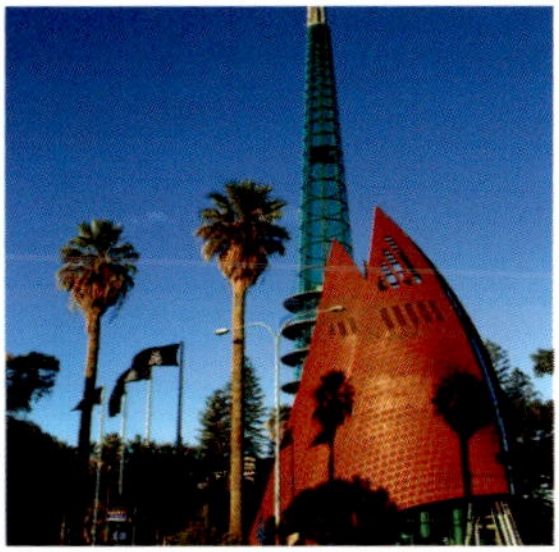
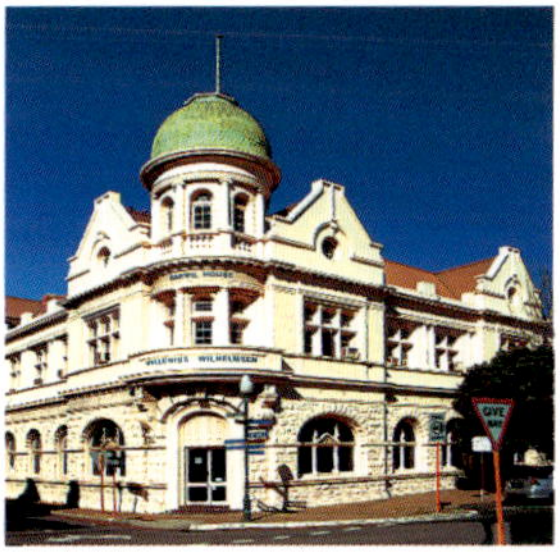
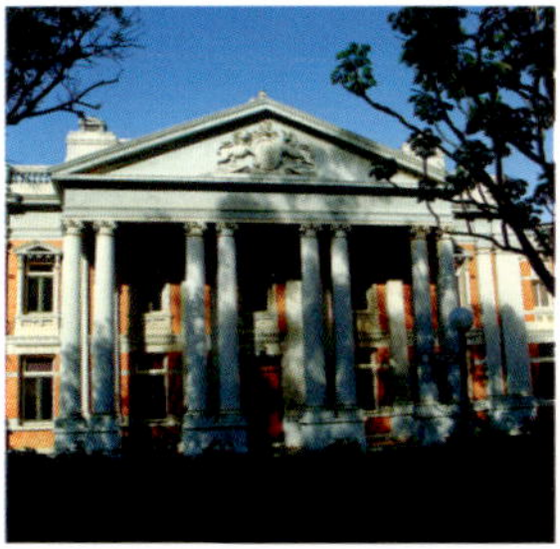
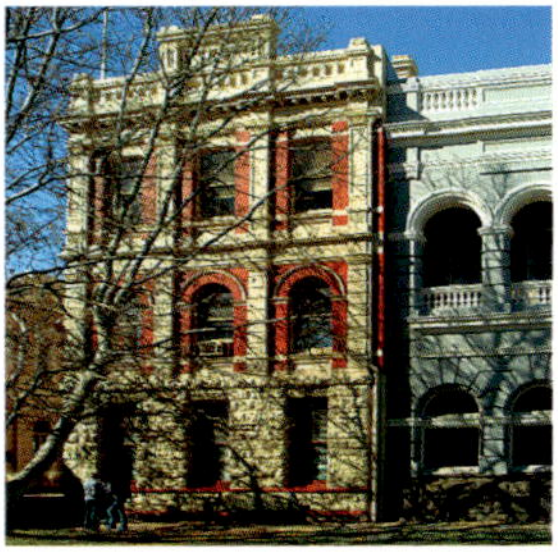
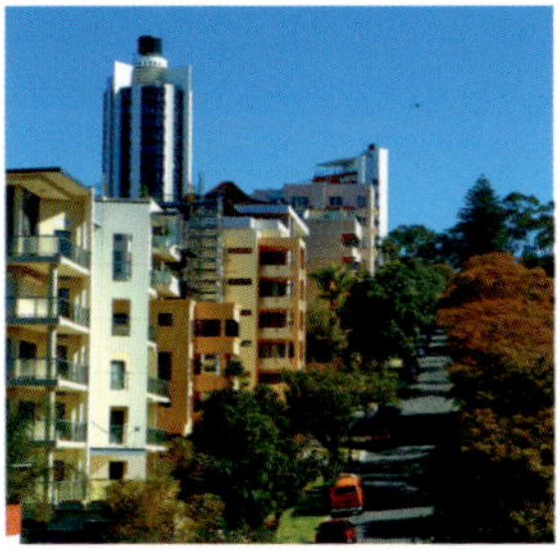
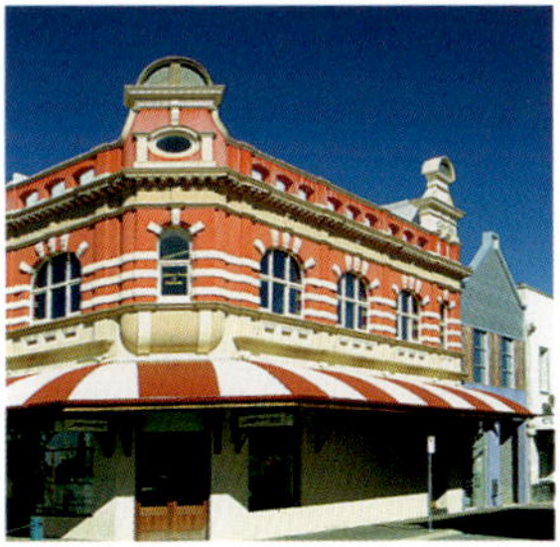
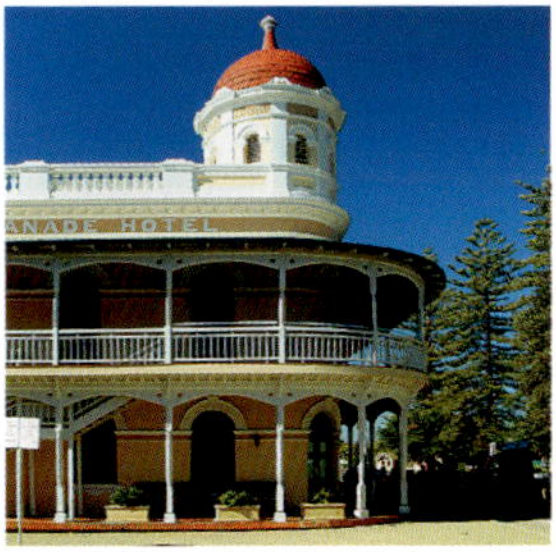

following page. adelaide, arts and convention centre with torrens river

a, b, d, f, h & i fremantle buildings c. bell tower e. supreme court g. mount street

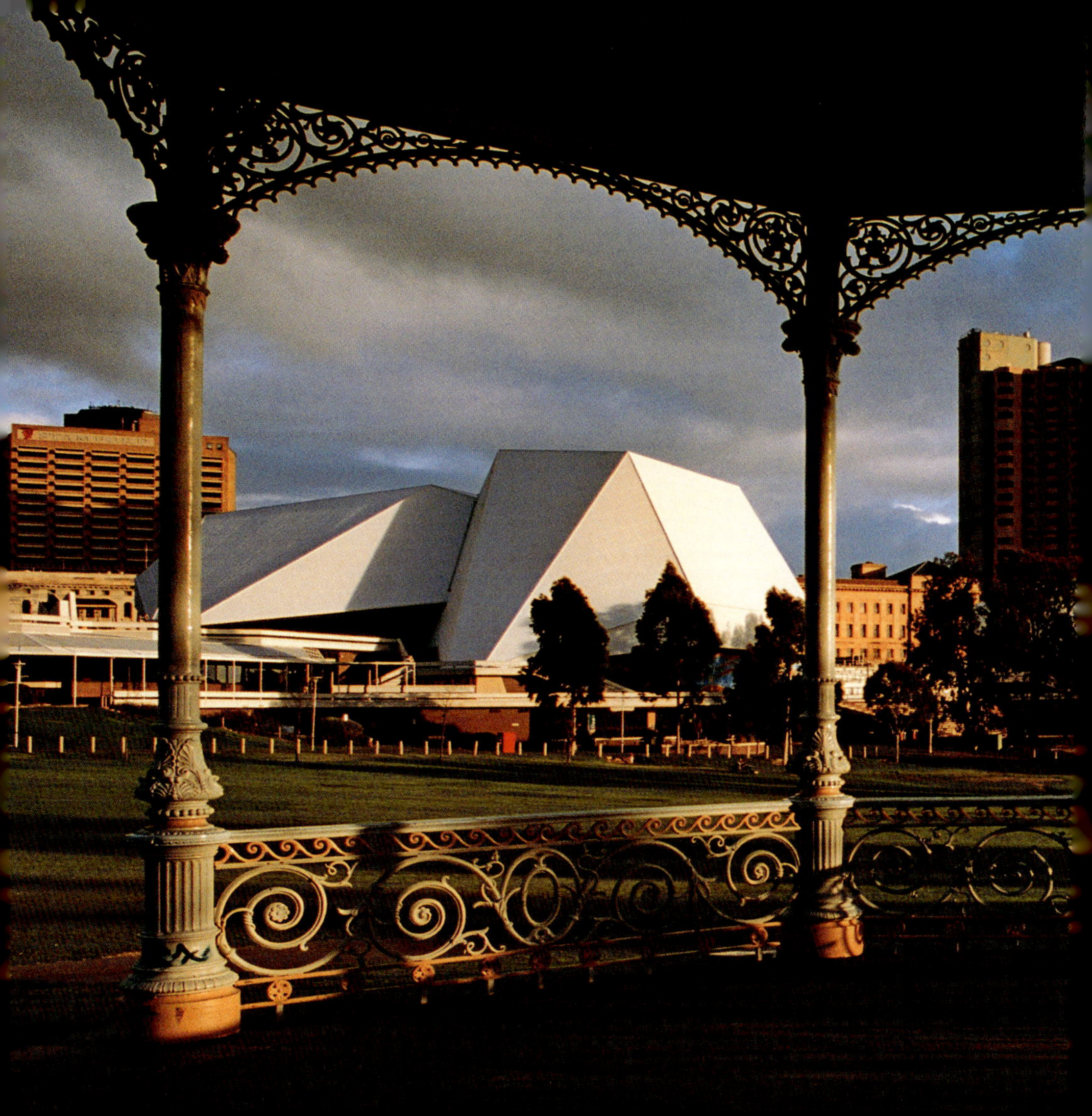

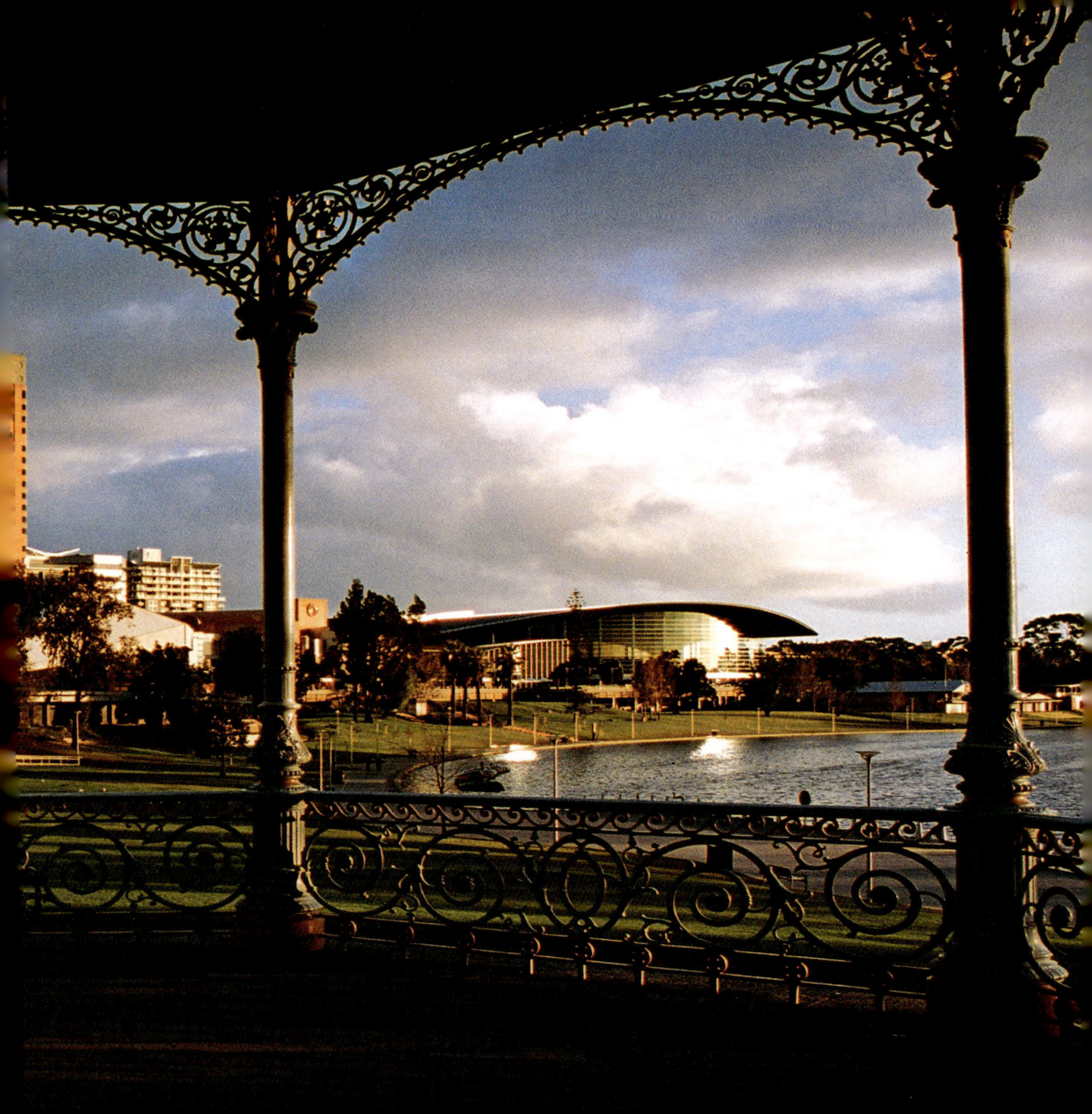

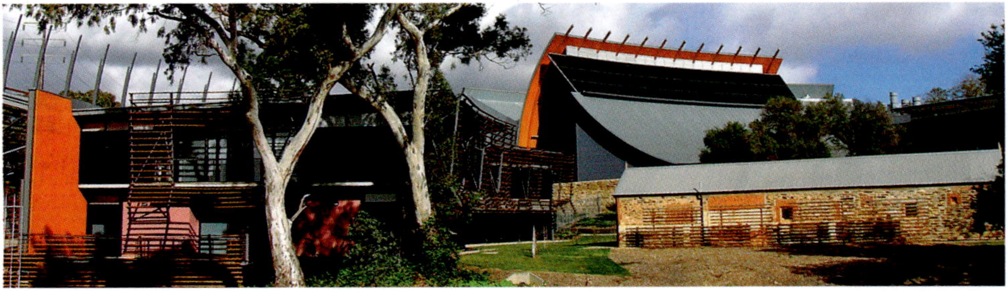

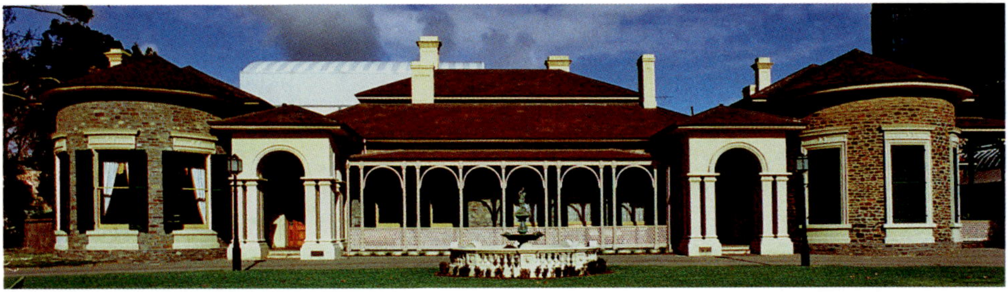

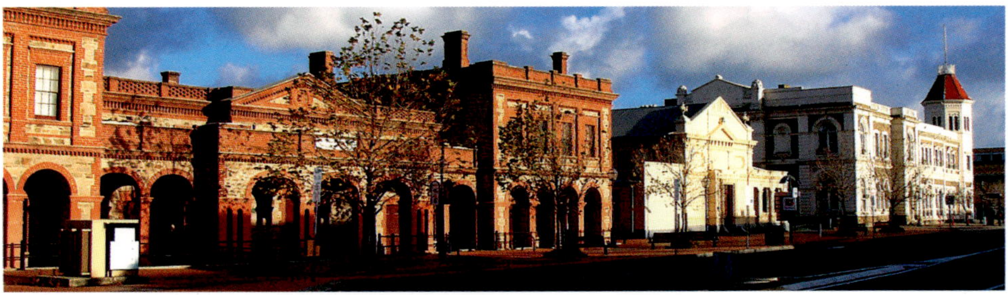

 a. national wine centre b. ayers house c. port adelaide

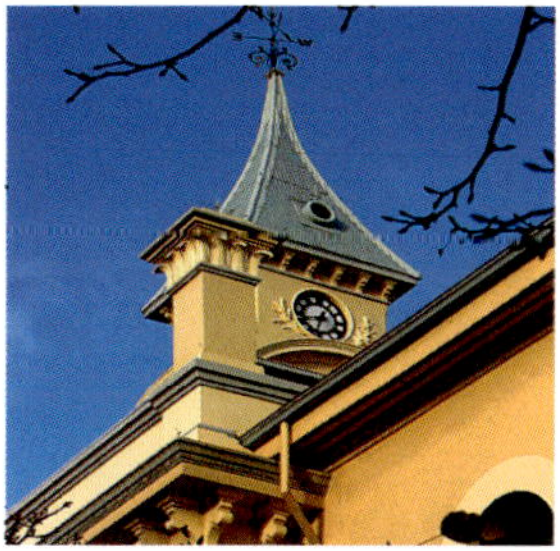

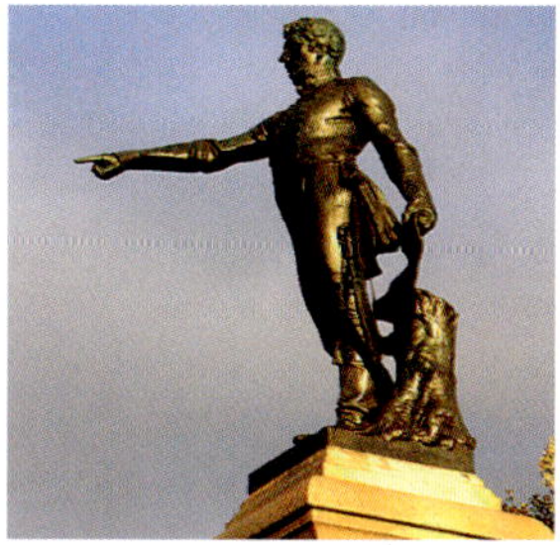

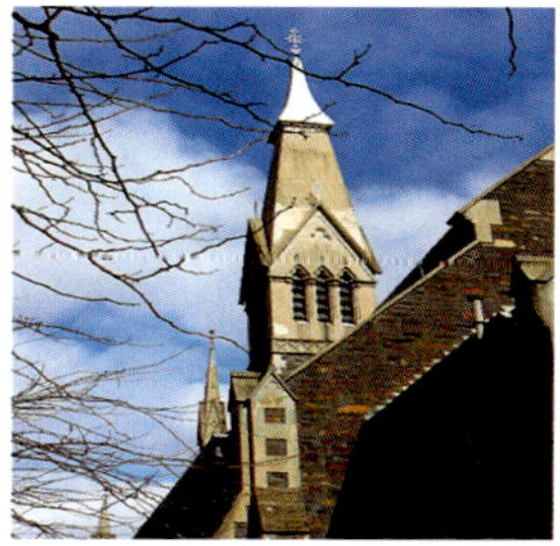

next page. middle flinders ranges

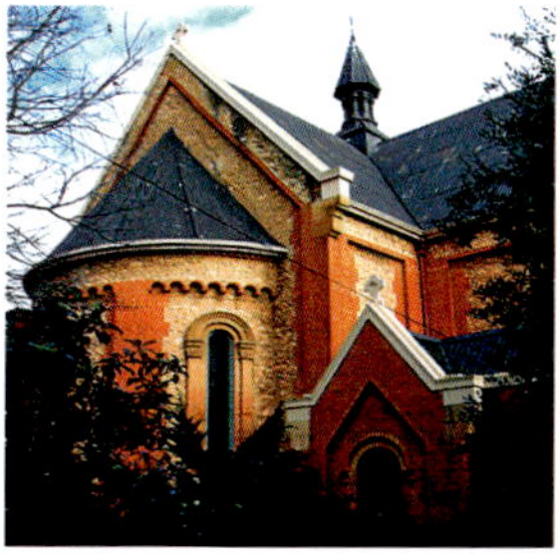

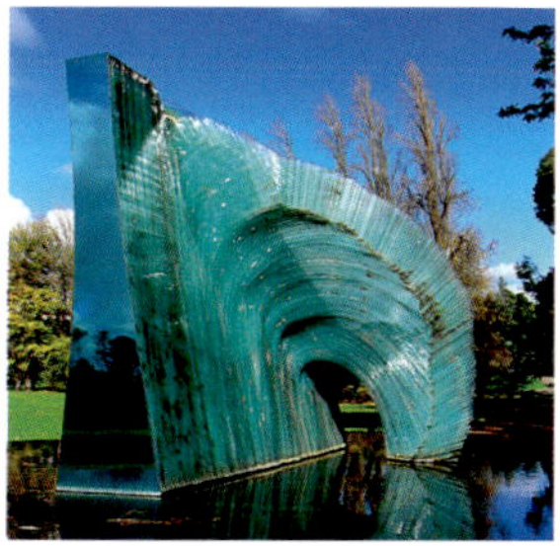

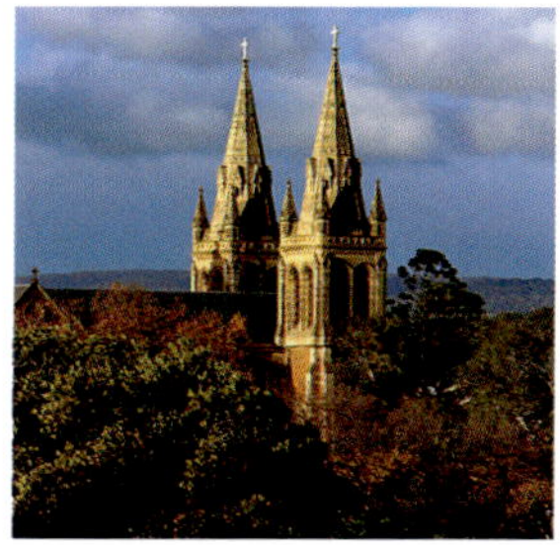

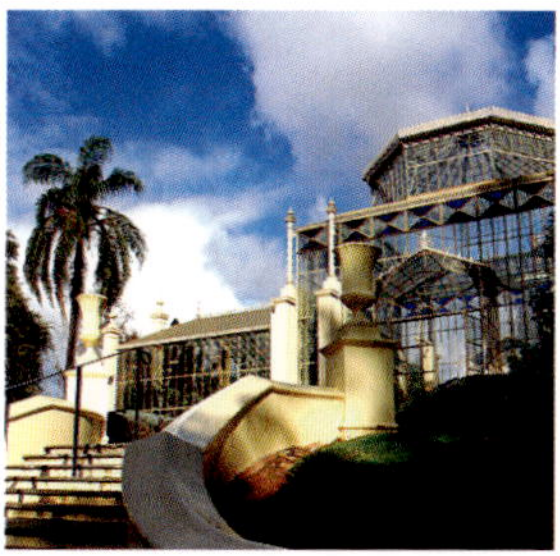

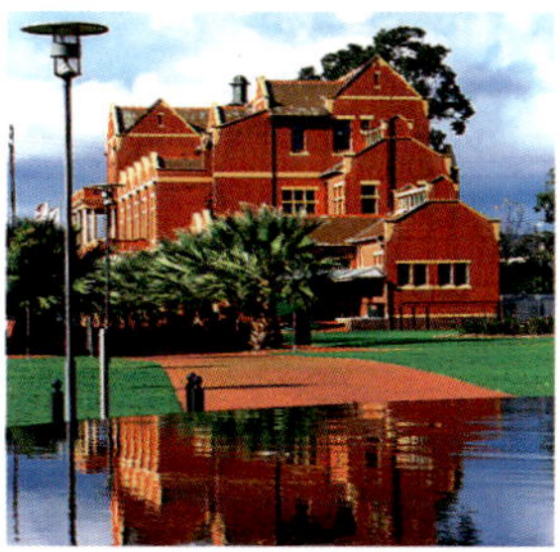

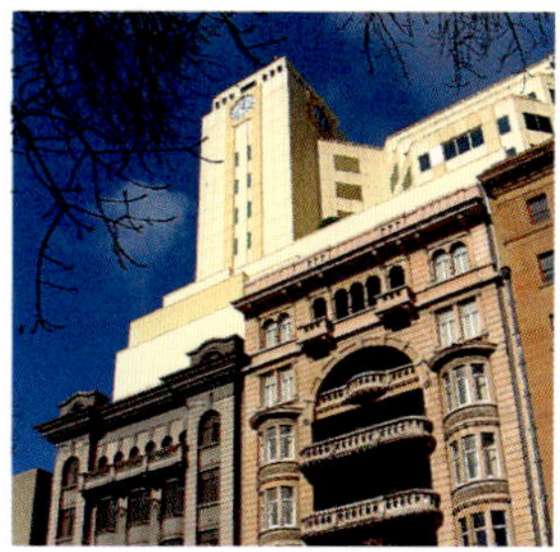

a. port adelaide b. lights vision c. st stephens d. christ church e & g & h. botanic gardens f. st peters i. north terrace.

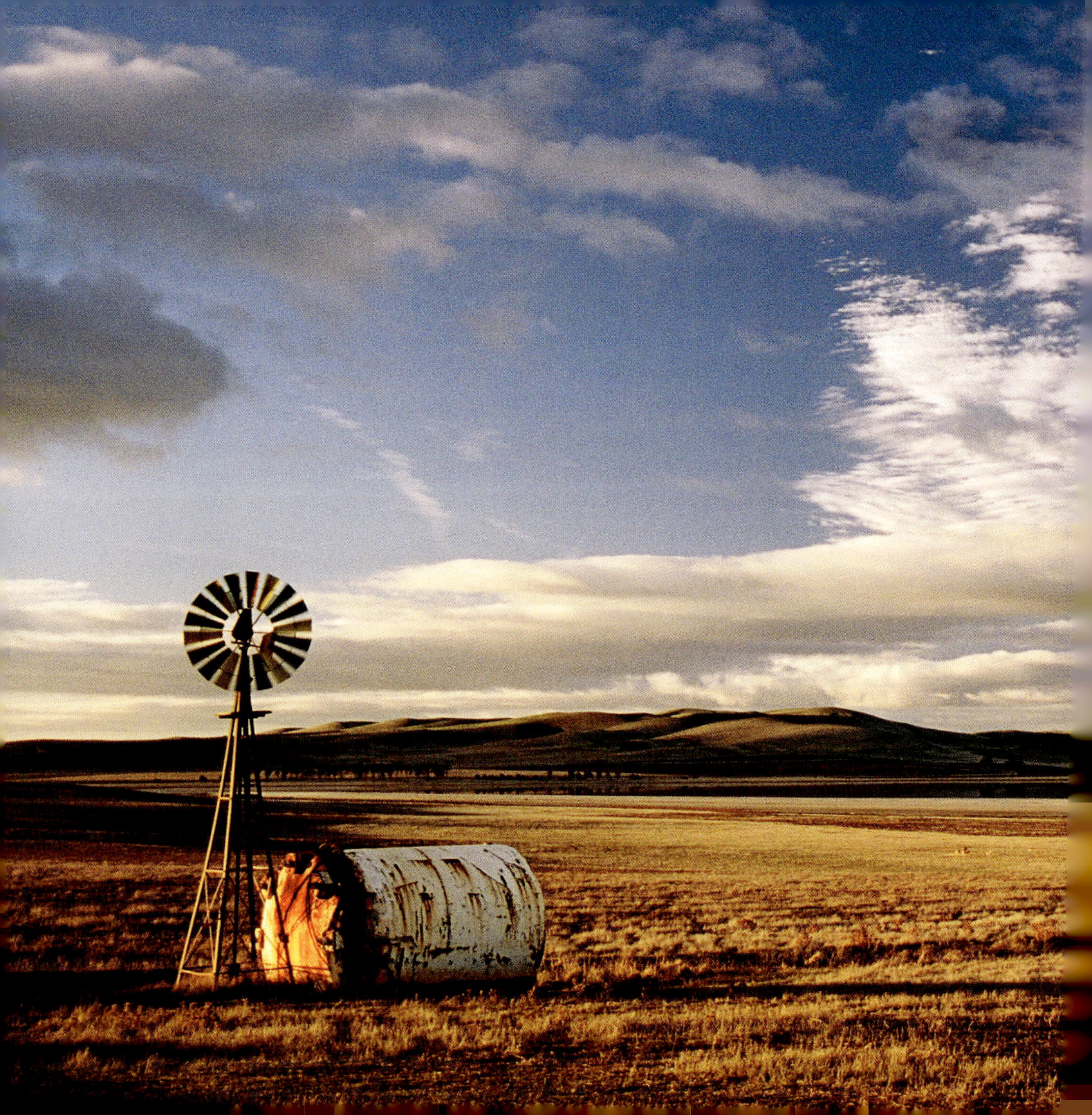

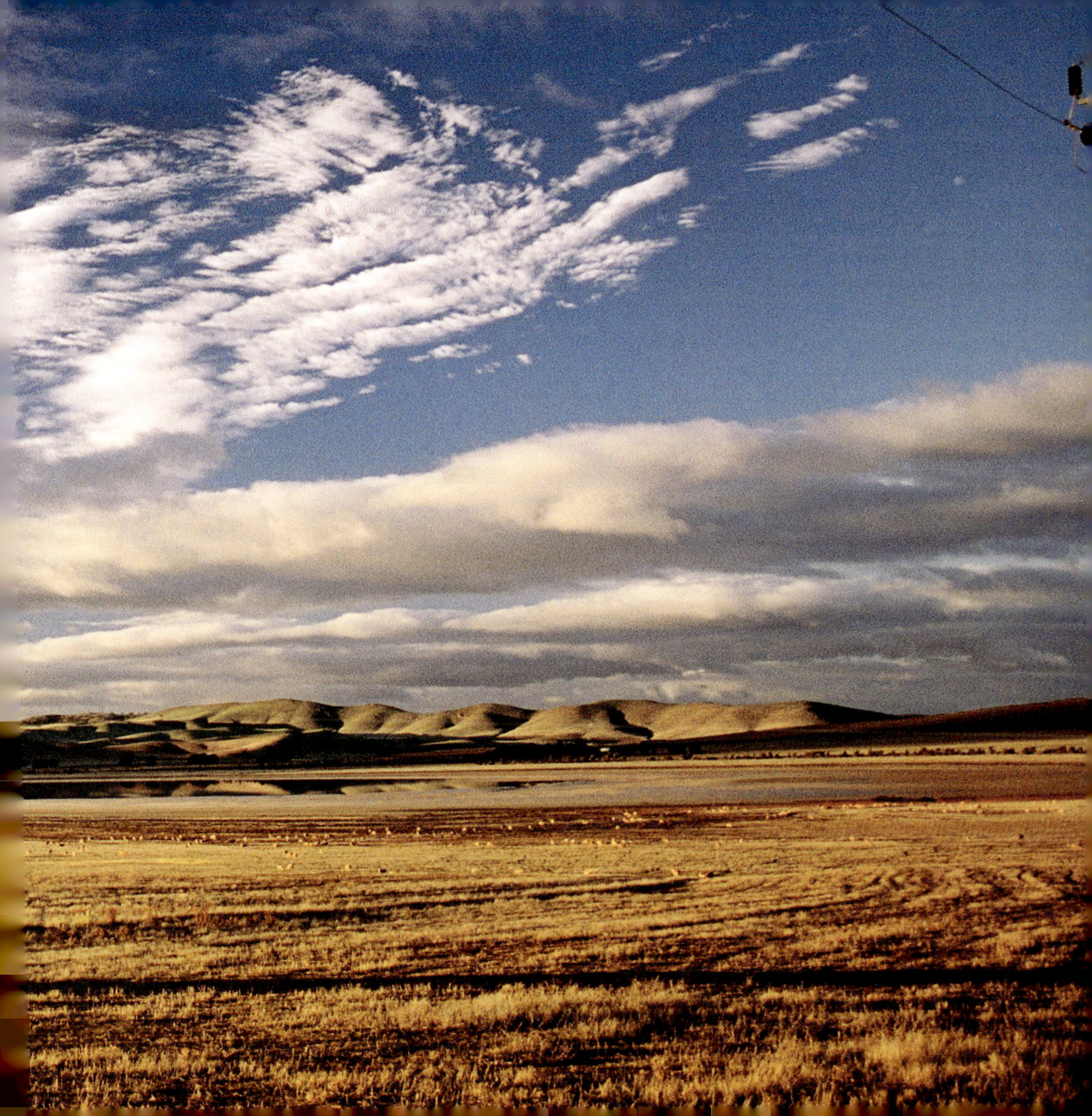

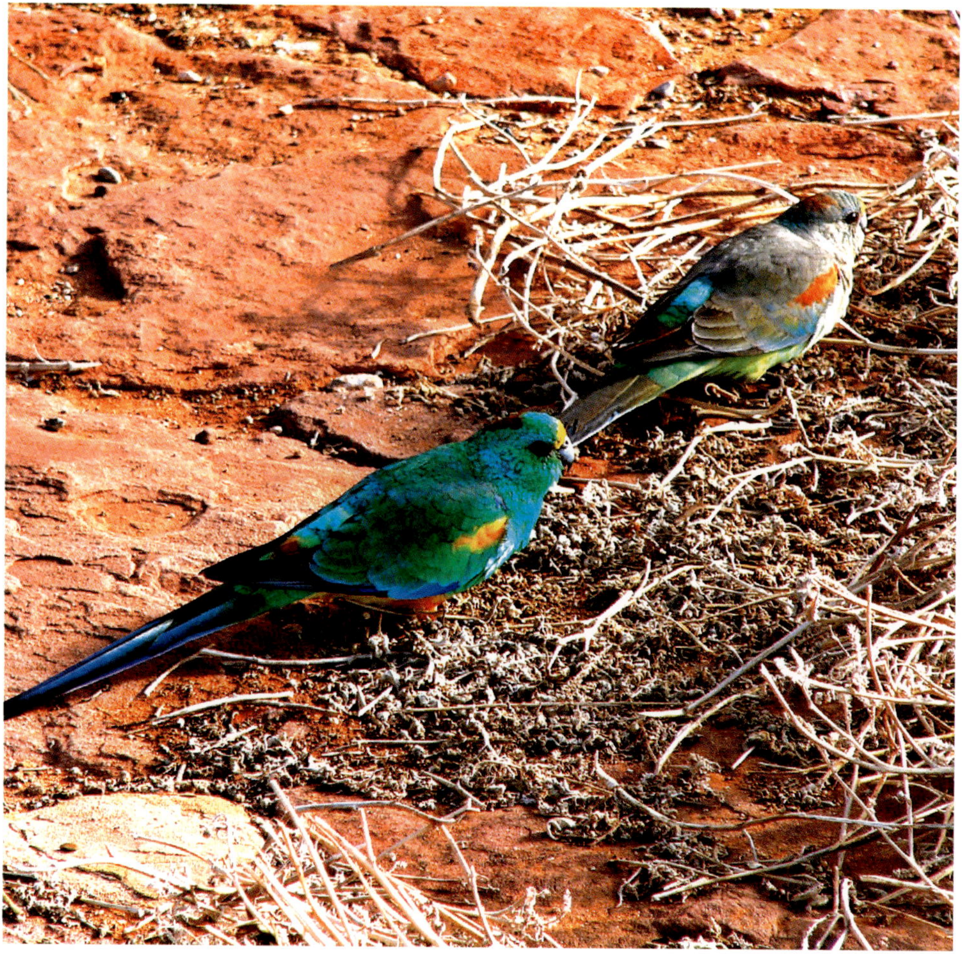

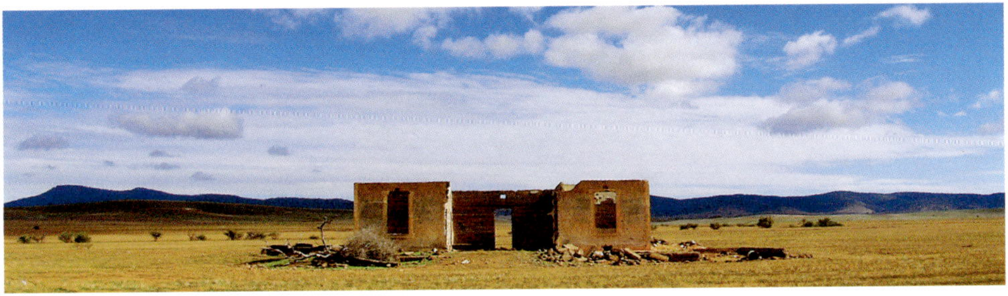

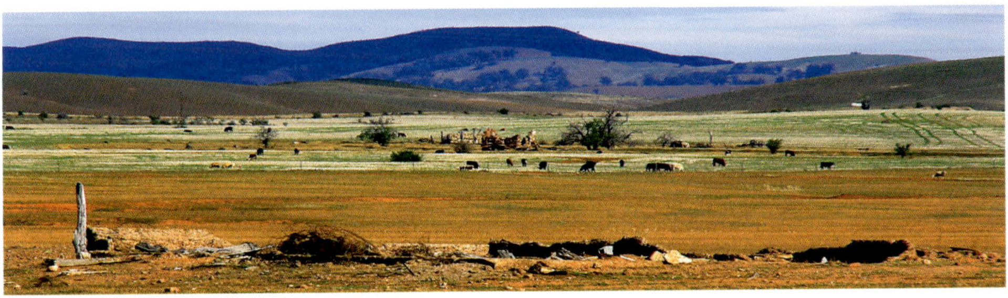

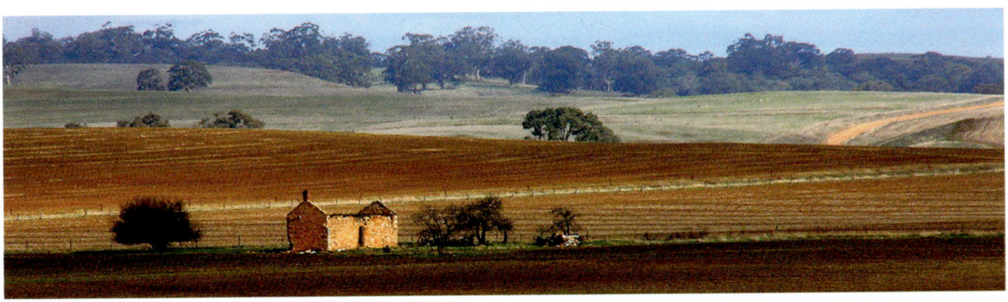

south flinders ranges

next page. palm valley

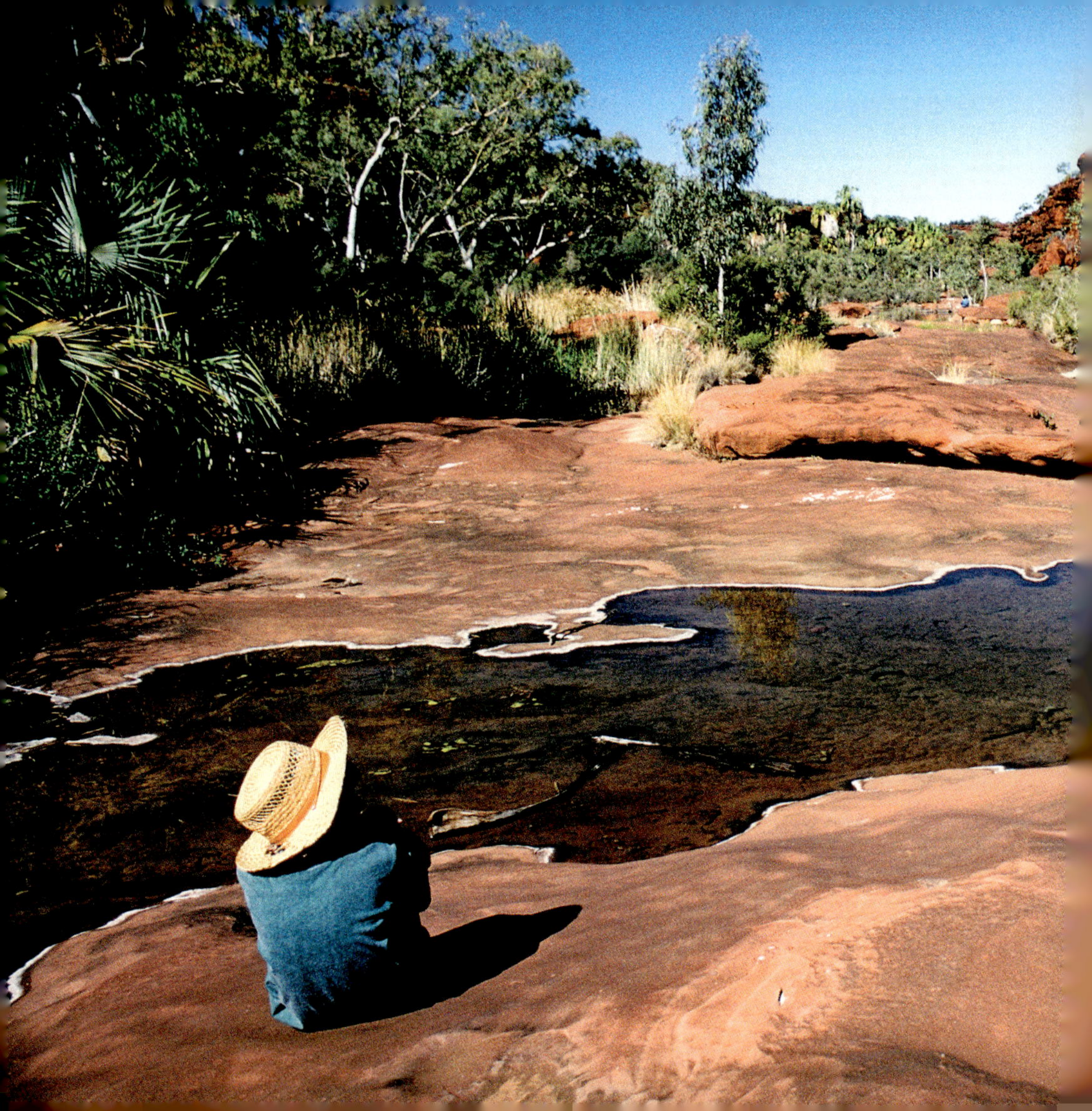

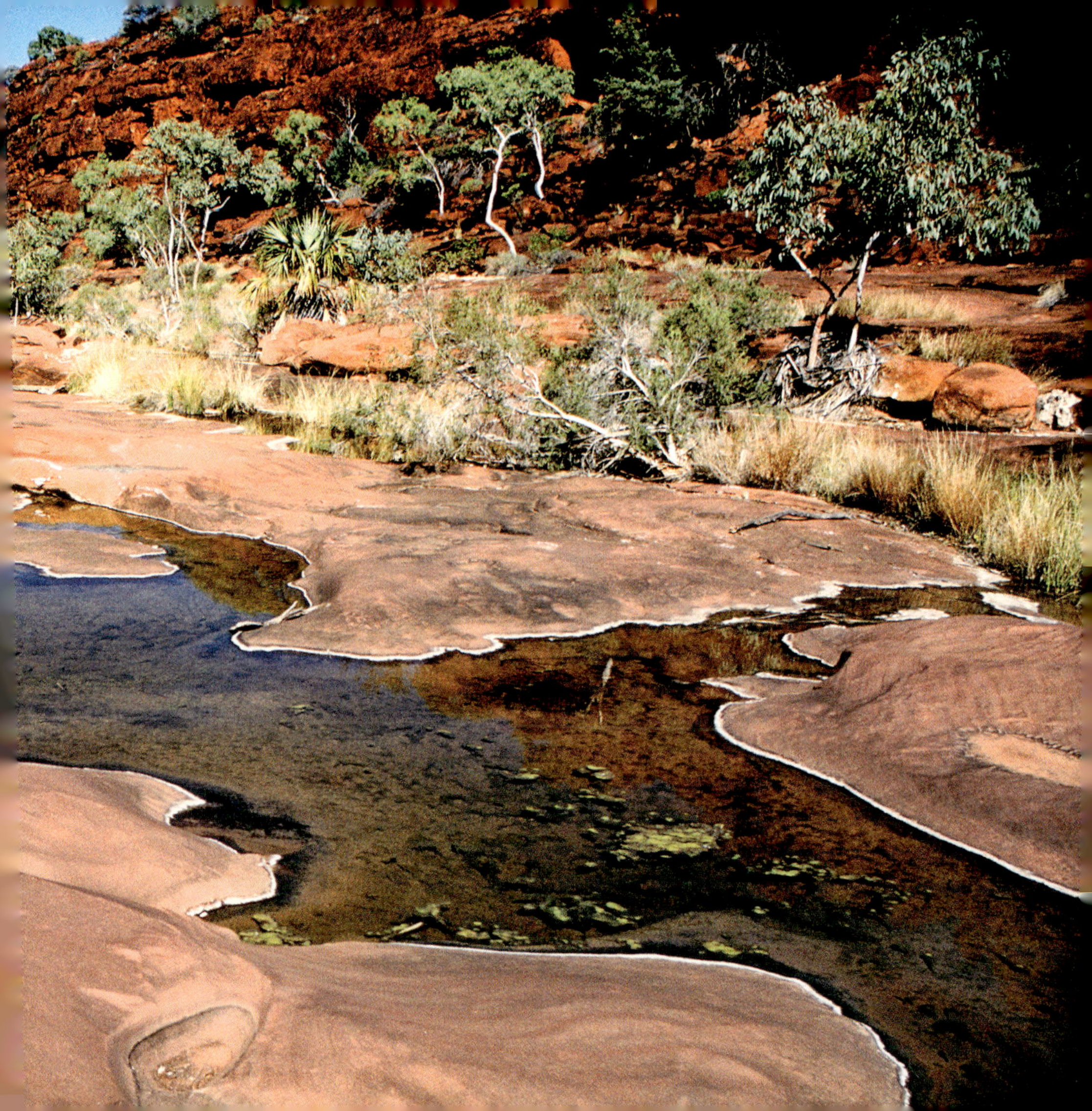

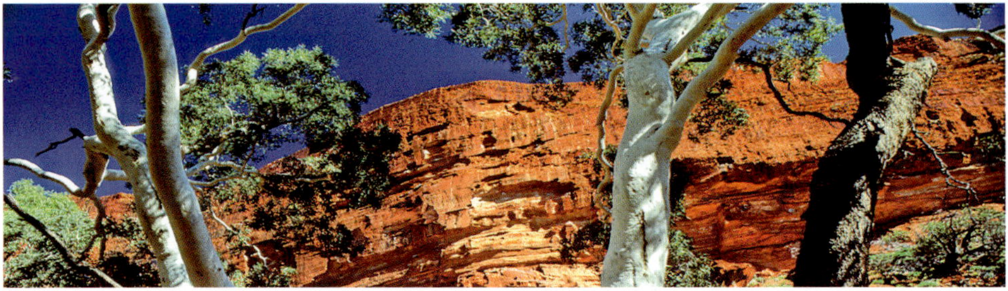

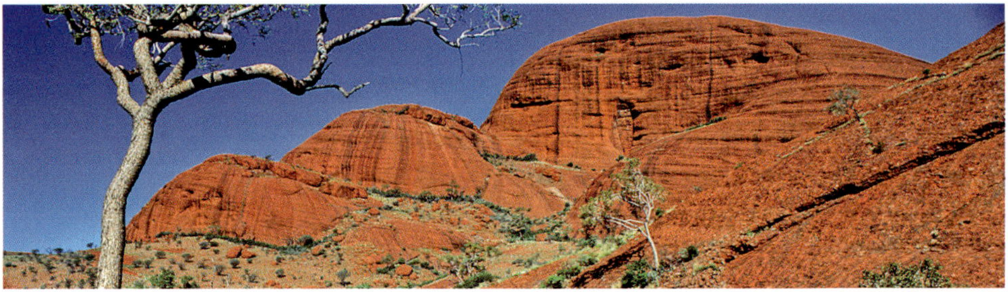

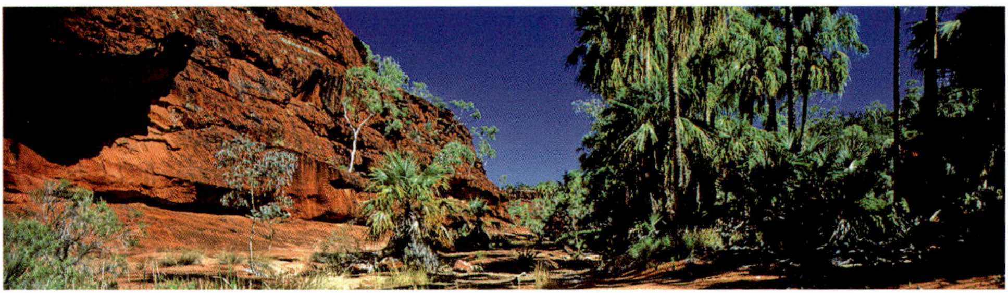

 a. kings canyon b. kata tjuta c. palm valley

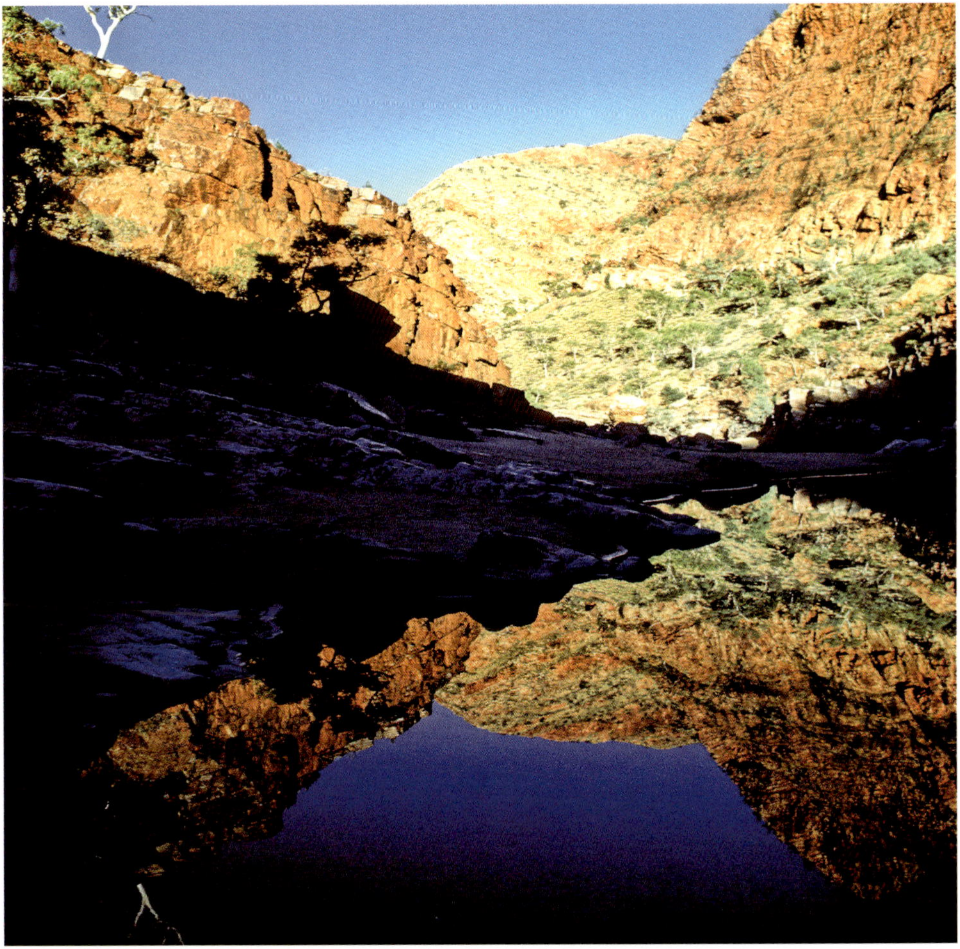

next page. kata tjuta national park

ormiston gorge

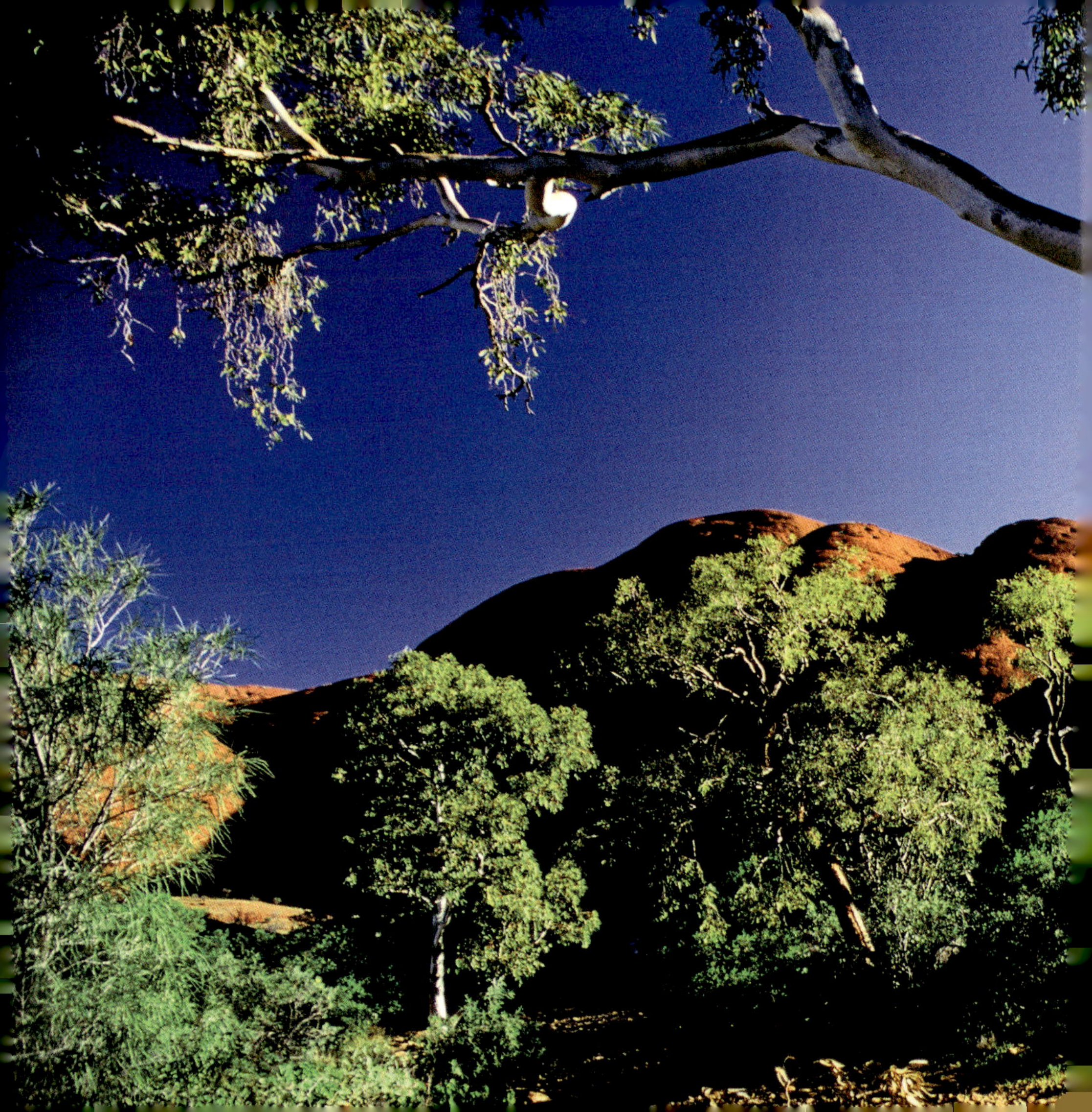

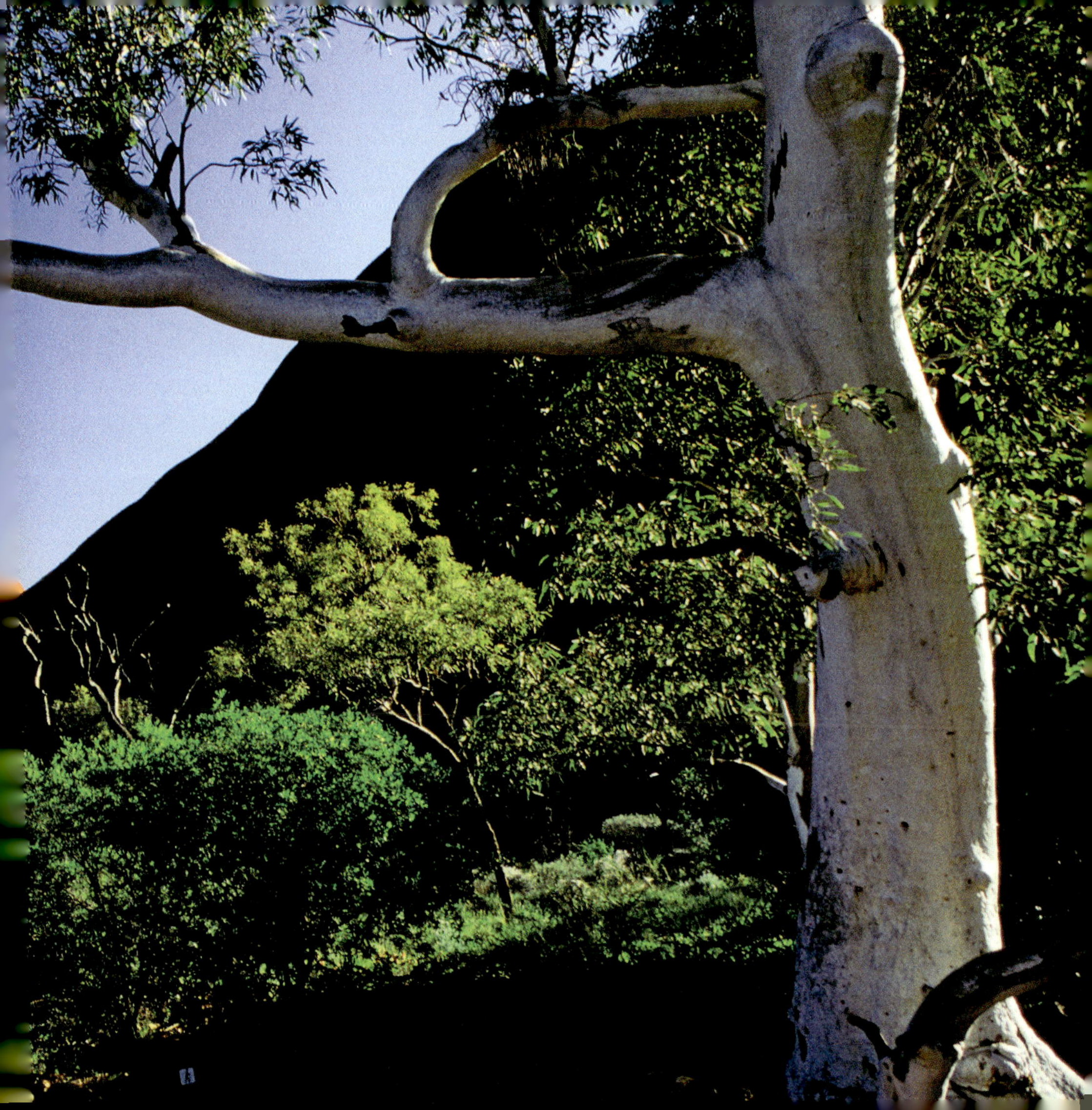

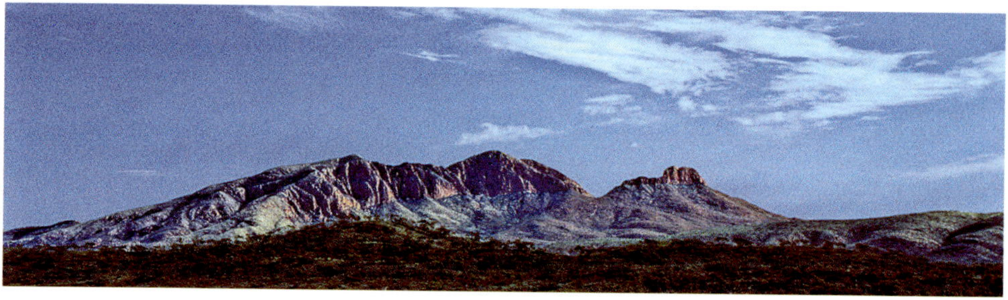

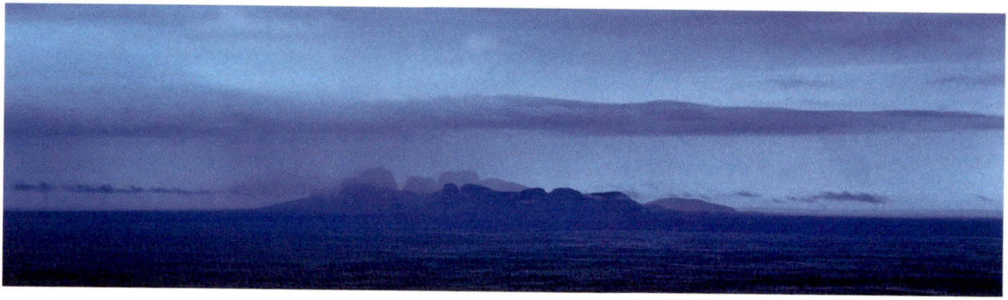

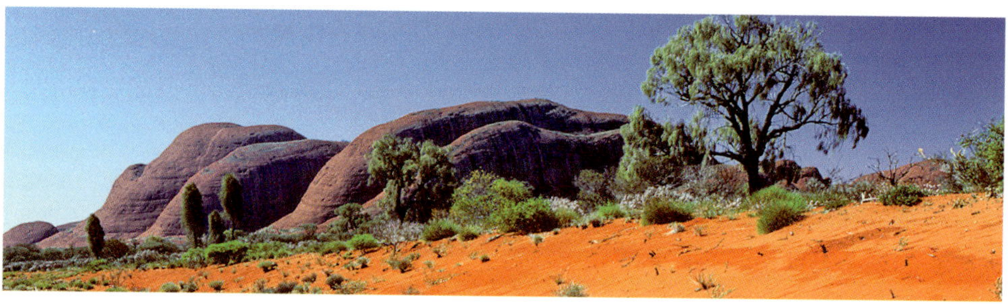

 a. kunparrka b&c. kata tjuta

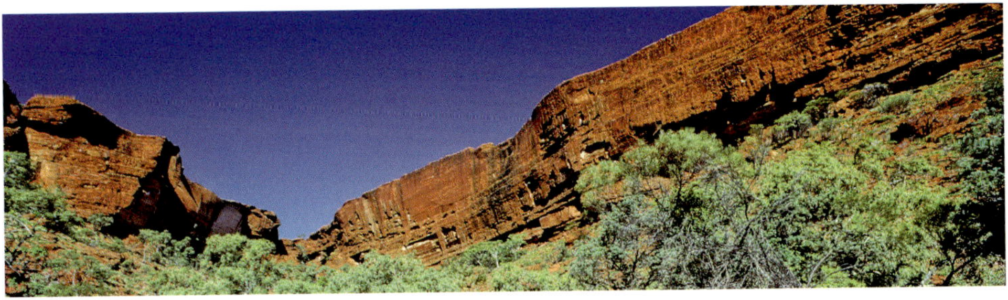

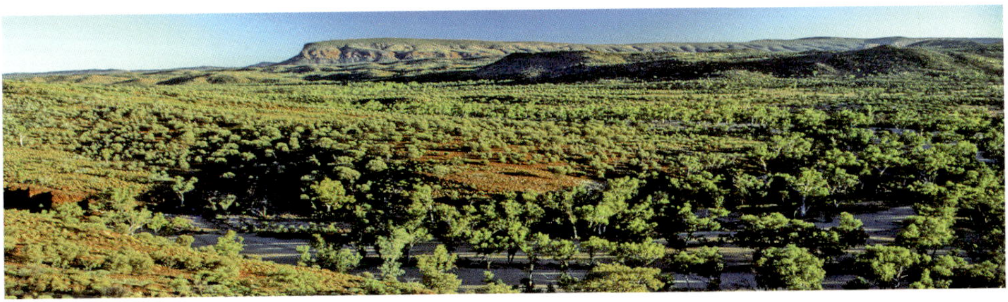

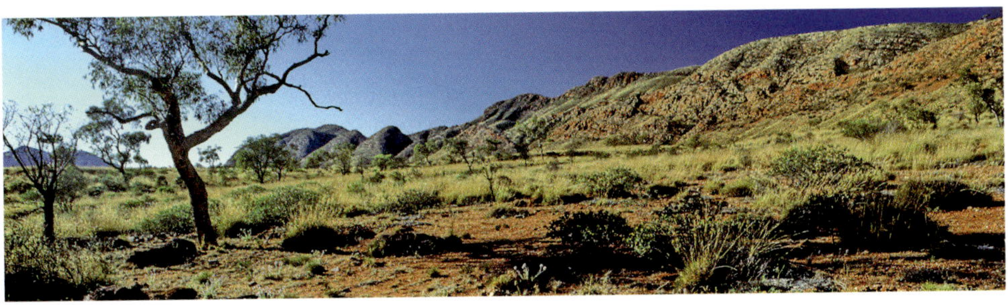

a. kings canyon b. east macdonnell range c. west macdonnell range

next page. devils marbles

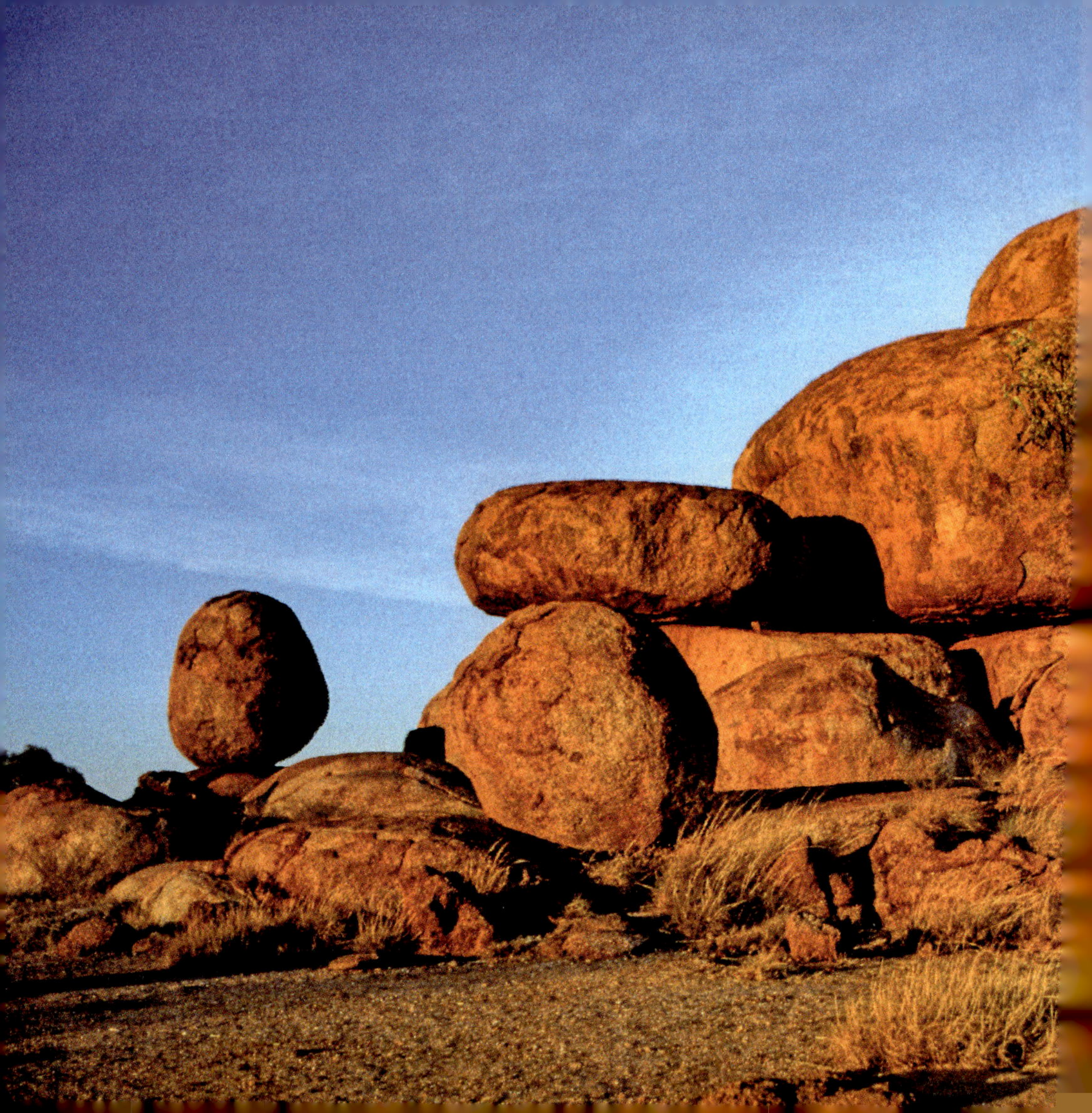

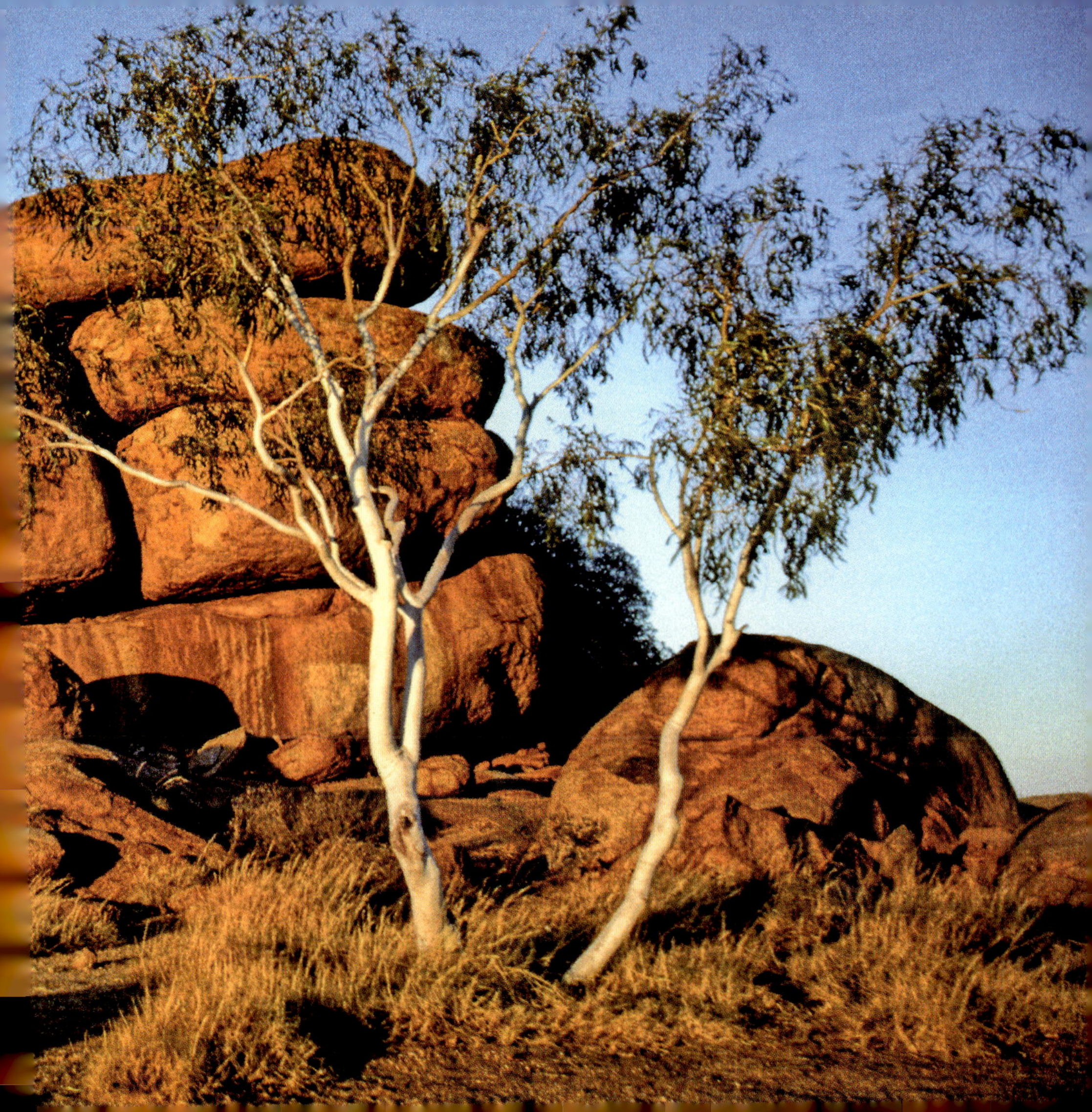

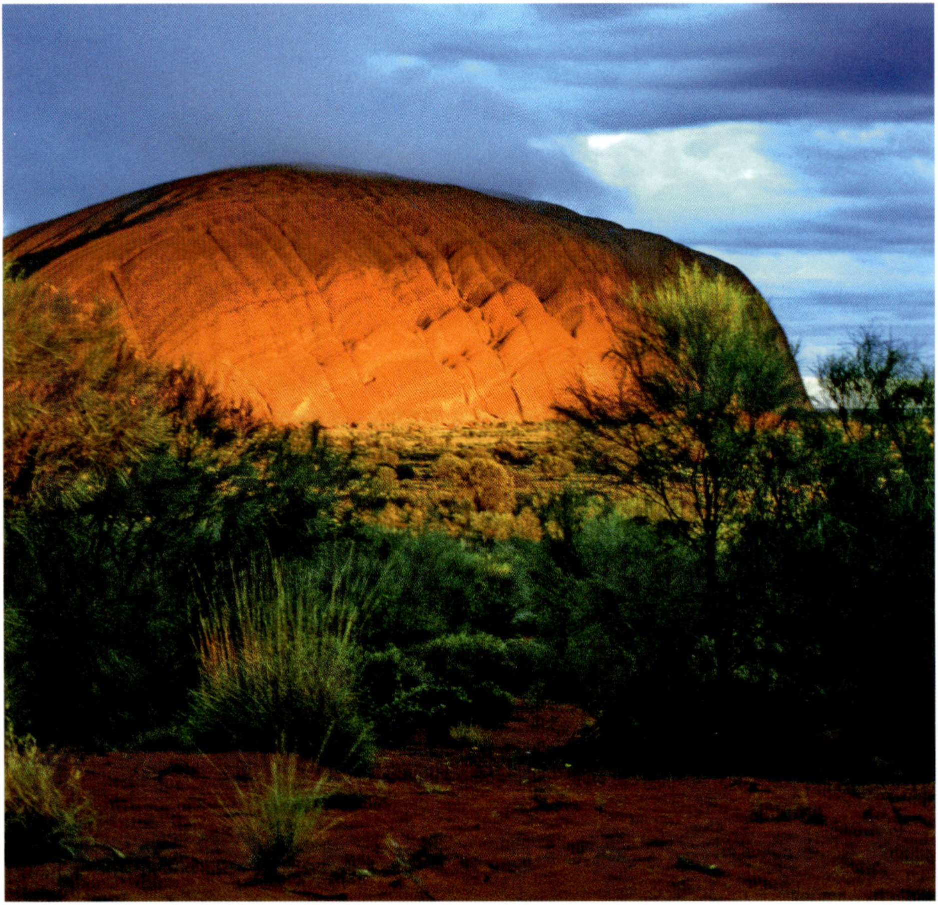

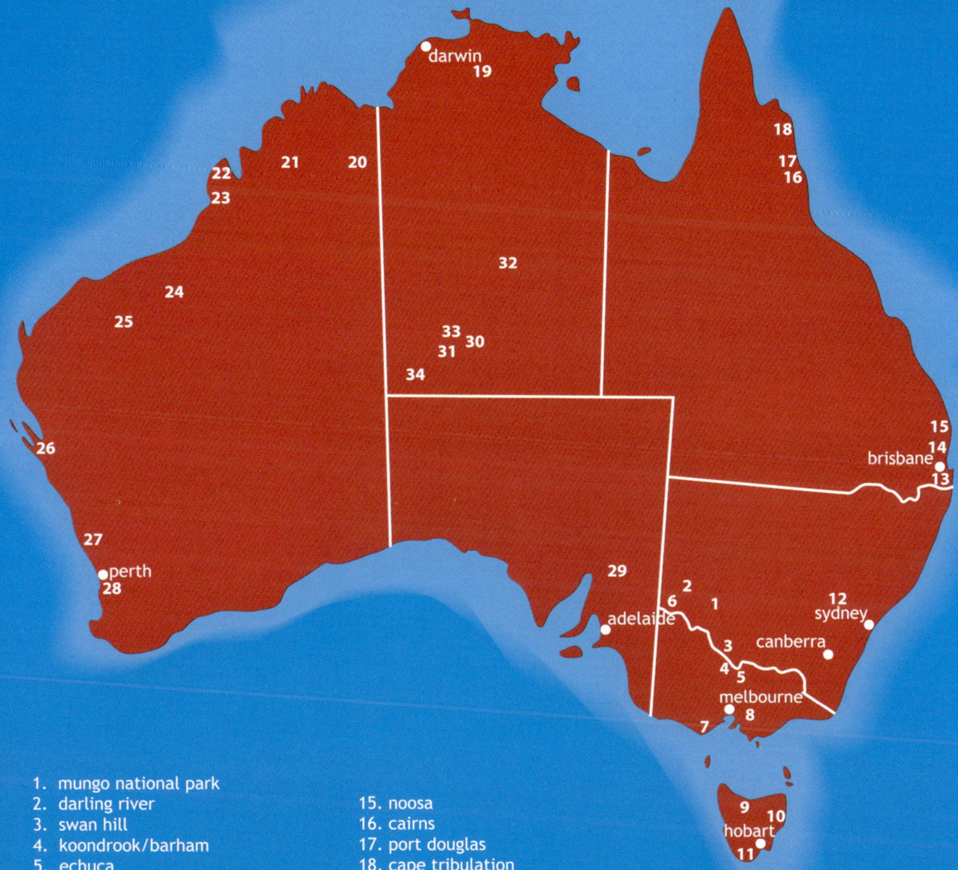

1. mungo national park
2. darling river
3. swan hill
4. koondrook/barham
5. echuca
6. wentworth
7. port campbell
8. dandenong ranges
9. cradle mountain
10. east coast, tasmania
11. surprise bay
12. katoomba
13. gold coast
14. sunshine coast
15. noosa
16. cairns
17. port douglas
18. cape tribulation
19. kakadu
20. purnululu
21. kimberley
22. cape leveque
23. broome
24. pilbara
25. karijini
26. cape leseur
27. pinnacles
28. fremantle
29. flinders ranges
30. palm valley
31. kings canyon
32. devils marbles
33. east macdonnell ranges
34. uluru & kata tjuta

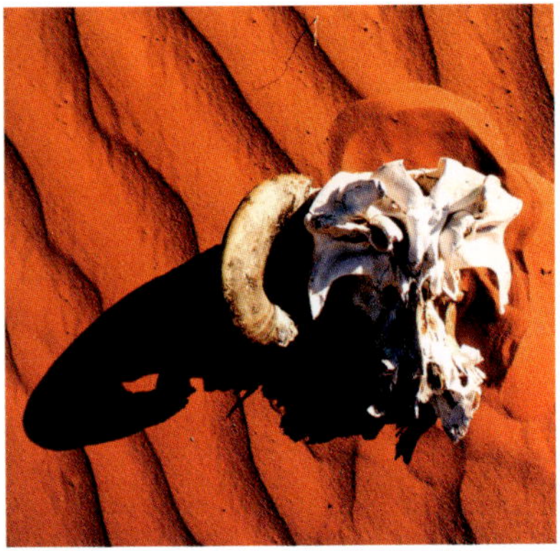

visit the peter emanuel galleries on line www.peteremanuel.com.au

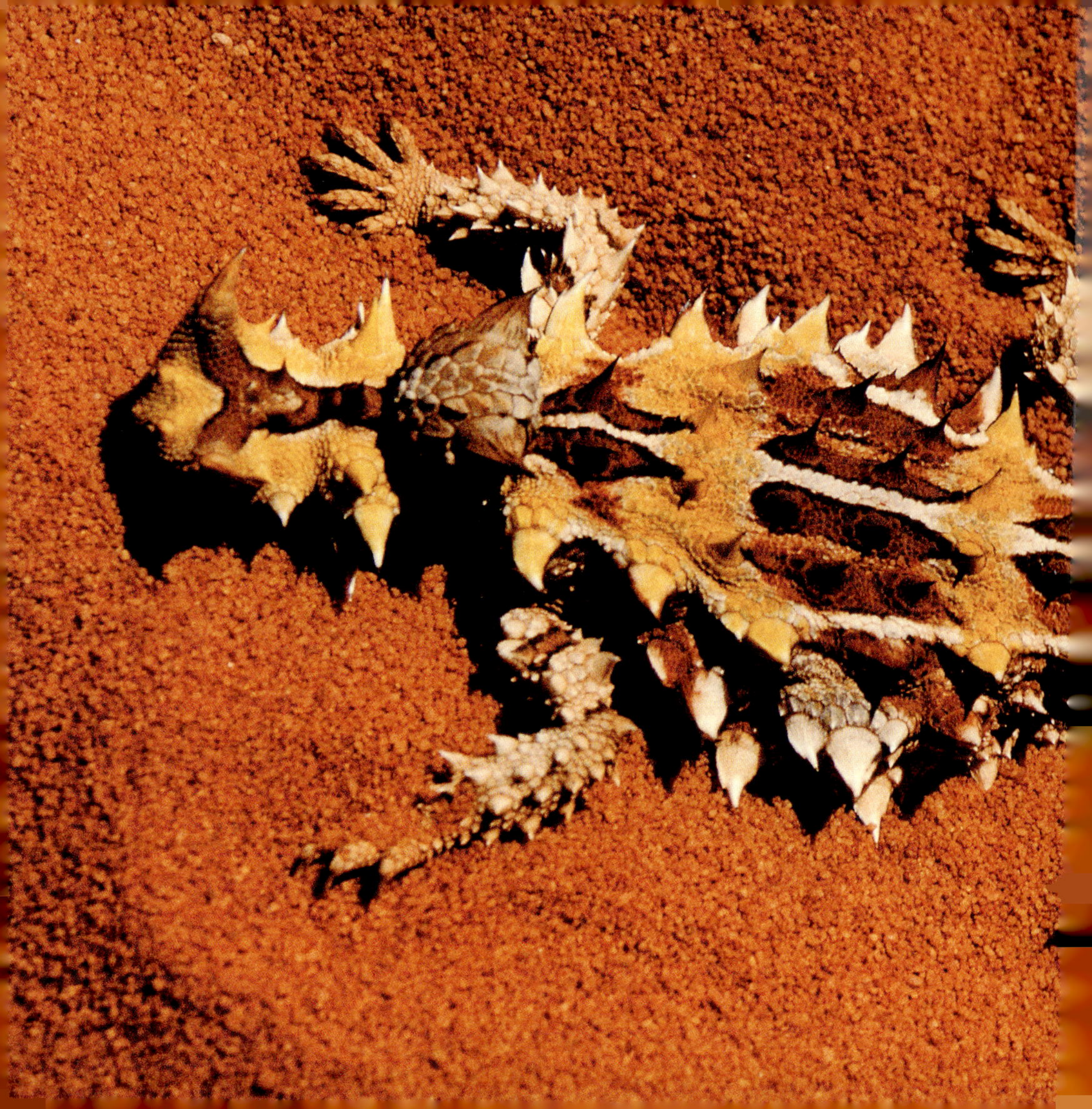